PRAISE FOR SPINSANITY

"The site has been scrupulously nonpartisan in its debunking of media myths and lancing of rhetorical hyperbole, from Michael Moore and Robert Scheer to Ann Coulter and Sean Hannity."

—Matt Welch, *Reason*

"There's no shortage of websites that purport to be beacons of truth, attacking the spin and propaganda of politics and celebrity, but usually they're only interested in attacking propaganda they don't agree with. Spinsanity is different. It'll point out half-truths and outright deceptions everywhere."

—Andy Ihnatko, *Chicago Sun-Times*

"Bipartisan bull detectors."

—Andrew Sullivan, AndrewSullivan.com

"One special source I recommend."

—Bill Press, author of *Spin This! All the Ways We Don't Tell the Truth*

"Great resource."

—Al Franken, author of *Lies and the Lying Liars Who Tell Them*

A TOUCHSTONE BOOK
PUBLISHED BY SIMON & SCHUSTER
NEW YORK   LONDON   TORONTO   SYDNEY

ALL THE PRESIDENT'S SPIN

GEORGE W. BUSH, THE MEDIA, AND THE TRUTH

BEN FRITZ,
BRYAN KEEFER,
AND BRENDAN NYHAN

TOUCHSTONE
Rockefeller Center
1230 Avenue of the Americas
New York, NY 10020

For information regarding special discounts for bulk purchases,
please contact Simon & Schuster Special Sales at 1-800-456-6798
or business@simonandschuster.com

Manufactured in the United States of America

10   9   8   7   6   5   4   3

Library of Congress Catalog Card Number 2004052205

ISBN 0-7432-6251-4

★ CONTENTS ★

★ PREFACE ★

Despite all that has been written about George W. Bush, something important is missing from conventional portraits of our 43rd president. While debate continues to rage over whether Bush is a liar, few have discussed the way he employs the insidious tools of public relations, which make selling a tax cut as slick and dishonest as the worst of corporate marketing. By using these tactics, Bush has promoted his policies in a remarkably deceptive manner and avoided serious consequences for doing so. This is the untold story of the Bush presidency.

During the 2000 election and subsequent Florida recount, the three of us saw how the national debate had been reduced to an endless barrage of spin. Politicians, pundits, and reporters twisted facts until they bore little relation to reality, compressing the election into a melodrama pitting Bush and his supposed lack of intelligence and gravitas against Vice President Al Gore's alleged arrogance and dishonesty. Rather than lifting up political debate, mainstream political institutions were dragging it down.

As a result, we founded Spinsanity (www.spinsanity.com) in early 2001 as a watchdog website dedicated to debunking political spin and fact-checking the media from a nonpartisan perspective. Though we started small, with a readership of only a few friends and family, major news outlets eventually began to take note of our work. Our criticism of commentators such as Michael Moore, Sean Hannity, and Ann Coulter has attracted national attention; our coverage of politicians and government officials has been cited by partisans of all stripes; and our debunking of falsehoods spreading through the press has helped prevent them from growing into conventional wisdom. Judging by the response we have received, we believe the public is hungry for nonpartisan criticism of a political system that is collapsing under the weight of deception.

All three of us were politically active in liberal or Democratic politics in the past, but our work is scrupulously fair. The citations, accolades, and hate mail we get from across the political spectrum attest to the fact that we effectively challenge the left and the right on a regular basis.

We will continue to hold both sides accountable on our site through the 2004 election and beyond. But after several years of de-spinning politicians and the media, we realized that things have only become worse since the 2000 election—and the man currently doing the most damage to our political debate is the President of the United States, George W. Bush. To fulfill our mission to counter those who spin and deceive, we must start at the top by holding the President accountable for the accuracy of his public statements. That is why we decided to write this book. When the chief executive can wield these tactics with little challenge, it is not surprising that other politicians so frequently mislead and dissemble.

Some readers may ask how we can claim to be nonpartisan if we have written a book that is critical of President Bush. We understand that many people, particularly conservatives, are skeptical of endless assertions from liberals that Bush is an inveterate liar, many of which boil down to little more than ideological disagreement.

Unlike those critics, our quarrel is not with Bush's policies or beliefs, but with the manner in which he sells them to the press and the public. The wisdom of his decisions is for others to judge.

Our goal is to show how Bush has attempted to deceive the nation and why he has escaped serious consequences for doing so. In the process, we hope to spur discussion about a political system under siege by the forces of public relations and spin. Bush may be the current leader of the arms race of deception, but his presidency reveals a deeper problem at the heart of American democracy.

★ INTRODUCTION ★

During the 2000 presidential campaign, then-Governor Bush liked to tell the story of a hypothetical waitress who would benefit from his tax cut plan. "Under current tax law," he said, "a single waitress supporting two children on an income of $22,000 faces a higher marginal tax rate than a lawyer making $220,000," adding, "Under my plan, she will pay no income tax at all." [1]

This wasn't much of a feat. What Bush failed to mention was that his hypothetical waitress probably already paid no federal income tax. [2]

In August 2001, President Bush announced a new policy on the use of stem cells in federally funded medical research. "More than sixty genetically diverse stem cell lines already exist," he told the nation in a televised address, concluding, "We should allow federal funds to be used for research on these existing stem cell lines."

Researchers eager to obtain access to these "existing" lines were quickly disappointed, however, when Tommy Thompson, Bush's Secretary of Health and Human Services, admitted that only twenty-four or twenty-five lines were actually "fully developed." Although sixty lines did *exist*, it was uncertain whether many of them would ever become available to researchers. [3]

In late 2001, Bush began pointing back to a statement he

claimed to have made during the 2000 campaign. As he put it in May 2002, "when I was running for president, in Chicago, somebody said, would you ever have deficit spending? I said, only if we were at war, or only if we had a recession, or only if we had a national emergency. Never did I dream we'd get the trifecta."[4]

It was a good story, but there's no evidence that the President ever made such a statement in Chicago or elsewhere. In fact, Vice President Al Gore was the candidate who had listed the exceptions in 1998 (though Bush advisor Lawrence Lindsey said at the time that they would apply to the Texas governor as well). Was this an innocent mistake? The answer is almost certainly no—Bush continued to repeat the "trifecta" story for months after it had been debunked.

Then, in a televised address to the nation in October 2002, Bush declared, "We know that Iraq and the al Qaeda terrorist network share a common enemy—the United States of America. We know that Iraq and al Qaeda have had high-level contacts that go back a decade. Some al Qaeda leaders who fled Afghanistan went to Iraq. These include one very senior al Qaeda leader who received medical treatment in Baghdad this year, and who has been associated with planning for chemical and biological attacks. We've learned that Iraq has trained al Qaeda members in bomb-making and poisons and deadly gases. And we know that after September the 11th, Saddam Hussein's regime gleefully celebrated the terrorist attacks on America."[5]

Each of these statements was true, but Bush's words were carefully constructed to leave a false impression. Without ever stating that there was a direct connection between Iraq, al Qaeda, and September 11, the President artfully linked them together with a series of carefully chosen phrases.

After the war, Bush told an interviewer from Polish television that "We found the weapons of mass destruction" in Iraq.[6] But he was not reporting the discovery of drums of chemical weapons or artillery shells filled with anthrax. Rather, Bush was referring to a pair of trailers that some analysts thought *might* have been used to produce biological weapons. While experts debated the purpose of the trailers, the President of the United States was falsely claiming that WMD had been found.

These examples might not be so troubling if the press had consistently called attention to them. But on most issues, with the possible exception of stem cells and the aftermath of the war in Iraq, he got away with little more than a slap on the wrist. Journalists deserve much of the blame for this, but one of the chief reasons these examples received so little attention is that many were based on a partial truth about a complex policy issue; after all, the waitress did end up with no federal income tax, there were sixty "existing" stem cell lines, and Iraq had some fragmentary connections to Al Qaeda . . . sort of.

Bush's record raises a number of questions. Just how often did the President deceive us? How did he do it? And why didn't anyone put a stop to it?

The answers are disturbing. George W. Bush has done serious damage to our political system. His deceptions span nearly all of his major policies, were achieved using some of the most advanced tactics from public relations, and were designed to exploit the failings of the modern media. In the process, Bush has made it even more difficult for citizens to understand and take part in democratic debate.

These deceptions are worthy of close attention for more than the insight they give us into the President himself. He is simply the highest profile carrier of a virus infecting our political system. Its symptoms are misleading public statements, a disregard for the value of honest discussion, and treating policy debates as little more than marketing challenges—a devastating combination for democracy.

BUSH'S TROUBLED RELATIONSHIP WITH THE TRUTH

Compared to other presidents, Bush's deceptions might seem unremarkable. He has certainly not been caught lying in a scandal comparable to Watergate or Bill Clinton's affair with a White House intern. Minor scandals have erupted during Bush's tenure, such as questions about his service in the Air National Guard and his administration's ties to Enron, but his behavior in these matters has been no different than that of previous chief executives. Nor do his statements about the conduct of military operations in Afghanistan and Iraq stand out compared to the great war-related deceptions of previous presidents like Lyndon Johnson or Richard Nixon.

George W. Bush's dishonesty is different. Rather than simply lying, he has subtly and systematically attempted to deceive the nation about most of his major policy proposals. On issues ranging from tax cuts to stem cells to the debate over the war in Iraq, he has consistently twisted the truth beyond recognition in order to promote his policies.

Remarkably, he has done so while generally avoiding obviously false statements. Instead, Bush consistently uses well-designed phrases and strategically crafted arguments to distract, deceive, and mislead. The result is that all but the most careful listeners end up believing something completely untrue, while proving the President has lied is usually impossible.

Unlike famous White House dissemblers of the past, Bush almost never explicitly claims that black is white or day is night. Instead, he deceives the public with partial truths and misleading assertions. So rather than saying day is night, George W. Bush will focus on an instance of a solar eclipse or remind Americans that people who work graveyard shifts are asleep. Both might be true, but without the proper context, they're highly misleading. Because Bush's statements are so often constructed in this way, he has walked away from one deceptive claim after another scot-free.

These tactics originate in public relations, a field that has become extremely skilled at promoting a message regardless of its factual accuracy. Previous presidents have also drawn on PR, of course, but Bush has gone far beyond his predecessors, systematically employing these dishonest strategies in nearly every major policy debate. At this point, the difference between corporate marketing and White House communications has largely disappeared.

THE RIGHT DEFINITION OF DISHONESTY

Before assessing Bush's dishonesty, however, we must answer an important question: What counts? One school of thought holds that any politician who contradicts his previous statements—like George H. W. Bush's decision to disavow his "no new taxes" pledge—is a liar. But violating a promise is not lying. This demeans the word and holds our leaders to an unrealistic standard that makes it impossible for them to compromise or adjust to changing circumstances. For instance, once he took office, Bill Clinton abandoned the middle-class tax cut he promised during the 1992 campaign, choosing instead to focus on reducing the federal budget deficit. Does this mean that he wasn't sincere when he first proposed the plan? We can't know for sure. That's not to say politicians should escape scrutiny for breaking a promise, but it's not a good measure of their honesty.

Similarly, some accusations of lying are based on little more than vague political rhetoric, such as George W. Bush's promise during his first year in office that veterans would be a priority for his administration.[7] He has since been accused of dishonesty for allegedly not spending enough on health care for veterans.[8] But spending on veterans has increased every year Bush has been in office.[9] Some may suggest that the budget has not gone up quickly *enough,* but there is no objective definition of a "priority." This sort of disagreement is hardly evidence that a politician's statement was misleading.

Rather than bickering over what counts as a priority or calling every broken pledge a lie, we need a different standard for political dishonesty. A better approach is to judge public officials' words against the known facts. We should focus on what the President and his top aides knew or should have known to be false or misleading at the time they made a public statement. By that standard, George W. Bush has been extraordinarily deceptive about public policy issues.

SETTING A NEW STANDARD?

The cumulative effect of these tactics is to blur and distort the truth so much that honest discussion is impossible. After all, if we can't agree on whether it's day or night, there's no way to figure out what time it is. By the same token, if we can't agree on whether the Bush administration justified the invasion of Iraq by saying Saddam Hussein possessed weapons of mass destruction, it becomes impossible to assess whether those statements were accurate.

That is why, after nearly four years of constant deception on major issues of public policy, the President must be held account-able. If we fail to do so, Bush's approach to political communica-tions threatens to become the new standard for politics in America. From its campaigns for tax cuts to the debate over war with Iraq, this White House has invented a new politics of dishonesty.

BUSH'S WHITE HOUSE:
THE VANGUARD OF SPIN

> The permanent campaign is the political ideology of our age. It com-
> bines image-making with strategic calculation. Under the permanent
> campaign governing is turned into a perpetual campaign. Moreover, it
> remakes government into an instrument designed to sustain an elected
> official's public popularity. It is the engineering of consent with a
> vengeance.
>
> SIDNEY BLUMENTHAL, *The Permanent Campaign*[1]

In 1980, liberal journalist Sidney Blumenthal was among the first to recognize the modern phenomenon of the "permanent campaign," which has obliterated the distinction between campaigning and governing. Elected leaders now use campaign-style tactics from the day they take office to try to win public support for themselves and their policies.

Blumenthal's analysis was prescient. Shortly after the release of his book, Ronald Reagan's administration broke new ground with its message discipline and image control. Years later, Bill Clinton (whom Blumenthal served as an advisor) would advance the trend even further, continually battling Republicans in Congress for public opinion.

George W. Bush, however, has opened a new chapter in the history of American politics. He has developed a communications strategy of unprecedented scope and sophistication centered on tactics borrowed from the world of public relations. These include emotional language designed to provoke gut-level reactions, slanted statistics that are difficult for casual listeners to interpret, and ambiguous statements that imply what Bush does not want to state outright. In his continual use of these tactics to mislead the public about his policies, Bush has escalated the war for public opinion, giving birth to what could be called a permanent campaign of policy disinformation.

In a democracy, such dishonesty about public policy is a fundamental betrayal of the public trust. Without accurate information about the reasons for and effects of proposed government policies, citizens can't reasonably assess the actions that officials are taking on their behalf. These public statements are critical to our ability to hold leaders accountable. Over and over again, George W. Bush has tried to subvert this process with a vast array of falsehoods, half-truths, and misleading implications that are straight out of the public relations playbook.

PRESIDENTS AND THE POWER OF PR

The modern presidency is largely defined in rhetorical terms, particularly those memorable moments that become embedded in the collective consciousness. John F. Kennedy's inaugural address in 1961, in which he said, "Ask not what your country can do for you—ask what you can do for your country," and Ronald Reagan's challenge to Soviet leader Mikhail Gorbachev in West Berlin during the Cold War to "tear down this wall!" helped define their presidencies. On the other hand, Richard Nixon, who resigned in shame after the exposure of the Watergate scandal, is remembered for saying "I am not a crook."

Presidents famously have the power to command national attention by manning the "bully pulpit" and demanding action from Congress on their legislative agenda, a style of leadership Theodore Roosevelt introduced in 1904.[2] But the bully pulpit has a dark side—the increasingly intensive use of PR tactics to manipulate political discourse.

The story begins in the early twentieth century, when the Progressive movement gave rise to a new model of informed public debate. As a national press took shape, politicians, corporations, and interest groups started to communicate directly with the American people through the media on a regular basis. This prompted the rise of a new class of public relations professionals dedicated to shaping news coverage and influencing the views of the public using social scientific methods.

Once presidents began to make direct appeals to the public, they quickly adopted the methods of PR. In 1917, Woodrow Wilson formed the U.S. Committee on Public Information to marshal public support for World War I. Unlike most previous public relations initiatives, the CPI devoted extensive effort to exploiting the emotional power of images using movies, posters, and other visual media.[3] Its success in building public support for the war spurred an emerging awareness of the power of PR and helped train a generation of practitioners.[4]

Walter Lippmann, a prominent newspaper columnist, was among the first to recognize the threat PR posed to democracy.

Lippmann believed that people are vulnerable to manipulation, arguing that they are primarily driven by emotion and unconscious forces, dependent on stereotypes, and limited in their ability to understand the world. "As a result of psychological research, coupled with the modern means of communication, the practice of democracy has turned a corner," he wrote in his book *Public Opinion,* adding that "Persuasion has become a self-conscious art and a regular organ of popular government."[5] This statement would prove to be prophetic.

PR experts like Edward Bernays had a disturbingly similar vision, though they sought to manipulate the public rather than protect it. Bernays, an ex-CPI employee, applied the lessons of wartime propaganda to domestic politics with tremendous success. In his book *Propaganda,* he wrote that "The conscious and intelligent manipulation of the organized habits and opinions of the masses is an important element in democratic society," displaying characteristic contempt for popular rule.[6]

Though PR never became as all-powerful as either Bernays or Lippmann might have imagined, politicians were quick to put such techniques to work in domestic politics after the war. In 1920, Warren Harding was elected to the presidency with the assistance of Albert Lasker, an advertising whiz known in part for his work promoting Van Camp canned pork and beans. Lasker helped direct Harding's "front-porch campaign" (conducted, literally, from his front porch) and made unprecedented use of film and photography to promote the future president. For instance, after footage of Harding golfing became a political liability, Lasker decided to build an association between the candidate and baseball by staging an exhibition game featuring the Chicago Cubs. Harding threw the first three pitches of the game and then gave a political speech wearing a Cubs uniform.[7]

The first public relations presidency, however, belonged to Franklin Delano Roosevelt. FDR, who described radio as helping to "restore direct contact between the masses and their chosen leaders," appealed directly to public opinion on a regular basis through broadcast addresses, including his famous "fireside chats." He also cultivated the Washington press corps, carefully exploited photography and newsreels, employed a number of publicity agents at New Deal government agencies to help promote his administration, and was the first president to study public opinion polling.[8] FDR's positive image today is partly a reflection of the communications savvy he displayed during his time in office, which helped him to win re-election three times.

Television changed the PR equation in politics. A turning point was the nationally televised debate between presidential candidates John F. Kennedy and Richard Nixon on September 26, 1960, which the haggard-looking Nixon was judged to have lost due to the contrast with the more telegenic Kennedy. Once in office, JFK held frequent televised press conferences to take advantage of his command of the medium and was also the first president to make polling a routine part of governing from the White House.[9] Communications expertise had become part of the job description.

Nixon learned from his loss to Kennedy in 1960 and hired H. R. Haldeman, a former advertising executive, to orchestrate television coverage during his successful 1968 presidential campaign.[10] Once elected, Nixon created the White House Office of Communications to coordinate his administration's efforts to shape the news, granted few interviews to the press, and put together the White House Television Office to stage media events.[11] He also introduced a series of new PR techniques, including a poll-driven "line of the day" coordinated across the administration as well as systematic efforts to bypass the Washington press and communicate directly with local and regional outlets.[12] As his aide Charles Colson later said, Nixon had "a fetish about wanting to try to dominate the news from the government."[13]

Ronald Reagan built on Nixon's approach, becoming the first president to exploit the full power of modern public relations, including visual imagery and poll-tested language, to shape public opinion and media coverage. The combination was extremely successful in pressuring Congress to pass Reagan's budget and tax cut after he took office. "[F]or the first time in any presidency," Reagan advisor David Gergen noted, "we molded a communications policy around our legislative strategy."[14] This integration of communication and legislative tactics developed into a standard part of the modern White House.

Reagan Deputy Chief of Staff Michael Deaver was especially perceptive in his understanding of the importance of visual imagery. As he said later, "What we did was strategize for periods of time what we wanted the story to be and created visuals to go with that story. I don't think television coverage will ever be the same."[15] Deaver frequently placed the president in front of backdrops designed to reinforce his intended message, while keeping the press at a distance and controlling the flow of information from the executive branch. When CBS correspondent Lesley Stahl ran a segment critical of Reagan's campaign, saying his photo opportunities contradicted his policy proposals, she expected complaints from the White House. Instead, Deaver thanked her, reportedly saying, "Lesley, when you're showing four-and-a-half minutes of great pictures of Ronald Reagan, no one listens to what you say."[16] The powerful visuals dwarfed the impact of news coverage even when it was intended to be critical.

More disturbingly, Reagan's administration employed propaganda tactics in the most sophisticated government effort to manipulate public opinion during the Cold War. In 1983, Reagan created a so-called "public diplomacy" program to build support for anti-Communist policies in Latin America that was shaped by the director of the Central Intelligence Agency, William J. Casey, and coordinated by a former CIA propaganda specialist.[17] The effort was concentrated in the State Department's Latin American Office of Public Diplomacy. Employing six Army specialists in psychological warfare, it planted fictitious leaks allegedly from U.S. intelligence with the media and placed op-eds written by government staff under the names of outside experts and political figures.[18] In 1987, the office was closed after the Comptroller General found that some of its actions constituted "prohibited, covert propaganda activities" that used State Department funding for "publicity or propaganda purposes" not authorized by Congress.[19]

George H. W. Bush largely eschewed polling, scripted rhetoric, and other PR staples while in office, but his administration's campaign for the 1991 Gulf War included a number of questionable tactics.[20] In the most egregious case, the Pentagon claimed that thousands of Iraqi troops and tanks were positioned in Kuwait near the border of Saudi Arabia, threatening a crucial ally. However, satellite photographs obtained from commercial sources revealed virtually no Iraqi presence in the area, a discrepancy that the White House never addressed.[21]

The Pentagon also tightly restricted press coverage of the war, using briefings and visual imagery to shape coverage. For example, it distributed video of precision-guided missiles hitting targets and Patriot missiles appearing to intercept Iraqi Scuds fired at Israel. However, only about 10 percent of U.S. bombs dropped in the war were precision-guided, and Patriot missiles reportedly destroyed incoming Scuds less than 10 percent of the time.[22] Once again, the powerful visuals overwhelmed the actual facts of the matter.

It was Bill Clinton, however, who first systematically integrated public relations tactics into every facet of the presidency. As a candidate, Clinton defeated Bush, Sr. in 1992 with a media-savvy campaign that prided itself on rapid response. After setbacks during the first months of his term in office, Clinton moved to an aggressive, campaign-style mode that prevailed for the rest of his presidency, using so-called "war rooms" inside the White House. He and his staff polled extensively to determine what rationales and language would be most effective in promoting his policies, tightly controlled the message coming from the White House and its supporters, and responded quickly to political opponents and the media to make sure the administration's viewpoint was included in every news story.

In particular, Clinton's push for health care reform in 1993–1994 was guided by public relations concerns, including poll-driven decisions to highlight a "health security card" and use the word "alliances" to describe so-called "health insurance purchasing cooperatives." Though passage of the bill was expected to be a difficult fight, Clinton's aides told scholars on a not-for-attribution basis that the administration believed it would be able to "lead public opinion" and thereby pressure Congress.[23]

The Clinton administration also made heavy use of public relations tactics to fight off political scandals. Officials parsed the meanings of words in disingenuous ways to protect the president, as when spokesman Mike McCurry appeared to deny during a White House press briefing that Clinton knew former advisor Dick Morris had an illegitimate child. McCurry was later forced to admit that his boss had learned about the child during the previous year.[24] Clinton himself, of course, took the same approach during the Monica Lewinsky scandal, saying he did not have "sexual relations" with the White House intern. And the White House employed a series of elaborate techniques for managing news about scandals, including the preemptive release of damaging documents.[25]

By the mid-1990s, both President Clinton and the Republican leadership were regularly deploying strategically chosen language and images to try to influence public opinion.[26] The White House polled extensively to determine what presidential initiatives to propose and what language to use in selling them to the public, even conducting a survey on the best place for the president to vacation.[27]

Meanwhile, public relations had grown to become a huge industry offering every sort of communication strategy imaginable to corporations and political groups, including crisis management, pressure campaigns designed to undermine critics, and fake grassroots lobbying campaigns known as "astroturf." The goals of these methods are clear. As the website of Burson-Marsteller, one of the world's largest public relations firms, once stated, "Perceptions are real. They color what we see . . . what we believe . . . how we behave. They can be managed . . . to motivate behavior . . . to create positive business results [ellipses in original]."[28]

It is these perceptions that politicians hope to manipulate. With campaigning and governing now virtually indistinguishable, PR has become integral to the conduct of politics.

THE BRAVE NEW WORLD OF PUBLIC DEBATE

While many assume that politicians use polls to follow public opinion obsessively, the opposite is true in most cases. Politicians and interest groups generally use polls to aid their efforts to shape the views of the public, especially as national politics has become more polarized and ideological. Opinion leadership is now the name of the game in Washington.

However, the conventional wisdom that the public is quick to change its opinions in response to persuasive messages is wrong. Collective public opinion on major policy issues is usually quite stable.[29] Because of this, generating support for proposals based on reasoned appeals is difficult. Instead, the more effective strategy for politicians has proven to be associating their preferred policies with values that the public already holds. For example, when debating campaign finance reform, conservatives frame the issue in terms of freedom of speech and liberals link it to the influence of big business on politics.

By the 1990s, these appeals began to incorporate the worst aspects of modern public relations techniques. PR strategies for manipulating perceptions are designed to make and break mental associations, often at a nonrational level. In the most benign cases, public relations experts use positive images or testimonials to portray an organization or product in a flattering light. On a more insidious level, they frequently employ tactics designed to simulate rational argument, developing a strategic message and manufacturing a set of "facts" to support it, even though they may be misleading or logically unrelated to the message. Often, the words themselves are tortured in Orwellian fashion, such as the sewage industry's efforts to rename sludge, the leftover material from sewage treatment plants, as "biosolids."[30] When words themselves are chosen for strategic advantage, the possibility of debating in good faith is lost.

As a result of the influence of PR, politicians now regularly select public rationales that they think will sell rather than discussing the true motivations for policy proposals. They manufacture factoids to support a chosen message regardless of their truthfulness, use strategically crafted language to make irrational appeals, and imply claims that they cannot prove or are reluctant to state explicitly. In this way, politicians can appear to stay within the accepted boundaries of debate, yet manipulate the press and the public. These tactics are the vanguard of twenty-first-century political spin—and President Bush has made their use in office routine.

THE BUSH SPIN MACHINE

The Bush White House features the most sophisticated communications apparatus in American political history. The idea that all politicians spin fails to do justice to this machine, which has repeatedly shattered expectations and crushed its rivals since Bush took office in 2001.

The team was initially led by Karen Hughes, a former reporter who worked for Bush in the Texas governor's office. Hughes was known for her relentless message discipline (reporters called her "Nurse Ratched" after the character in the book *One Flew Over the Cuckoo's Nest*), and during her fifteen months in the White House, she exerted near-total control over the administration's communications and media strategy.[31]

One insider report on her influence comes from conservative journalist David Frum, who worked as a speechwriter under Hughes. Frum recounts how Hughes insisted that Bush use softer, female-friendly language, such as "employers" instead of "business," "moms and dads" in place of "parents," and "tax relief" rather than "tax cuts." She also disliked verbs, Frum wrote, because they "conveyed action, not feeling" and "[a]bove all things, she hated the word 'but,' a word that suggested harsh choices, conflict, even confrontation."[32] Hughes, the prototypical PR operative, systematically shaped the language of the administration down to the smallest level of detail in order to enhance Bush's appeal.

After Hughes' departure from the White House (she continued to consult for the administration from her home in Texas), Dan Bartlett, a long-serving Bush loyalist, assumed responsibility for White House communications. Both he and Hughes have worked closely with Karl Rove, a former political consultant who serves as the chief White House liaison to conservative groups and directs the Office of Strategic Initiatives, which conducts long-term political planning.

The daily voice of the administration was originally Ari Fleischer, who served as White House press secretary until May 2003. Dubbed the "flack out of hell" for his previous work on Capitol Hill, Fleischer was undoubtedly the most stubborn and combative press secretary in modern history. His particular talent for answering questions only when he could repeat his talking points helped ensure that Bush's message got into the press day after day. When Fleischer resigned, he was succeeded by his deputy Scott McClellan, an understated Texan who has proven to be nearly as unyielding in his spin as his predecessor, though far less effective.

The talented production team responsible for staging Bush's appearances for television has included Scott Sforsza, a former producer for ABC News; Bob DeServi, who worked as a cameraman for NBC; and Greg Jenkins, an ex–Fox News producer.[33] In her book *Ten Minutes from Normal*, Hughes describes Sforsza's hire as crucial, saying it was "perhaps the best decision of all" in setting up the White House communications office. She writes, "My own days in television had reminded me of the truth of the adage 'a picture is worth a thousand words,' and that has proven true time and again as Scott creates powerful backdrops to showcase the President and his policies."[34] The trio's combined expertise in television news has been a powerful asset for the White House.

The administration has also staffed key executive branch agencies with an all-star team of political operatives who synchronize their daily message with the White House. Chief of Staff Andrew Card emphasized this coordination. "I make sure our communications team is not just a team in the White House," he said. "It is a communications team for the executive branch of government."[35] The lineup has included Victoria Clarke, press secretary for the 1992 campaign of George H. W. Bush, at the Department of Defense; Mindy Tucker, the press secretary for the 2000 Bush-Cheney campaign, at the Department of Justice; and Barbara Comstock, the former head of research at the Republican National Committee, as Tucker's successor at Justice. The administration also placed public relations professionals in charge of shaping international perceptions of the United States after the September 11, 2001 terrorist attacks, including Charlotte Beers, a top advertising executive who served as Undersecretary for Public Diplomacy and Public Affairs at the Department of State from October 2001 to March 2003.

This focus on the PR skills of appointees extended beyond communications operatives. In 2001, Mitch Daniels, a former political operative and pharmaceutical executive, was appointed director of the Office of Management and Budget, a position he held from January 2001 through June 2003. His selection was a surprise because Daniels lacked expertise in the details of the federal budget. He explained his rather different set of credentials to the *Wall Street Journal* in August 2001: "To the extent I bring anything . . . to this job, maybe it's an ability to think about how a product, whether it's Prozac or a president's proposal, is marketed [ellipsis in original]." [36]

Similarly, when John Snow was chosen to replace Paul O'Neill as Treasury Secretary, administration officials told the *Washington Post* that he was picked primarily for what the paper described as his "ability to communicate Bush's policy clearly on television and Capitol Hill," a skill that O'Neill lacked.[37]

The head of the Office of Management and Budget and the Secretary of the Treasury are two of the most important policy officials in the United States government. In the Bush White House, however, their primary role was advocating for the President's agenda.

MANAGING IMAGE AND INFORMATION:
WHAT BUSH LEARNED FROM REAGAN

The Bush White House has borrowed and improved upon two key strategies from the Reagan administration: controlling the flow of information and creating powerful visual imagery. Michael Deaver, Reagan's former deputy chief of staff and image manager, described conversations with Bush advisor Karl Rove "over a period of years, a couple of years" to ABC News in 2001, saying they focused on "strategic message development and tactics on getting that message across visually and hammering it home." [38] Clearly, Rove and the White House staff understand the approach that Deaver pioneered—the former Reagan advisor has since called Bush's administration "the most disciplined White House in history" and said, "They understand the visual as well as anybody ever has." [39] As a result, the administration has been able to generate a substantial amount of positive coverage.

The White House is open about its focus on message-driven

imagery. "We pay particular attention to not only what the President says but what the American people see," Bartlett told the *New York Times* in 2003. "Americans are leading busy lives, and sometimes they don't have the opportunity to read a story or listen to an entire broadcast. But if they can have an instant understanding of what the President is talking about by seeing sixty seconds of television, you accomplish your goals as communicators." [40]

This attention to visuals has taken two forms. First, the Bush White House has a special flair for elaborately staged events, such as the President's jet landing on the aircraft carrier USS *Abraham Lincoln* declaring the end to major combat operations in Iraq. Sforsza reportedly spent days planning the event, creating the perfect lighting and backdrop for television camera shots, including the now-infamous "Mission Accomplished" banner. On another occasion, the administration placed three rented barges of powerful stadium lights at the foot of the Statue of Liberty to create a dramatic visual behind Bush for his speech on Ellis Island commemorating the one-year anniversary of September 11. White House handlers even aligned Bush's head with those of the presidents who are carved into Mount Rushmore during a speech there. [41]

The administration devotes similar attention to the details of lower-profile appearances. Sforsza specializes in made-for-TV backdrops repeating a word or phrase that the administration wants to highlight, an innovation borrowed from Deaver. Anything that distracts from this message is carefully excluded. In one instance, when Bush gave a speech at a Missouri trucking company, volunteers used stickers to cover up labels on boxes around him saying they were "Made in China." Behind him, the White House put up a backdrop with images of boxes that said "Made in U.S.A." [42] Television viewers, of course, were none the wiser.

Like Reagan, Bush has also practiced tight message control. The

White House understands that disciplined repetition of a series of talking points is the best way to control its coverage in the media. Members of the administration engage in detailed long-term communications planning to guide this effort. Before Bush even entered office, for example, Rove had developed a 180-day plan that guided the President's first months in the White House, including his communications strategy.[43]

These plans help coordinate a so-called "message of the day," which gives Bush enormous leverage over the media. "The idea is to give the press one thing to cover," said one unnamed White House aide.[44] As *Washington Post* White House correspondent Dana Milbank said, the administration develops "talking points that they email to friends and everyone says exactly the same thing. You go through the effort of getting Karl Rove on the phone and he'll say exactly the same thing as Scott McClellan."[45] Such monomaniacal devotion to the official message gives the White House press corps little else to report.

Bush's "economic forum" held in August 2002 illustrates the administration's disciplined efforts to control its public image. The heavily stage-managed event—purportedly an open discussion of the nation's economy—was actually an homage to Bush and his policies. According to the *Washington Post,* the "rigorously screened" group of attendees "lauded Bush's policies and urged him to pursue his previously announced proposals," even reading speeches prepared by supportive interest groups. In fact, as the *Post* reported, the forum was so carefully scripted that "White House officials even had talking points about their talking points. 'We're really pushing that this isn't a PR deal,'" one official laughably claimed.[46] Yet this simulated news received a great deal of coverage from the national press.

In some cases, Bush has also gone further than recent predecessors in politicizing official government communications. For example, after the 2001 tax cut, the Internal Revenue Service mailed letters to taxpayers informing them whether they would get a refund. The mailings included controversial political-style language stating that the tax cut "provides long-term tax relief for all Americans who pay income taxes." Those taxpayers receiving a refund got a version that also praised the law for providing "immediate tax relief in 2001," language that was omitted for those who did not receive a refund.[47] It's unlikely that this difference was a coincidence.

THE WAR ROOM STYLE AND CLINTONESQUE LANGUAGE

After pledging during the 2000 campaign to "restore honor and dignity to the White House," a direct attack on Clinton's conduct while in office, Bush and his team are loath to admit that their tactics have anything in common with those of their immediate predecessors.[48] It is clear, however, that they have mirrored the Clinton White House in their development of an integrated, round-the-clock communications infrastructure and heavy use of strategic language that has been tested in polls or developed by PR professionals.

One administration insider has already admitted as much. John DiIulio, a Bush aide who headed the Office for Faith-Based and Community Initiatives, wrote a long letter to *Esquire* reporter Ron Suskind describing a July 2001 senior staff retreat in which "an explicit discussion ensued concerning how to emulate more strongly the Clinton White House's press, communications, and rapid-response media relations."[49] In this sense, Bush actually aspired to meet the standard for spin that was set by Clinton. (After criticism from Fleischer, DiIulio later retracted his statements, calling them "groundless and baseless.") [50]

In addition, the administration consults public opinion surveys despite Bush's pledge on the campaign trail not to rely on polls as Clinton had.[51] The President has created an extremely low profile operation—a Republican National Committee official working with Rove supervises the polling, insulating Bush from direct contact, and results are held closely inside the West Wing. The exact amount of polling conducted by the White House and the way the results are used is unknown. In an early analysis, *Washington Monthly* estimated that Bush spent about half as much on polling in his first year as President Clinton did in 1993—approximately $1 million versus $2 million for Clinton.[52] But in the fourth year of his term, an anonymous Bush advisor told the *New York Times* that the administration had used polls and focus groups to decide that an apology for previous actions would be a mistake—a classic example of the sort of poll-driven decision Bush had foresworn.[53]

Another indicator of the influence of PR comes from the administration's language itself, which is obviously shaped by polls and strategic calculation. During a single May 2001 press briefing, for instance, Press Secretary Ari Fleischer called Bush's energy plan "comprehensive" or suggested the need for a "comprehensive" energy plan twenty times.[54] The White House also frequently gives PR-influenced titles to major proposals and actions, including its "Clear Skies" and "Healthy Forests" initiatives (on air pollution and forest management, respectively) and "Operation Enduring Freedom" in Afghanistan, which was followed by "Operation Iraqi Freedom." By repeating such phrases, the administration hopes to dominate the very terms of the debate—who, for example, could oppose "Iraqi freedom" or "clear skies"?

BUSH'S CHARACTERISTIC BRAND OF POLICY DISHONESTY

Although the origins of George W. Bush's deceptive tactics date back to his predecessors, the Bush White House's dishonesty is ultimately different, and more insidious, than that of Reagan or Clinton. Reagan was known for his use of apocryphal stories and false claims made off the cuff. Clinton famously told the country that he "did not have sexual relations" with Monica Lewinsky—one of the most bald-faced lies told by a politician in recent memory—and misrepresented his relationship with her under oath. When it came to matters of substance, however, Reagan and Clinton did not attempt to mislead the public about the policies they were proposing on the same scale or with the same sophistication as Bush does.

Bush uses five major strategies to spin the press and the public, ranging from outright falsehood to subtle half-truths and suggestive language. None are truly original, of course, but no other modern president has used them so frequently or in such effective combination. As a result, it is now much more difficult for the public to understand the relevant facts in current policy debates and to hold the President accountable for his actions.

First, Bush has made a few claims that are factually incorrect, such as the "trifecta" story discussed earlier and his false assertion that weapons of mass destruction had been found in Iraq.[55] However, such statements are relatively few and far between.

More frequently, Bush and his aides have used unrepresentative examples that are presented as typical. These include "tax families" and assertions about the "average" benefits of his tax cut proposals. In both cases, the claims were technically true but did not accurately represent the benefits most taxpayers could expect to receive.

Bush also often makes claims that rely on questionable information or offers assertions that go far beyond the available evidence. For example, the administration asserted that aluminum tubes purchased by Iraq could only be used to enrich uranium for nuclear weapons, ignoring significant debate in the intelligence community about their purpose.[56] The President and his aides made similarly controversial claims about economic policy and global warming that were contradicted by the administration's own analysts and other experts. Because such claims can be difficult for journalists to evaluate, however, they often receive little attention from the press.

In the months after September 11, the Bush administration used another approach—attacking those who raised questions in an attempt to quash or discredit legitimate dissent. The President and other White House officials suggested several times that opponents' views were illegitimate or that they aided the nation's enemies. Politicians have always tried to associate their opponents with unpopular causes, perhaps most notably during the Cold War. But rarely have the president or his aides been willing to go so far as to accuse their rivals of helping the enemy during a time of war.

Perhaps the most troubling—and most effective—tactic has been President Bush's strategic use of language to imply controversial conclusions or outright untruths he wouldn't dare state publicly. Using this public relations strategy, Bush and his aides have suggested things that are at best unprovable, such as Iraqi involvement in the September 11 attacks, while still being able to plausibly deny they did so when challenged. To truly understand Bush's assault on honesty, you have to look at the implications of what he says, not just the words themselves.

POLITICS AND PR UNITE

George W. Bush has created a White House that draws on techniques pioneered by Reagan and Clinton but goes far beyond them
in making unprecedented use of professionalized, strategic dishonesty to sell his proposals. His exploitation of these tactics has
become so routine that it threatens to make dishonest policy campaigns the norm in American politics.

Yet Bush would not have succeeded if the media had fulfilled its
responsibilities. To understand why these tactics have been so effective, we must examine why the press—the institution charged with
monitoring the actions of government and providing political information to the public—has not effectively challenged the White
House.

★ 2 ★

FROM WATCHDOG TO LAPDOG:
HOW BUSH HAS EXPLOITED THE PRESS

The press is the primary institution connecting the public to national politics. Americans have little direct interaction with politicians; much of what they know about government policy and the people who make it comes from reading or watching news accounts.

The media, however, serve not only as a source of information but as the primary check on our public officials. Americans expect reporters to scrutinize the actions of politicians and government on their behalf—and they hope that the vigilance of the press will serve as a deterrent not only to illegal or unethical behavior, but to dishonesty as well. By acting as both information providers and watchdogs, journalists are critical to the health of American democracy.

The Bush White House has largely succeeded in undermining both of these functions. The administration makes little secret of its disdain for the press, going so far as to openly question the legitimacy of the media's role in American politics. As White House Chief of Staff Andrew Card told the *New Yorker,* "They don't represent the public any more than other people do. In our democracy, the people who represent the public stood for election. . . . I don't believe [the press has] a check-and-balance function."[1] Rather than viewing journalists as performing a public service, the White House sees them as a hostile force chasing the next headline regardless of fairness or accuracy.

This viewpoint guides the administration's approach to relations with the media. Modern presidents have always complained about news coverage and wished they could bypass the filter imposed by reporters. But George W. Bush's disdain for the press goes further than any president since Richard Nixon. By denying the need for democratic accountability in word and deed, the White House has subverted the notion that the government should have to answer for its actions and statements through any mechanism other than the ballot box.

The Bush administration has been able to get away with this in large part because public esteem for the media has declined significantly since the Watergate scandal. Like the White House, most Americans now see the press as more of a special interest than a democratic watchdog, allowing the Bush administration to manipulate it virtually without consequence.

One would expect that reporters would return the favor by treating Bush with corresponding hostility. For his first years in office, however, the opposite was the case. Bush's affable personality, which charmed much of the press corps during the 2000 presidential campaign, and a general deference to the President in the wake of September 11 helped to protect him. Yet these explanations miss the most important aspect of Bush's relations with the press: his ability to exploit its blind spots and structural problems. More than any other factor, this strategy has prevented journalists from exposing his deceptions and falsehoods.

PRESIDENTS AND THE PRESS

The media first emerged as a muscular watchdog of the government in the late 1960s and early 1970s, particularly during the Vietnam War. Reporters came to see their job as providing a check on powerful leaders and institutions.

The Watergate scandal proved to be the apex of this trend. Richard Nixon had always harbored a deep distrust of the media, and his administration fought the press for public opinion throughout his presidency. He went even further behind the scenes, ordering IRS audits of journalists, tapping their phones, and directing the FBI to investigate CBS reporter Daniel Schorr.[2] When the *Washington Post* and other papers discovered that the White House had been involved in illegal activities, including a break-in at Democratic National Committee headquarters, it set in motion a crisis that led to Nixon's resignation. By bringing down a presidential administration, the press demonstrated that it was a powerful institution in Washington. This crusading coverage also spawned a good deal of resentment against journalists, however, particularly among those who felt that coverage of Nixon and the Vietnam War was biased and unfair.

As competition from cable television, the Internet, and other outlets has increased, the media has moved toward a focus on entertaining stories, known as "soft news."[3] In particular, cable news channels, with their emphasis on speed and saturation coverage of major stories, have helped move the press in this direction.

In terms of political news, these trends toward speed and entertainment have translated to wall-to-wall coverage of scandals and dramatic confrontations, such as the Senate hearings on Clarence

Thomas' nomination to the Supreme Court and Bill Clinton's affair with Monica Lewinsky. The slightest whiff of scandal sends reporters into a frenzy. This strategy can drive up ratings; it ultimately decreases the public's respect for journalism.

The question facing modern presidents is how to handle a press corps with an endless need for compelling stories and controversy. Ronald Reagan's administration carefully restricted reporters' access to the president while creating dramatic photo opportunities and playing up Reagan's amiable personality. This strategy largely succeeded. Reagan Deputy Chief of Staff Michael Deaver stated that until the Iran-Contra scandal, his boss had "enjoyed the most generous treatment by the press of any president in the postwar era."[4]

By contrast, the press quickly turned against Bill Clinton, who spent almost his entire time in office enmeshed in scandal and controversy. To manage the media, Clinton created an elaborate White House operation modeled on his campaign war room. Though this hardly put an end to negative coverage, Clinton's consistently high approval ratings after 1996 proved that politicians could defy the press and survive.

By the end of Clinton's term, public regard for journalists had dropped precipitously. The media's antagonistic relationships with Reagan, Clinton, and other presidents helped feed the perception that the press is politically biased and prone to inaccuracy. Between 1985 and 1999, the number of Americans saying "news organizations get the facts straight" dropped from 55 to 37 percent, while the number saying the media are "politically biased in their reporting" rose from 45 to 56 percent.[5] The press's sensationalism and fascination with personal scandals had taken its toll.

HOW BUSH EXPLOITS THE WEAKNESSES
OF THE MEDIA

Bush's White House has broken new ground in its press relations strategy, exploiting the weaknesses and failings of the political media more systematically than any of its predecessors. The administration combines tight message discipline and image management—Reagan's trademarks—with the artful use of half- or partial truths and elaborate news management—Clinton's specialties—in a combination that is near-lethal for the press.

These techniques are effective precisely because they prey on four key weaknesses of contemporary journalism. First and foremost, reporters are constrained by the norm of objectivity, which frequently causes them to avoid evaluating the truth of politicians' statements. In addition, because reporters are dependent upon the White House for news, the administration can shape the coverage it receives by restricting the flow of information to the press. The media are also vulnerable to political pressure and reprisal, which the Bush White House has aggressively dished out against critical journalists. Finally, the press's unending pursuit of scandal and entertaining news often blinds it to serious issues of public policy.

By aggressively deploying its communications strategy against a media establishment wary of giving credence to charges of liberal bias and fearful of challenging a self-described "war president" after September 11, Bush has successfully dissembled about public policy on a far more consistent basis than his predecessors. Do President Bush's tax cuts primarily benefit the wealthy or the middle class? Was there clear evidence that Iraq was attempting to produce nuclear weapons or was connected to al Qaeda? What role have tax cuts played in the recent growth of federal budget deficits? There are answers to all of these questions, but the media are frequently reluctant to point out the misinformation in Bush's statements about such controversial policy issues. By using every advantage it can muster against the media, the Bush administration has dedicated itself to transforming the press from a watchdog to a mouthpiece for its spin.

THE WEAKNESSES OF "OBJECTIVE" JOURNALISM

The gold standard of American journalism has long been "objective" reporting. Journalists at news outlets are expected to present the public with an unbiased account of the facts rather than their own views on the issue at hand. This is a laudable goal, but the expectation that reporters will present both sides of the story too often translates into the mistaken belief that they should refuse to sort out competing factual claims. This is the media's greatest weakness in dealing with political dishonesty.

While the press generally does a reasonable job of pointing out the most blatant instances of political deception, reporters attempting to remain objective often fail to evaluate claims that are misleading but not obviously wrong. This is especially true when it comes to politicians who are generally seen as honest. As a result, Bush has frequently gotten away with misleading claims and language. Perversely, this strategy of dissembling and denial leaves journalists in the position of appearing to be "taking sides" if they point out deception.

Objectivity emerged as the guiding principle of news journalism in the late nineteenth and early twentieth century. As the press moved from open partisanship toward professionalized news reporting, the principle that reporters should remain neutral about the subjects they covered became the norm. The American Society of Newspaper Editors codified "objectivity" in 1923 as reporting that is "free from opinion or bias of any kind," setting the tone for the news media for the rest of the century.[6]

The idea of objectivity has done much to improve journalism, but it also has serious flaws. It is obvious to any observer that news stories are inherently subjective. Reporters cannot present every fact they observe or gather in their reporting; they decide what is "news" and focus their story on that angle. Likewise, decisions about what to cover and what not to cover are guided not by clear standards but by the decisions of individual editors and reporters.

Despite signs that some journalists recognize the problems with the ideal—the Society of Professional Journalists removed "objectivity" from its code of ethics in 1996—it still holds sway over most of the profession.[7] Journalists continue to suggest that objectivity, if not completely attainable, can be approximated in practice: 79 percent of national print journalists and 80 percent of national TV and radio journalists polled by the Pew Research Center in 1999 said that it was possible to create a "true and accurate account of an event that most journalists could agree on," and 72 and 69 percent, respectively, said that it was possible "to develop a systematic method to cover events in a disinterested and fair way."[8]

The pressure to remain objective frequently reduces reporters to little more than stenographers transcribing the latest spin from politicians. Rather than sort out competing factual claims, they typically give equal play to both sides—even if one is misleading. This "he said/she said" form of journalism allows politicians to enter deceptive statements into the public record and leaves citizens with little or no basis to evaluate the truth of the matter at hand.

Coverage of the debate over the war in Iraq provides a particularly telling example of this sort of thinking. *New York Times* reporter Judith Miller, who has come under fire for her generally credulous reporting about the Bush administration's case for war, told Michael Massing of the *New York Review of Books,* "My job isn't to assess the government's information and be an independent intelligence analyst myself. My job is to tell readers of the *New York Times* what the government thought about Iraq's arsenal." (Miller later claimed in a letter to the editor that she had actually stated, "I could not be an independent intelligence agency." Massing disputed that claim, stating he read Miller her quote for approval and the reporter signed off.) [9]

In a May 12, 2004, interview on MSNBC's *Hardball,* veteran journalist Jim Lehrer, the host of PBS's *The NewsHour with Jim Lehrer,* expressed similar deference to the claims of government leaders. When asked by host Chris Matthews whether journalists had explored the issue of how Iraqis would respond to Americans running their country after the war, he responded, "The word 'occupation,' keep in mind, Chris, was never mentioned in the run-up to the war. It was 'liberation.' This was a war of liberation, not a war of occupation. So as a consequence, those of us in journalism never even looked at the issue of occupation." When Matthews asked why reporters weren't able to go beyond the Bush administration's framing of the war as one of "liberation," the answer was astonishing: "It just didn't occur to us," Lehrer said. "We weren't smart enough to do it."

In fact, Miller and Lehrer's job (and the job of other reporters) is to go beyond government claims and uncover the truth. Their statements demonstrate an all-too-typical reluctance to sort out the facts for readers and a deference to authority that is troubling coming from any reporter, let alone two at prestigious national news outlets.

George W. Bush has exploited the media's reluctance to dispute presidential claims through his habitual use of misleading technical or partial truths. This sort of spin is hardly unique to Bush, but he and members of his administration have made it their trademark. Examples include unrepresentative "average" benefits he has repeatedly suggested his tax cuts would offer; the dubious assertion that the 2001 tax cut reduced the deficit; and strategically ambiguous language, such as the links he implicitly drew between Saddam Hussein and the September 11 attacks. Constrained by the need to maintain the appearance of impartiality, it is difficult for reporters to point out that such claims are heavily disputed or misleading without appearing to be editorializing. As a result, all three of the claims just listed drew little critical attention.

The White House also preempts critical reporting by almost always refusing to concede error. Bush and his aides understand that political reporters are often reluctant to report on deception without some corroboration from the administration. For instance, the President received the harshest coverage of his first three years in office after White House officials stated in July 2003 that the claim that Iraq was seeking uranium in Africa should not have been included in that year's State of the Union address.

The media feeding frenzy that followed apparently taught the administration a lesson. In February 2004, White House officials told the *Washington Post* it had been a mistake to back down on the uranium claim: "The admission of error, they say, made Bush appear weak and encouraged more skeptical coverage than if the White House had refused to budge." [10] Since the uproar, the Bush administration has refused to concede ground to reporters or critics on any but the most obvious misstatements.

Reporters' concern about appearing balanced has protected

Bush in other ways. First, journalists tend to vary the amount of scrutiny they give to factual claims depending on who is making the statements and who is contradicting them. One important factor is criticism from political allies, which often legitimizes continuing coverage of a story. For example, Democratic criticism of President Clinton's affair with Monica Lewinsky helped feed press coverage that was highly critical of his administration. By contrast, Bush benefited from a relatively united Republican Party and a divided Democratic Party during the first three years of his term. The absence of dissent within his party made it far more difficult to criticize the sort of subtle dishonesty that the Bush administration has regularly practiced.

In addition, reporters claiming to be objective are especially vulnerable to charges of media bias, even if many such allegations are trumped-up or bogus. Certainly, a substantial amount of reporting is unfair or slanted, but many bias critics have made a practice of manufacturing ideological attacks against reporters to advance their own causes. In the last twenty years, this sort of criticism has largely come from conservatives, though liberals are starting to play the game as well. After years of such attacks, many journalists have become unwilling to face the fallout that tough factual reporting can bring. This appears to be a factor in coverage of Bush, who made a show of publicly carrying *Bias,* a book by a former CBS reporter alleging a liberal slant in news coverage.

There is little question that these attacks can have a chilling effect on the willingness of journalists to produce stories critical of the administration. For example, *Washington Post* reporter Dana Priest told the *New York Review of Books* that when the paper ran articles examining parts of the Bush administration's case for war in Iraq, "We got tons of hate mail and threats, calling our patriotism into question."[11] By attacking the motivations of reporters, critics of media bias can undermine the media's willingness to scrutinize government action, particularly in a tense wartime atmosphere.

REPORTERS' DEPENDENCE ON THE WHITE HOUSE

The nature of the White House beat is that reporters depend on the officials they cover for access and information. If the administration decides to stonewall them, there is often little they can do. By controlling the flow of information available to the press, the White House can shape news coverage. Despite the media's tendency to focus on negative stories, the absence of damaging information usually preempts critical coverage and creates a news vacuum that reporters must fill. If they are offered nothing other than the White House's chosen message of the day, coverage tends to focus on that message.

To an even greater extent than Clinton or Reagan administration officials, Bush and his aides have taken advantage of this reality. Most importantly, they rarely leak to the press, often forcing journalists to repeat their message because there is no other news to report. The press depends on such leaks not just as a source of information about the administration, but to legitimize inquiry into the truthfulness of the White House's claims. Without these sources, critical stories wither on the vine.

As *Washington Post* reporter Dana Milbank said, "this White House has been remarkably good about keeping its internal deliberations under wraps, then announcing it with unified voice."[12] Without a steady diet of juicy tidbits about internal debates in the White House—something reporters feasted on during Clinton's term in office—reporters have had a much harder time pursuing critical stories.

The White House, with some justification, feels no remorse about refusing to dish to reporters. Chief of Staff Andrew Card summed up Bush's views to the *New Yorker,* telling Ken Auletta that "It's not our job to be sources" and "Our job is not to make your job easy."[13] This leak-prevention strategy has enabled Bush to avoid the sort of critical coverage that was prevalent during the Clinton administration.

The flip side of this (and one that is hardly unique to the Bush White House) is that the administration often makes news at strategically valuable times, forcing the press corps to cover relatively positive events or announcements in place of more damaging stories. The White House can also put out damning information when it will get the least attention. For example, knowing that Saturday papers have the lowest readership of any day of the week, it released a number of documents regarding Bush's Air National Guard service on a Friday afternoon.

Of course, the White House does provide more access to some reporters—those it expects will provide favorable coverage and help create positive storylines. The administration grants these journalists extensive interviews with Bush and senior officials, who provide vivid minute-by-minute accounts of major events that reflect the White House's preferred take on events. Two examples are Bob Woodward of the *Washington Post* and Bill Sammon of the *Washington Times,* both of whom wrote books in the aftermath of September 11 portraying the administration in a flattering light.[14] (Indeed, Woodward called the White House "more responsive" to him than any administration he has ever covered, and President Bush urged officials to cooperate on his next book.)[15]

The White House can also use reporters' need for access to control the message that they report down to the smallest detail.

Jonathan Weisman, an economics writer for the *Washington Post,* described his experience covering the Bush administration in a March 16, 2003 letter posted on the website of the Poynter Institute's James Romenesko. Weisman recounted how, in the process of writing a story about White House economic advisor Glenn Hubbard, he was forced to conduct an interview with an administration economist off the record. To use any statement made during the interview, he had to submit the quote to the press office, which would then approve its publication sourced to an unnamed White House official. As a result, Weisman ended up allowing the economist from whom he obtained the statement to alter the quote, a move the reporter came to regret. He said this had become "fairly standard practice" and concluded that "it is time for all of us to reconsider the way we cover the White House." Weisman's note speaks to the frustrations and compromises the Bush administration has forced on the press corps.

The administration also makes frequent use of background briefings, another tactic employed by previous administrations but taken to extremes under Bush. During these briefings, White House officials, whom reporters cannot identify by name, ostensibly speak with reporters more candidly than they might if they knew they would be named in print. The Bush administration has taken this practice and turned it on its head, frequently using background briefings as an occasion for the vacuous recitation of talking points. As one reporter asked an official after a particularly empty but upbeat briefing, "I'm just wondering what possible reason there is why all this isn't on the record?" [16] Even when administration officials are on background, their adherence to the White House message is unstinting, depriving the media of one more source of information. (In early 2004, both the *New York Times* and the *Washington Post* altered their policies on granting anonymity to sources because of perceptions that the practice was being abused.)

To fill the news vacuum, the Bush administration offers reporters an unending supply of carefully scripted talking points, a standard public relations tactic that the White House has elevated to an art. When talking points are all officials will repeat, it gives reporters literally nothing else to quote.

For instance, during the July 2003 controversy over Bush's claim that Iraq had attempted to obtain uranium from Africa, National Security Advisor Condoleezza Rice and her deputy Stephen Hadley pounded the spin point that the statement in question was only "sixteen words" long, repeating it six times each during an interview on CNN and a press briefing, respectively.[17] This focus on a scripted message often defeats reporters' attempts to provide coverage of topics other than administration talking points.

Two internal memos from the Treasury Department's public affairs staff to Secretary Paul O'Neill graphically illustrate the disciplined message that the administration tries to enforce.

First, to prepare O'Neill for a February 2001 press conference announcing the President's fiscal year 2002 budget, Assistant Secretary of the Treasury for Public Affairs Michele Davis wrote a memo telling O'Neill, "This event, more than anything you've participated in to date, requires that you be monotonously on-message." Her advice was frank: "Roll-out events like this are the clearest examples of when staying on message is absolutely crucial. Any deviation during the unveiling of the budget will change the way coverage plays out from tomorrow forward. . . . Your remarks should be very focused and your answers during the Q and A should only repeat your remarks."[18] (This memo is reproduced in full in appendix A.) Davis's comments demonstrate the strategic approach the Bush administration takes to its public statements.

The memo clearly had the desired effect on the often spontaneous O'Neill. During the press conference, the Secretary largely stuck to his message save for a testy exchange with reporters over the percentage of the tax cut going to the wealthiest Americans.

In a second memo to O'Neill, Davis gave him advice for a January 6, 2002 appearance on NBC's *Meet the Press*. (See appendix B.) This time, she encouraged him to aggressively insert the administration's talking points into the interview. Davis advised O'Neill to disregard host Tim Russert almost entirely: "FIRST ANSWER, no matter the question: We must act to ensure our economy recovers and people get back to work." She later stated that "You need to interject the President's message, even if the question has nothing to do with that." [19]

As she predicted, Russert's first question concerned the state of the economy, not Bush's agenda. When the host asked, "How bad is this recession?" O'Neill gave a short answer before turning to his talking points as Davis suggested, saying, "We need to get people back to work in this economy." The memo also listed "key lines" and "word choices," such as "economic security" (a phrase O'Neill used five times), and advised him to say that "the terrorist attacks and the recession caused the deficit," which he did. In this way, the administration turned the interview from a spontaneous exchange into something closer to a prepared speech.

The public face of the White House—the press secretary—has been just as obstinate throughout Bush's term. Former White House Press Secretary Ari Fleischer and his successor Scott McClellan have proven to be unstinting in their devotion to the White House message. Fleischer in particular was one of the most talented spinners ever to stand at the podium of the White House briefing room. His particular genius for stonewalling the press went far beyond simple deceptions and falsehoods (which are relatively difficult to pull off in front of a large group of reporters looking for such statements). Instead, Fleischer treated the press corps to patronizing recitations of the legislative process, denials that he had the expertise to answer various questions, disputes over the premises of questions, and what the *New Republic*'s Jonathan Chait called "a complex, arbitrary, and constantly shifting set of rules governing what questions he can answer."[20] When Fleischer did choose to answer a question, his adherence to the administration's talking points was relentless.

Though members of the press resented Fleischer for being so unhelpful, Bush praised him for his message discipline and loyalty, saying in 2002 that his then–press secretary "understands the fine line between the need to know and the need to say."[21] McClellan was just as stubborn as his predecessor in pushing White House spin and hardly more responsive. Reporters began to complain in early 2004 that, as CBS correspondent John Roberts put it, "We don't get our questions answered most of the time."[22]

In addition, Bush rarely submits himself to intensive questioning from the press. By January 1, 2004, he had held just eleven solo press conferences, far fewer than predecessors ranging from Reagan (21) to Clinton (38) to his father, George H. W. Bush (71), at the same point in their presidencies.[23] McClellan explained this by saying that Bush is skeptical of "peacocking" by reporters who play to the cameras and prefers "more informal encounters with the press." Dan Bartlett, Bush's communications director, was more explicit: "At press conferences, you can't control your message."[24] For a White House that so carefully manages its public image, free-ranging press conferences simply provide too many opportunities for journalists to chip away at the façade.

The shorter "availabilities" and joint press conferences Bush holds restrict the number of questions he can be asked and make it more difficult for reporters to follow up on his answers. Without those follow-ups, reporters have little opportunity to puncture the President's talking points. And even when Bush has held formal press conferences, he has tightly restricted the format and the order in which he calls on reporters. While hardly unprecedented—presidents have traditionally called on a reporter from one of the wire services for the first question—the Bush administration has gone further than any other, including apparently scripting the entire order for a prewar press conference on March 6, 2003.[25] By early 2004, reporters became so desperate to get the President to talk to them that they began calling to his dog Barney as Bush got off the presidential helicopter, hoping to make him come get the terrier and answer some questions in the process.[26]

Taken together, these strategies create what Bush adviser Mark McKinnon calls a "funnel for information."[27] No wonder the administration has been so successful at protecting its image in the media.

CHARM, PRESSURE, AND REPRISAL

The President's personality and popularity also influence how the press covers the White House. Both have helped the Bush administration to limit the amount of critical coverage it receives.

While administration officials such as Fleischer may treat the press with open hostility (and vice versa), President Bush's personal relationship with some members of the press is far more cordial. From chatting and joking with reporters in the back of his campaign plane to bestowing nicknames on them, candidate Bush launched a charm offensive that helped endear him to much of the press corps. This helped Bush generate more sympathetic coverage than Vice

President Al Gore, whose traveling press team reportedly despised him.[28] This dynamic appeared to hold during the first part of Bush's term, although it has eroded over time.

Bush has also benefited from the fact that the press tends to be particularly deferential to the executive during popular wars because there is strong pressure to avoid criticizing the commander in chief. As a result, he was often given the benefit of the doubt by the press after September 11, an advantage he exploited for some time. The ongoing nature of the "war on terror," which has no defined time frame, created a chilling effect on media scrutiny that extended well into 2003.

Journalists clearly felt this pressure. *New York Times* reporter Elisabeth Bumiller said of the March 6, 2003 presidential press conference before the beginning of the war in Iraq that, "I think we [the media] were very deferential because . . . it's live, it's very intense, it's frightening to stand up there. Think about it, you're standing up on prime-time live TV asking the President of the United States a question when the country's about to go to war. There was a very serious, somber tone that evening, and no one wanted to get into an argument with the President at this very serious time."[29] But the pressure reporters face from critics and government officials is no excuse for failing to perform the vital democratic function of questioning our elected leaders.

When journalists do challenge the White House, administration officials can retaliate. For example, the Clinton administration directly pressured antagonists in the press, with spokesman Mike McCurry telling ABC News producer Chris Vlasto "You're never going to work in this town again" and complaining to Vlasto's boss after he publicized a document that the White House claimed had been given to him on a not-for-attribution basis.[30] There is always a chance that these tactics may backfire, leading to more negative coverage. However, such attacks can also serve to limit the scrutiny that government receives. Jody Powell, the former press secretary for Jimmy Carter, observed that Reagan's presidency had proven that "the press's bark is much worse than its bite. They'll huff and puff around, but in the end you can cut severely into the flow of information and manage it with a much firmer hand than we were able or willing to do." [31]

The Bush administration has put this lesson to good use. The *Post*'s Milbank, the most prominent member of the press to devote sustained attention to Bush's dishonesty, has been a major target of White House retaliation. When Milbank, a former staffer at center-left magazine *The New Republic,* was first assigned to cover the White House, Rove reportedly called the *Post* to complain. [32] Since then, the administration has repeatedly attacked Milbank for his critical reporting and Hughes and Fleischer have complained to his editor. [33]

The most direct attack came in October 2002, when Milbank wrote a broad and powerful indictment of the Bush administration's dishonesty on a number of different issues. In it, he reported on Bush's pattern of deceptive and misleading statements, ranging from the suggestion that Iraq had unmanned aircraft that could attack the United States to the claim that the International Atomic Energy Agency found that Iraq was six months from developing a nuclear weapon in 1998. In response, an administration official called ABC News political insider newsletter *The Note* to denounce him, stating that the story was "cooked and ready to go before any due diligence of the facts" and adding that Milbank "is more interested in style than substance." [34] Such attacks send a message to the press corps that the White House takes note of critical coverage and will fight back.

Thomas Ricks, the *Washington Post*'s defense correspondent, has also faced the ire of the administration for his use of nonofficial sources. Ricks claims a military press officer told him he was not allowed to cover a special forces operation because "We don't like your stories, and we don't like the questions you've been asking." [35] In December 2003, Lawrence Di Rita, spokesman for the Department of Defense, filed a letter with the *Post* complaining about Ricks' coverage and then met with his editors to press the case—a step *Washingtonian* magazine called "unusual, if not unprecedented." The complaint against Ricks suggested that he was soliciting comments from too many people and giving too little weight to official statements.[36] This, of course, is simply a case of a reporter trying to do his job—and an administration trying to shut him down.

SENSATIONALISM OVER SUBSTANCE

Another reason the press has largely ignored Bush's dishonesty is because it concerns the least sexy aspect of politics: the details of public policy. In recent years, the political press has come to focus more on the style of candidates—the flashy sound bite, the attention-grabbing catchphrase, a candidate's clothing—than on policy. Scandal-driven news and cartoonish storylines have come to trump substance. With news organizations competing for eyeballs, the pressure to produce entertaining coverage is immense, and political scandals and made-for-TV showdowns provide more compelling stories for the press than disputes over the details of the tax code. As a result, media fact-checking tends to focus on scandal and personal peccadilloes—when it happens at all.

Ironically, although many of Bush's most deceptive statements have concerned public policy, the sustained negative coverage he has received has focused on style and scandal. Examples include the Harken Energy controversy, scrutiny of his past ties to Enron and its former CEO Ken Lay, and investigations of his service record in the Air National Guard during the Vietnam War. (The lone exception before early 2004 was Bush's claim about Iraq's alleged pursuit of uranium in the 2003 State of the Union, which drew extra attention because the administration uncharacteristically admitted error. The story also contained unusually colorful details about forged documents, former Ambassador Joseph Wilson's trip to Niger, and the outing of his wife as a CIA operative.) Because these scandals often provide vivid details, they tend to be covered by hordes of journalists for a few days before being abandoned. This "boom-and-bust" coverage veers from one extreme to the other, rarely balancing tough scrutiny with fair-minded restraint.

The pressure to generate an entertaining narrative also drives reporters toward stories that fit with existing stereotypes of political leaders. Such reports can help engage the public, but they also serve as a filter on what information is included in news reporting and how it is presented. Once these storylines take shape, they quickly become entrenched and often give rise to haphazard coverage. Thus Nixon and Clinton were portrayed as dishonest, Reagan and George W. Bush as dumb, Carter as ineffectual, and Gerald Ford as bumbling, with facts that reinforced these portraits given wide attention and contradictory ones discarded. Reporters are also frequently seduced by false or misleading claims that fit these narratives, such as the erroneous claim that former Enron CEO Ken Lay was one of many political donors to sleep in the Lincoln Bedroom of the Clinton White House.

Most important, once a national leader begins to be portrayed as dishonest, the narrative becomes self-perpetuating. Politicians whom journalists view as slippery come in for intense scrutiny; those seen as honest often receive far less. For example, Vice President Al Gore and then-Governor George W. Bush both made a number of misstatements during the 2000 campaign. Gore, however, was often portrayed as a liar, generating a number of inaccurate and misleading news reports that fit the facts into that storyline. Bush's misstatements were treated as verbal gaffes by the press (when they were reported at all), who generally portrayed him as dumb but honest.

The same pattern persisted once Bush took office. Though the narrative of Bush as a verbal bumbler who lacked intellectual gravitas cut against the President, the media's view of him as honest persisted until at least the beginning of the war in Iraq despite enormous evidence to the contrary. Even when journalists did take note of deceptions, such as Bush's false claim that he listed exceptions justifying deficit spending during the 2000 campaign, the reports failed to become major news. Absent a storyline that places each falsehood in an overall context, claims that Bush has said something deceptive or misleading are not perceived as "news." The result is that the press has become Bush's enabler.

THE MEDIA AND BUSH: DEMOCRATIC DYSFUNCTION

The Bush White House's philosophy that the media serve no particular democratic function guides its relationship with journalists. Because it sees them as a hostile force in search of the next headline, the administration has no reservations about employing an arsenal of public relations and news management tools to try to shape coverage. These include half-truths and strategically ambiguous language that are difficult for "objective" reporters to expose, relentless message discipline, restrictions on press interaction with Bush, direct pressure on journalists, and dishonesty about policy issues that the media find boring. By wielding these tactics against reporters reluctant to criticize the President after September 11, Bush was able to neuter the press corps for most of his first three years in office.

This media management strategy debuted on the national stage during the 2000 campaign, when the public got its first taste of what it could expect from a Bush White House.

★ 3 ★

CAMPAIGN 2000:
THE ORIGINS OF THE BUSH PLAYBOOK

Going into his first debate with Vice President Al Gore, George W. Bush was the presumptive underdog. The media expected that Gore, with his command of policy and debating experience, would wipe the floor with the Texas governor, who was known for his verbal gaffes.

The debate, however, proved to be a turning point in the campaign. Faced with criticism of his tax and budget proposals from the Vice President, Bush dismissed them with the suggestion that Gore was practicing "fuzzy math." The clever phrase indirectly accused the Vice President of lying without making a specifically disprovable assertion.

The strategy worked brilliantly. Media coverage the next day focused not on the substance of the claims made by either candidate but on Bush's catchy retort, which played into the narrative that Gore was dishonest. Hundreds of reports included the phrase in the next day alone.[1]

"Fuzzy math" is far from the most deceptive statement ever made by a presidential candidate. It is, however, typical of how Bush conducted his campaign, relying on a sophisticated, PR-driven media strategy. Led by a trio of advisors—Campaign Manager Joe Allbaugh, Communications Director Karen Hughes, and chief strategist Karl Rove—the Bush camp carefully controlled information, used vague catchphrases, and made artfully crafted misleading claims about the candidate's policies. In particular, the ways in which candidate Bush attempted to deceive the public and the press about his economic proposals would prove remarkably similar to the tactics he would later deploy while in office. With the benefit of hindsight, Bush's campaign can be understood as a primer for the presidency to come.

THE BUSH COLLECTION OF VAGUE CATCHPHRASES

The media's coverage of the 2000 campaign demonstrated some of the worst tendencies of political journalism. Simplistic storylines dominated press coverage of the candidates. Many in the media portrayed Gore as robotic, prone to reinvent himself for political advantage, and a frequent liar who liked to give himself more credit for accomplishments than he deserved. There was some evidence for each charge, but this trio of character flaws became the dominant narrative. In particular, misleading reports suggesting Gore had claimed to have "invented the Internet" and discovered the Love Canal toxic waste site fed these charges.[2] For his part, Bush was often portrayed as jocular but dim, thanks in part to a much-hyped November 3, 1999 interview with Boston TV station WHDH in which reporter Andy Hiller quizzed him on the leaders of various foreign countries and the Texas governor was able to name only one of four.

How prevalent were these stories? A study by the Project for Excellence in Journalism found that between February and June 2000, charges that Bush lacked intelligence accounted for 26 percent of all assertions by journalists in stories about the future President, and 34 percent of assertions about Gore concerned his alleged tendency to lie or exaggerate.[3] Rather than going beyond the conventional wisdom, reporters were largely reinforcing it.

The Republican National Committee played a role in hyping Gore's alleged exaggerations, and Bush also skillfully reinforced and amplified this portrayal of the Vice President by attacking him with language like "fuzzy math." For instance, during the first presidential debate on October 3, 2000, Gore claimed that the Texas governor's plan would "spend more money on tax cuts for the wealthiest 1 percent than all of the new spending that he proposes for education, health care, prescription drugs, and national defense, all combined." The Vice President's claim was accurate. The liberal Citizens for Tax Justice found that approximately $554 billion of the $1.3 trillion ten-year cost of Bush's tax cut proposal (not including increased interest payments on the national debt) went to people in the top 1 percent of the income distribution.[4] This total easily exceeded the $475 billion in new spending Bush had proposed in the areas Gore cited.

Instead of addressing Gore's argument on the merits, however, Bush implied it was untrue without providing any evidence to back up his claims. After an exchange about Medicare, Bush returned to the topic and retorted, "It's fuzzy math. It's to scare them, trying to scare people in the voting booth." He went on to use the phrase three more times during the debate. "The man's practicing fuzzy math again," he said when the Vice President argued that the portion of Bush's tax cut that would go to the top 1 percent far exceeded the new spending Gore proposed for health care or education. Similar exchanges led to Bush stating, "This man has been disparaging my plan with all this Washington fuzzy math" and "I can't let the man continue with fuzzy math." His frequent repetition of the catchphrase suggested that the Vice President was not being honest even though Bush never provided any evidence to refute Gore's claims.

"Fuzzy math" is the most famous line Bush used to evade criticism from Al Gore during the debates, but it is not the only one. Bush also responded to Gore's initial budgetary salvo about "tax cuts for the wealthiest 1 percent" by saying, "Well, let me just say, obviously tonight we're going to hear some phony numbers about what I think and what we ought to do." "Phony numbers" allowed Bush to suggest that Gore's numbers were wrong without directly calling the Vice President a liar, although the phrase clearly implied it and drew on the existing storyline that he was dishonest. And as with his "fuzzy math" responses, Bush followed up "phony numbers" with facts that didn't rebut Gore.

Rather than scrutinize the candidates' claims, the press was generally content simply to transcribe the exchanges, passing on Bush's retort as if it were a substantial response to the Vice President. *Atlanta Journal-Constitution* readers learned the next day that "Gore repeatedly criticized Bush's tax cuts as primarily benefiting 'the wealthiest 1 percent' of the population" while "Bush repeatedly countered that Gore was using 'fuzzy math' and 'phony numbers.'" The *Providence Journal-Bulletin* wrote that "Bush appeared irritated, accusing Gore of distorting his plans and questioning Gore's arithmetic, calling it 'Washington fuzzy math.'" And the *San Francisco Examiner* reported that Bush "complained repeatedly about Gore's 'phony' statistics and 'fuzzy math.'"[5] Rather than sorting out the facts, newspapers often simply passed along the spin. Readers were left to choose their favorite catchphrase, rather than getting facts that might help them sort through the issues at hand.

Some in the media betrayed a remarkable disregard for the policy issues at stake in the debate. On CNN, Larry King asked ABC *Nightline* host Ted Koppel about the matter. "Were you impressed with this 'fuzzy [math],' top 1 percent, 1.3 trillion, 1.9 trillion bit?" Koppel responded with a declaration of ignorance. "You know, honestly, it turns my brains to mush," he said. "I can't pretend for a minute that I'm really able to follow the argument of the debates. Parts of it, yes. Parts of it, I haven't a clue what they're talking about."[6] Not all journalists were as overwhelmed by substantive questions as Koppel, but his lack of interest helps demonstrate why candidate Bush was so effective at framing his message.

Over the course of the race, Bush would use a number of similar catchphrases to define himself and his opponents. These well-designed sound bites also helped to focus the attention of the press on political conflict and away from the facts and issues. The Texas governor was hardly alone in his use of such loaded phrases; Gore, for instance, often borrowed a line from his acceptance speech at the Democratic convention that "They're for the powerful, and we're for the people." But Bush wielded language in a far more subtle manner, positioning himself with insinuations rather than direct claims.

The most familiar of these was "compassionate conservative." The phrase implied moderation while reinforcing Bush's conservative political stance. After he was defeated in the New Hampshire primary by Arizona Senator John McCain, who described himself as an outsider who would change Washington, Bush added a second slogan to his arsenal in mid-February: "reformer with results."[7] Designed by Karen Hughes, the phrase played on McCain's appeal while focusing attention on Bush's record. The then-governor debuted the new line in a February 7, 2000 speech, pointing to his legislative record in Texas and stating, "I'm going to remind people that of the two of us running, I'm the reformer with results."[8] The two phrases would come to define his candidacy.

After McCain left the race and Bush became the presumptive nominee, his campaign also picked up a phrase the Arizona senator had used: "restoring honor and dignity" to the White House (or the variant "honor and integrity"). It served as a way of indirectly criticizing President Clinton, who famously tarnished the presidency during the Monica Lewinsky scandal. The phrase also associated Gore with Clinton and played on accusations that the Vice President had violated campaign finance laws and that he lacked ethical standards.

Once again, Bush was able to reinforce an important campaign message—his contrast with the alleged ethical misdeeds of Bill Clinton and Al Gore—without making any direct allegations that he would be forced to defend. He simply introduced the theme, confident that by quoting his catchy phrases, the press would pass his message on to the public. Many journalists, looking to provide context for their readers, even filled in the blanks about Bush's implicit criticism of Gore and Clinton.

POLICY DISINFORMATION

The Bush campaign also debuted a strategy that would become a staple of his time in office: misrepresenting his tax and budget plans. The candidate inaugurated the claim that his tax cut plan would benefit "all" taxpayers (a misleading implication since only those who paid federal income tax would benefit) and began touting the first of many slanted statistics that misrepresented the benefits of his plan for lower-income taxpayers.

Likewise, Bush's media strategy during the campaign foreshadowed his communications philosophy once in office. Examples included limiting the distribution of information about his plan to ensure positive coverage, providing deceptive figures about the distributional effects and cost of his plan, and the use of unrepresentative "tax families." In retrospect, it was a disturbing preview of how George W. Bush would sell his policy proposals from the White House.

CONTROLLING THE TAX FACTS

From the very beginning, Bush's campaign aggressively spun his tax cut plan. One part of the strategy was to manage the news cycle to generate positive coverage. When the campaign released the details of the first five years of Bush's tax cut proposal in December 1999, it required reporters to agree not to share its details with independent budget experts before publishing their articles. One Bush aide told a journalist, "This is between you, me, and your typewriter." [9] As a result, reporters largely repeated the description of the plan fed to them by Bush's press apparatus—that it primarily benefited the middle class.

The idea, of course, was to avoid reports questioning Bush's spin. It worked perfectly. The *Washington Post* headline the next day stated that under Bush's plan, "Working Poor, Middle Class Would Get Much of Relief." According to the paper, the plan would "focus its deepest reductions on the working poor and middle class." It added, "While the five-year Bush tax plan would benefit wealthier Americans, roughly half of the overall relief would be targeted to middle- and lower-income families, according to campaign aides."[10] The *Post* report carried exactly the message the Bush team wanted.

Those who read that story, however, were in for a surprise if they read the next day's *Post*. It noted that an initial analysis by the liberal Citizens for Tax Justice based on leaks from the Bush campaign showed that two-thirds of the benefits of the tax plan would go to the top 10 percent of income earners, while the bottom 60 percent would get only 11 percent of the benefits.[11] If the bottom 90 percent of Americans would receive only one-third of the plan's benefits, there's no way that "middle- and lower-income families" would receive "roughly half of the overall relief," as Bush officials had told the *Post*.

At that point, however, readers had already been given the Bush campaign's line, and the storyline surrounding the tax cut was established. Remarkably, the press had agreed not to gather expert opinion about a presidential candidate's policy proposals in its initial reporting, instead serving as a conveyor belt of campaign spin.

MISLEADING TAX CUT FIGURES

Bush was equally deceptive about who would benefit from his plan. He frequently suggested that his tax cut would help those with lower incomes more than those with higher incomes. During the primary campaign, for instance, the Bush campaign asserted that about half of every dollar "returned to taxpayers would finance changes that help low-income families."[12] In the third presidential debate, he stated that the "top 1 percent will end up paying one-third of the taxes in America, and they get one-fifth of the benefits" under his plan, while "a family of four making $50,000 in Missouri" would "get a 50 percent cut in [their] federal income taxes." [13]

As is so often the case with Bush, these claims have a germ of truth but are ultimately misleading. For example, although half of every dollar in Bush's tax cut would have gone to provisions that benefit low-income families, many of these provisions would also benefit middle-income and wealthy people.[14] Far less than half of his tax cut actually went directly to low-income families.

Furthermore, Bush's assertion that the top 1 percent would have received just one-fifth of the benefits of his plan was true only if his proposed elimination of the estate tax were not included. An analysis of all the provisions of Bush's plan by Robert McIntyre of Citizens for Tax Justice found that it would have given 42.6 percent of its benefits to the top 1 percent of filers, more than twice what Bush had claimed.[15]

By ignoring significant aspects of his plan and offering carefully spun statistics to the press and public, the Bush campaign exaggerated the tax cut's benefits for people at the lower end of the income spectrum. On the rare occasions when this spin was contradicted, press reports were usually structured as "he said/she said" debates, leaving readers to figure out who was being honest.

THE WAITRESS AND THE TAX FAMILIES

The Bush campaign used a number of misleading examples to help sell his tax cut. One favorite bit of campaign spin was the example of a hypothetical waitress who, he said, would have her federal income taxes lowered to nothing under his tax plan. According to Bush, who debuted the talking point at an Iowa campaign stop, "a single waitress supporting two children on an income of $22,000 . . . will pay no income tax at all."[16] Bush's speechwriters had come up with the example as an icon of hard work who would put a sympathetic face on the tax plan.[17] He cited it throughout the campaign (and would continue to do so once in office).

Bush neglected to mention a crucial fact, however: the hypothetical waitress probably had no tax liability already and would not get a large refund under Bush's tax plan.[18] At times, the Bush campaign displayed some awareness of this; Bush economics advisor Lawrence Lindsey suggested that the goal of his boss's tax plan was to allow such a single mother of two to avoid paying taxes on up to $31,000 in income.[19] But the implication that this waitress would receive a substantial tax cut at her current income was simply deceptive.

The future president also liked to point to individual families at campaign events who would benefit from his plan. These "tax families" were low- and middle-income families from around the country who had been carefully selected because they would benefit disproportionately from the tax plan compared to other households with similar incomes. Though these families took advantage of provisions, such as the increased child tax credit and reduced "marriage penalty," that many others of their income levels would not have received, the administration suggested that they represented how the majority of the general public would benefit.

Bush used families like these on the campaign trail frequently (as did Gore on occasion). It was an extension of a tactic developed by President Clinton, who often pointed during his State of the Union addresses to individuals in the crowd who had benefited or would benefit from his policies and proposals. They helped Bush create the impression that most American families would save as much as those he was highlighting.

The future president had decided to make use of such families in December 1999 while reassessing his campaign with top advisors. To fend off opponents like McCain and Steve Forbes, Bush and his campaign team worked out an approach to connect his tax plan to working people.[20] He debuted the strategy at a January 7, 2000 Republican primary debate, at which he contrasted his tax-cutting plan with McCain's by stating, "Let me see if I can put it in human terms for you. Chris and Beth Bradley came to the airport today. They make $42,000 a year in income. Under the plan that you laid out, Mr. Senator, here in South Carolina, they will receive a $200 tax cut. Under the plan that I proposed and will get through the United States Congress, they'd receive a $1,852 tax cut."

In fact, these families were completely atypical—and they were selected precisely for that reason. A *Washington Post* reporter uncovered an email sent by the Bush campaign in September 2000 seeking to find such families for an appearance in New Hampshire. The families had to make between $30,000 and $70,000 per year, itemize their deductions, have no children in college or day care, no family member in night school, no children under one year old, and no substantial savings besides a 401(k) plan.[21]

Looking at IRS data, a professor at Harvard's Kennedy School of Government found that only 15 percent of American families making between $30,000 and $70,000 would meet the Bush "tax family" qualifications.[22] Moreover, individuals in the middle 20 percent of the income distribution would see an average tax cut of $453 under Bush's plan, according to an analysis by Citizens for Tax Justice's McIntyre.[23] But the families served as easy anecdotal and visual hooks for journalists, who often mentioned them in reports without discussing how unrepresentative they were.

Bush also repeatedly misrepresented the percentage of the federal budget surplus that would go to finance his tax cut. Most often, this occurred during an illustration of his plans for the projected $4.6 trillion federal budget surplus. In appearances such as one in Naperville, Illinois, on Labor Day in 2000, Bush would hold up four $1 bills for the audience and the assembled media, telling them that the bills represented the surplus. He then took two bills away, saying they represented money he would use to preserve the Social Security system by paying down the national debt. Another bill, he said, would be used for spending, such as "making sure that our defense is strong." Finally, he handed the last dollar to someone in the crowd, stating, "I want 1 trillion, roughly a quarter of the surplus, to go back to the people that pay the bill."[24]

If grocery store cashiers did math like this, they'd be fired. Liberal columnist Paul Krugman demonstrated that a more accurate division of the dollars according to Bush's proposals would give $1.40 to the tax cut and 45 cents to new spending, with the rest devoted to the Social Security and Medicare program surpluses.[25] In short, rather than devoting about 25 percent of the surplus to new spending and 25 percent to tax cuts, Bush would actually have devoted approximately 35 percent to tax cuts and 10 percent to new spending, differences representing billions of dollars in inaccuracy. Yet Bush repeated the same numbers on a regular basis, including during a presidential debate on October 7, 2000. Bad math proved no impediment to the future president when it made for a good talking point.

A TAX CUT THAT COSTS LESS THAN THE SUM OF ITS PARTS

Bush's campaign also misrepresented the ten-year price tag of his tax plan. Vice President Gore repeatedly attacked the plan as costing more than $2 trillion over ten years. Using estimates from the Congressional Joint Committee on Taxation, however, Bush economic adviser Lawrence Lindsey told the press in May 2000 that Bush's plan would cost $1.3 trillion, saying "The Joint Committee on Taxation proves that Vice President Gore was badly mistaken." [26] That analysis only covered the nine years from 2002 to 2010, however, and completely excluded additional interest costs to the Treasury that would result from higher government debt.[27]

Adding the tenth year and interest costs raised the total cost of the tax cut to $1.9 trillion. In addition, the Bush plan would have pushed millions of Americans into a different tax rate under the alternative minimum tax, reducing the impact of the Bush tax cuts. Fixing that problem would have increased the cost to $2.2 trillion, according to CTJ's McIntyre.[28]

As they had done with the exclusion of estate tax, the Bush team was using an analysis of part of the tax cut proposal and presenting it as complete.

"COUNTING AND RECOUNTING" IN FLORIDA

In the aftermath of the November 2000 election, Americans were left with the spectacle of a legal battle to determine the winner of Florida's electoral votes—and the presidency. An initial count gave Bush a victory in the state by 1,655 votes.[29] Bush's narrow win triggered an automatic machine recount, and within days his lead had shrunk to only 960 votes, with continued recounts generally shifting that number downward. The two candidates' legal strategies in requesting and attempting to block recounts were highly disputed and have since been argued over endlessly by analysts and pundits. Regardless of one's opinion of the outcome, it's indisputable that during the public debate surrounding the recount, the Bush campaign once again used expertly crafted rhetoric to spread its message through the media.

First, when Vice President Gore requested manual recounts in four Florida counties, Bush's campaign sought to block them. To do so, Bush campaign aides brazenly suggested that manual recounts were somehow less accurate than machine counts, turning the normal practice in contested elections on its head. There was little evidence for this claim—hand recounts had long been the standard in determining the outcome of close elections, including in Bush's home state of Texas, where he signed a law in 1997 providing for hand recounts in close elections. Machine counts are prone to errors of up to 1 percent or more, which experts have found is typically higher than the human error rate.[30]

Instead of addressing the issue, the Bush campaign relentlessly repeated its talking point that hand counts were inaccurate. In a November 12 appearance on NBC's *Meet the Press,* James Baker, a veteran of the first Bush administration who represented then-Governor Bush during the election dispute, said, "hand recounts, as we've pointed out over and over again, are not as accurate as machine recounts because under this statute here in Florida, you have this procedure whereby the electoral officials look at the ballots and simply divine the intent of the voter. They divine the intent of the voter. That's extraordinarily inaccurate." In his November 15 press conference, Bush pushed the same line: "Unfortunately, what the Vice President proposed is exactly what he has been proposing all along: continuing with selective hand recounts that are neither fair nor accurate."[31] With these vague claims about inaccuracy, Bush and his aides managed to call expert opinion into question without engaging in a substantive challenge. And once again, by quoting the Bush team's response to Gore as part of a back-and-forth debate, journalists often suggested it was an equally valid position.

The Bush team also attacked the idea of recounting the votes at all. Rather than make an argument about why those additional counts were unnecessary, Bush and his aides simply noted that there had already been machine recounts. In his first press conference on November 10, Baker had this to say about the dispute: "to suggest that we should keep counting ballots that have been counted once, and even twice, over and over again, I think is not a fair position to take, nor a responsible position to take." The line was repeated by Bush and his aides throughout the controversy. Speaking on November 18, Bush aide Karen Hughes said, "Florida's votes have now been counted and recounted, and in some areas recounted three or four times."[32] Vice presidential nominee Dick Cheney kept it up near the end of the recount, stating on December 5 that, "with respect to the vote in Florida, the votes have been counted and recounted and now certified."[33] The Bush team's strategy in Florida was the same as it had been during the campaign: repeat something often enough, and people will start to believe it.

These talking points skirted the issue. Nobody disagreed that the ballots had been recounted by machines. The Gore team wanted hand recounts in certain counties, arguing that the machine recounts were inaccurate. The Bush campaign dodged the question of whether this request was legitimate by suggesting that multiple recounts had already been completed. The Bush team was yet again making an implicit argument—that Gore wouldn't accept the final outcome of an election—while appearing to respond to the question at hand.

The recounts and legal challenges continued into December. On December 8, in response to a challenge by the Gore team, the Florida Supreme Court ordered a statewide recount of all "undervotes," or ballots that didn't record a vote for president. On December 12, however, a divided U.S. Supreme Court decided in a highly controversial ruling that the Florida Supreme Court had erred and recounts could not continue. Gore conceded the election to Bush the following day.

PROLOGUE TO PRESIDENCY

If George W. Bush had lost his run for president, his campaign would not be remembered as particularly remarkable. He had helped to advance the use of public relations tactics, such as talking points and heavily spun statistics, but this was an ongoing trend to which Vice President Gore had also contributed. And while Bush had misled the press and the public about several of his policy proposals, his campaign would have disappeared into history if he had been defeated.

However, Bush won. And because his deceptions during the campaign received little attention, few observers anticipated the way that he would revise and expand his playbook after taking office. Tactics that may have once seemed harmless suddenly took on new significance. "Fuzzy math" led to "class warfare" and suggestive rhetoric linking Iraq and al Qaeda; arguments that manual recounts were less accurate than machine recounts foreshadowed claims that it was an open question whether human activities play a significant role in causing global warming; and a dishonest sales effort for his main economic proposal foreshadowed Bush's first major effort in office: a remarkably sophisticated and deceptive publicity campaign for his tax cut.

★ 4 ★

TAX AND SPIN:
SELLING THE 2001 TAX CUT

One of the centerpieces of George W. Bush's 2000 campaign was what he billed as a $1.3 trillion tax cut. He repeatedly emphasized that the primary motivation for the plan was to give back a portion of the sizable projected budget surplus to taxpayers.

"America has a strong economy and a surplus," he said in his convention speech accepting the Republican presidential nomination. "Now is the time to reform the tax code and share some of the surplus with the people who pay the bills." Bush made a similar statement during a debate with Al Gore on October 3, saying that the surplus was "the hard-working people of America's money, and I want to share some of that money with you, so you've got more money to build and save and dream for your families." According to candidate Bush, his tax cut plan was essentially a refund.

By the time Bush entered office on January 20, 2001, the dot-com boom had given way to a slowing economy. With the ground shifting under his feet, the newly elected President continued to support the same plan he introduced back in 1999 but changed his rationale for it. What he had called the "huge debate" of the campaign—what to do with the surplus—suddenly wasn't so huge anymore.[1] Instead, Bush went to work advertising his tax cut as what the economy needed to avoid recession.

The shift began just before Election Day. In one of his rare comments during the campaign about the need for tax cuts to boost the economy, Bush said in early November that "One of the interesting things we're beginning to see is there's some kind of grumblings about the economy. And one of the reasons why I'm so strong for tax relief is to provide a second wind to economic growth."[2] He began pushing this line harder after the election. On December 15, Bush spoke of his "concerns about a possible slowdown" and said they were "one of the reasons I feel so strongly about the need to reduce marginal rates in our tax cut."[3] After taking the oath of office, Bush promised in his inaugural address to "reduce taxes to recover the momentum of our economy and reward the effort and enterprise of working Americans"—an argument he would continue to make throughout the spring.

As time went on, Bush's chameleon-like sales campaign took on another form. In response to Democratic proposals for a smaller tax cut focused on immediate economic stimulus, he began to emphasize the long-term benefits of his plan. On March 27, he told a Kalamazoo, Michigan crowd, "We must put more money in the hands of consumers in the short term, and restore confidence and optimism for the long term," saying, "We need an immediate stimulus for our economy and a pro-growth environment for years to come."[4] By piling rationale on top of rationale, Bush managed to tie his plan to the latest economic news and eventually win its passage.

Of course, each of the arguments Bush made was perfectly reasonable on its own. What's notable is the cavalier way he slip-slided from one rationale to the next as circumstances changed. Until the economy started to struggle, he rarely discussed the need for a short-term stimulus. But, by early 2001, Bush and his aides hardly talked about anything else.

The audacity of this maneuver was stunning, but it was really just an opening act. After he took office, the President and his team embarked on a months-long campaign to mislead the public about the beneficiaries of his proposal and the size of the tax cut a typical family would receive. The White House bag of tricks included slanted information about the distributional effects of the plan; deceptive suggestions that everyone who paid taxes would receive a tax cut; and distorted "average" statistics and unrepresentative examples that exaggerated the benefits of the plan to middle-income Americans.

Though this went on for months in plain view, the President generally received a pass from the supposed watchdogs in the press. Reporters covering Bush were largely uninterested in the policy issues at stake, wedded to the narrative that he was an honest man, and deferential to a newly elected president in the "honeymoon" phase of his term. In addition, the administration carefully phrased most of its deceptive claims in technically true but highly misleading terms that did not meet "gotcha!" standards of reporting on dishonesty.

For many presidents, the first months of their term often set the tone for their entire time in office. Bush's victory on the 2001 tax cut showed that he would take the "permanent campaign" to new lows in order to enact his agenda.

MISLEADING CLAIMS ABOUT THOSE
WHO WOULD BENEFIT

The tax cut proposal Bush offered in 2001 mirrored the plan he touted during the campaign. It would have made a number of significant changes to the tax code as it was phased in, including consolidating the five federal income tax brackets to four rates of 10, 15, 25, and 33 percent; doubling the child tax credit; reducing the so-called "marriage penalty" in which couples pay more when filing jointly than they do when filing individually; and eliminating the estate tax. This combination of changes ensured that nearly all Americans who paid federal income or estate taxes would receive a tax cut.[5]

Bush faced a marketing challenge in promoting the plan, however. Because the American income tax system is progressive (those who earn more pay higher rates), most tax cuts that reduce income tax rates across the board will deliver the greatest dollar benefits to those who make the most money and pay the most in taxes. Also, the estate tax disproportionately impacts wealthy Americans, so the benefits of its elimination flow almost exclusively to those with the highest incomes.[6] The child tax credit increase and marriage penalty reduction delivered more of their benefits directly to middle-income Americans, but they represented a relatively small portion of the total value of the tax cut.

As a result, the benefits of Bush's plan primarily went to wealthier Americans. The liberal Citizens for Tax Justice analyzed Bush's initial proposal using a tax model from its sister organization, the Institute on Taxation and Economic Policy, and found that if Bush's plan had been fully enacted in 2001, approximately 72 percent of the benefits would have gone to the top 20 percent of Americans by income, with 45 percent going to the top 1 percent.[7]

Regardless of one's opinion of the merits of the plan, these distributional effects are undeniable. Instead of attempting to refute these numbers, however, Bush and his aides consistently obscured the effects of the plan, presenting a tax cut that gave the majority of its absolute benefits to wealthier Americans as one that would primarily help people in the lower and middle classes.

"THE GREATEST HELP FOR THOSE MOST IN NEED"

One way the White House did this was by focusing on percentage reductions without explaining the size of those tax cuts in dollars and cents or how they compared between income groups. In principle, percentage reductions are a valid way to describe the impact of a tax cut proposal, but Bush used these statistics to imply that his plan was designed to give most of its financial help to the poor, which was simply not true.

To illustrate this idea, consider what the President said in an executive summary of his plan: "These are the basic ideas that guide my tax policy: lower income taxes for all, with the greatest help for those most in need. Everyone who pays income taxes benefits—while the highest percentage tax cuts go to the lowest income Americans."[8] Out of context, "higher percentage tax cuts" for the "lowest income Americans" sounds like a description of a plan focused on helping the poor.

It was a line he repeated frequently. Responding to a reporter's question about Democratic criticism that the plan favored the wealthy, Bush said on February 5, 2001, that "the bottom end of the economic ladder receives the biggest percentage cuts."[9] In his

February 17 radio address, he stated that "the greatest benefits, the largest percentage reductions" of his plan "will go to those who need them most." And after Congress passed his plan in May, the President said, "This tax relief helps all taxpayers. It especially helps those at the low end of the economic ladder." [10] Again, the impression left was that the tax cut delivered the largest benefits for those most in need.

As we just demonstrated, however, the majority of the Bush tax cut's benefits would have gone to those at the top of the income scale. So how could the President make this claim?

The key is the phrase "percentage cuts." Because lower-income people typically pay little in federal income taxes, Bush's claim was technically accurate. By this logic, a low-income person whose income tax liability was reduced from $100 to $50 (a 50 percent cut) would have benefited more from the tax cut than someone whose income taxes fall from $100,000 to $75,000 (a 25 percent cut). Because the President never discussed the size of the tax cuts received by those at the bottom, this was hard to figure out.

Thus, while Bush's statements about percentage tax cuts were usually accurate, he used them to suggest that most of the plan's benefits were directed to low-income Americans. With these out-of-context statements, the President obscured who actually received the largest tax cuts from his plan.

A TAX CUT FOR "ALL TAXPAYERS"

In addition to selling his tax cut as a boon for people with low incomes, Bush also liked to brag that it would help everyone, rich and poor. He frequently claimed that his tax cut would help "all taxpayers," broad language that made it sound as though everyone who paid federal taxes would get a cut. In reality, workers with no federal income tax liability who paid only payroll taxes (a category that includes millions of Americans with relatively low incomes) would not have benefited.[11]

However, as with his claims about the tax cut being targeted at the poor, Bush's spin was partially correct—his proposal did cut taxes for everyone who paid federal *income* taxes. The President's vague language often omitted this key qualifier, however, exaggerating the number of people who would benefit from his plan. For instance, Bush said that the cut would lower "the rate for all taxpayers" (February 17), that "everybody who pays taxes ought to get tax relief" (February 20, March 23), and that it would "reduce taxes for everyone who pays taxes" (April 16).[12] Again and again, the President left out relevant facts that might hurt his case.

All too often, reporters complacently passed on Bush's claims without providing additional context. In a February 17, 2001 dispatch, for instance, Associated Press reporter Alan Fram practically transcribed Bush's radio address from that day, writing that the President "said on the radio that his plan was fair and would help all taxpayers."[13] A week later, CNN reporter Kelly Wallace did the same thing in reporting on another radio address, saying Bush stated that his proposal "would give everyone who pays taxes a tax cut."[14] As a result of this sort of coverage, Bush received little flak for his potentially misleading language.

CLAIMING TO HELP SMALL BUSINESSES

Bush didn't just exaggerate the benefits of his plan for low-income workers, however. Small business owners came in for the same treatment.

The President liked to point out that many small business owners (about 17.4 million) paid taxes at individual income tax rates. He frequently cited the fact that some paid the top rate of 39.6 percent as a reason to reduce it. In fact, virtually the only group of people Bush ever mentioned benefiting from the proposed cut in the top rate were small business owners. But a Citizens for Tax Justice analysis using the Institute on Taxation and Economic Policy model and IRS data found that most small businesses would not have benefited. The group estimated that only 1.4 percent of small business owners with positive business incomes (about 180,000) would pay the top rate in 2001, a result that was consistent with a finding by the Treasury Department.[15]

Bush consistently ignored these facts, presenting a cut in the top rate as a boon to small businesses. During a March 9, 2001, speech in South Dakota, for instance, the President stated that "many small businesses are unincorporated, many are what they call Subchapter S, and they pay the highest marginal rate in the tax code."[16] While 180,000 is a significant number, Bush's use of the term "many" suggested that they were a far higher portion than 1.4 percent.

The President went even further in a March 16 meeting with small business owners, where he stated, "The Treasury Department released a report earlier today on small business owners who pay personal income taxes, and small businesses which pay at the highest rate of 39.6. According to the Treasury Department, nationwide there are more than 17.4 million small business owners and entrepreneurs who stand to benefit from dropping the top rate from 39.6 to 33 percent." He then cited figures for three states, saying there were "one million small businesses and entrepreneurs who will benefit when we drop the top rate" in Florida, "more than

630,000 small business owners and entrepreneurs who will benefit" in Ohio, and "55,000 small business owners and entrepreneurs . . . who will benefit from dropping the top rate from 39.6 to 33 percent" in South Dakota. This language implied that millions of small business owners (including all of those Bush listed in the three states above) would have received a tax cut due to the reduction in the top rate.

The Treasury Department press release Bush was citing said something quite different, however. It noted that 17.4 million small business owners "stand to benefit from the President's tax relief plan," which "reduces all marginal tax rates," but specified that "many" (not all) of them paid the 39.6 percent rate.[17] (This language was also misleading, of course: the term "many" again implied a much higher percentage than 1.4 percent.) The state-by-state figures Bush cited included anyone who filed a tax return with positive nonfarm business income in 1999, not just those who paid the top rate.[18]

Again and again, Bush pointed out that "many" small businesses paid the top rate while failing to specify how small the actual percentage was, leaving the impression that most or even all small businesses would benefit.

Not surprisingly, the media often presented the President's misleading statements without clarifying how many small businesses would be helped. For instance, a March 15 Knight Ridder story on a New Jersey speech said, "[Bush] added that the [top-rate] reduction would help many small-business people that pay individual rather than corporate income taxes."[19] And at least one outlet took the President's statement about 17.4 million small business owners at face value. The *Columbus Dispatch* reported on March 17 that "Bush cited a study released yesterday by the U.S. Department of

the Treasury that concluded that 17.4 million small-business owners would save taxes if the top rate falls to 33 percent."[20] In today's
politics, this sort of credulous reporting amounts to journalistic
malpractice.

MISLEADING EXAMPLES

When he wasn't abusing statistics, Bush frequently trotted out a series of hypothetical and real sample beneficiaries of his tax plan (including the "tax families" he continued to bring up on stage with
him during speeches). But the stories Bush told about the people he
presented were often demonstrably false or misleading.

THE WAITRESS

One of Bush's favorite examples from the 2000 campaign, the famous waitress/single mom with two children, got a raise. Although
Bush occasionally continued to describe her salary as $22,000 when
speaking off the cuff, he and the White House began to describe her
as making $25,000 instead in prepared speeches.[21] The reason for
this was simple: she would have received very little from Bush's tax
cut if she made $22,000, a fact confirmed by White House Press
Secretary Ari Fleischer during a February 9, 2001 press briefing.
After joking that the President is "raising incomes for [the] American people since he was elected," Fleischer acknowledged that
$25,000 was a better example because "That person would receive a
tax cut." (This rare admission of error passed with little fanfare from
the press at the time.)

However, even after Bush's midcourse correction, the example was still misleading. Though his plan would have reduced the marginal rates the waitress would pay on income above her $25,000 salary, it probably would have provided her with little or no tax cut if she didn't get a raise. Yet Bush suggested she would have received a substantial benefit. "For the waitress," he bragged in his February 3, 2001 radio address, "our plan will wipe out her income tax bill entirely." However, as the liberal Center on Budget and Policy Priorities showed, the most that he could "wipe out" was $447, a figure that assumed the waitress, a single mother, spent nothing on child care for two children. If she had child care expenses of more than $100 per month, her tax cut would have dropped to less than $200, and it would have been zero if she spent more than $170 per month.[22] Like the percentage reductions he touted, Bush presented a benefit that was likely to be very small as one that was much larger by omitting the relevant details.

Nevertheless, the waitress example made it into many press reports on the tax cut without any sort of qualification or context. For example, the *Philadelphia Inquirer* wrote that Bush "stressed [in his February 3 radio address] that the tax cuts would help people at both ends of the economic ladder, from a lawyer making $250,000 a year to a waitress making $25,000 a year," providing no assessment of the accuracy of that statement.[23] Without such information, the example could only mislead.

A NOT SO "TYPICAL" FAMILY

Another administration spin point was that "the typical family of four will be able to keep at least $1,600 more of their money when the plan is fully effective," as the President's budget proposal stated in February 2001.[24] Bush repeated this line frequently in his public statements over the next few months, including a number of radio addresses and speeches.[25]

Of course, such examples can help to highlight the benefits of a policy proposal when used appropriately. But as it turned out, the tax cut received by this "typical" family was not representative of the benefits that most taxpayers would have received, though Bush presented it as though it was. The majority of the family's tax cut, $1,000, came from a $500 increase in the tax credit it received for each child. Families without enough income tax liability to qualify for the credit or without multiple children under 17 would have received a much smaller tax reduction. An analysis by Citizens for Tax Justice using the Institute on Taxation and Economic Policy model found that 89.6 percent of taxpayers would have received a smaller tax cut than $1,600.[26] In reality, the tax cut received by Bush's "typical" family was quite unusual.

Yet a broad cross section of media outlets blindly repeated the President's unrepresentative example with little or no critical context, including New York *Newsday*, the *New York Times*, and the Minneapolis *Star Tribune*. When most of these reports were written, figures on the distribution of benefits from Bush's plan were widely available. But these outlets and many others often repeated Bush's "typical family of four" tale nearly verbatim. *Times* reporter Katherine Seelye, for instance, described Bush as saying that "his plan will return $1,600 to the typical family of four in one year when fully phased in" while failing to provide a single figure not included in the President's speech.[27]

SAVING THE FAMILY FARM OR BUSINESS

Another favorite Bush parable was intended to illustrate his case for repealing the estate tax, which he often called the "death tax." To do so, he employed yet another misleading example intended to pull on the heart strings: the hard-working owners of small family businesses and farms.

Though the White House often ignored the estate tax when calculating who would benefit from his plan, Bush loved to tell stories about its impact on small businesses. For example, in his February 3, 2001 radio address, Bush said, "We will eliminate the death tax, saving family farms and family-owned businesses." The claim was that the families of the owners of these businesses often could not afford estate tax on business or farm assets and had to sell them to pay the tax bill.

In reality, however, owners of farms and businesses who were asset-rich but cash-poor made up a very small percentage of the people who would have benefited from repealing the estate tax. The Center on Budget and Policy Priorities noted that farms and other family-owned business assets represented less than 4 percent of assets in taxable estates worth less than $5 million.[28] In other words, the smallest estates subject to the estate tax included a minimal amount of farm and family business assets. An IRS study of 1999 tax returns corroborated this finding, showing that only a few people whose wealth was concentrated in farm assets and property paid estate taxes. In fact, an Iowa State University economist and tax expert failed to find a single case in which a farm had been lost because of the estate tax despite conducting an extensive search.[29] It was very unclear who Bush's plan would save.

As always, President Bush did not accurately portray the beneficiaries of his plan. The strategy was obvious: sell the tax cut using misleading examples that would win over the public.

THE USE AND ABUSE OF STATISTICS

Bush's sales pitch also depended on deceptive statistics that did not fairly represent the costs or benefits of his proposal. In particular, the White House issued a study in March 2001 of the distributional effects of the tax cut intended to counter criticism that it favored the wealthy. However, this analysis turned out to be just as deceptive as much of the administration's rhetoric.

The study came from the Treasury Department, which was known for reliable analysis. Under Bush, however, the department was co-opted by a White House with a flexible definition of honesty. The press release announcing the analysis was titled "Treasury Releases Distribution Table for the President's Tax Relief Plan." But as the table's small print revealed, Treasury had looked at just *part* of the Bush tax plan, which the text of the release called "major individual income tax provisions." It omitted several parts of the plan, most significantly the elimination of the estate tax.[30]

Not coincidentally, the estate tax was the part of Bush's plan that delivered the greatest proportion of its benefits to the wealthy. The exclusion made the numbers look much more progressive than would otherwise have been the case. Treasury reported that 25.4 percent of the individual income tax cuts in Bush's plan went to those making over $200,000, but Citizens for Tax Justice found that 45 percent of the overall tax cut, nearly twice as much, went to those making over $373,000 (the top 1 percent).[31]

This table was more than a shift in judgment by the department—it was a change in policy for transparently political reasons. Since 1998, Treasury analyses had included all aspects of proposed changes in the tax code, including estate taxes.[32] But that policy was abandoned soon after Bush took office.

BUSH'S FIRST MARKETING TRIUMPH

On June 7, 2001, George W. Bush signed a tax cut into law that was remarkably similar to the one he had proposed during the 2000 election campaign. In a striking reversal from typical presidential practice, he had won the day with a series of misleading campaign-style tactics that were arguably *worse* than those he had used in his race against Al Gore only months before. Bush and his aides had embarked upon a troubling new approach to governance, and they were just getting warmed up.

THE NATURE OF THE TRUTH:
SCIENCE AND THE ENVIRONMENT

Spinning science is as old as public relations itself. In 1913, Edward Bernays, one of the founders of PR, staged his first promotional campaign for a play called *Damaged Goods*. The actor who was producing the show feared that its sexually explicit content would trigger a police raid, so Bernays, who was then editing a magazine called *Medical Review of Reviews,* organized a group to rally public support that he called the "Medical Review of Reviews Sociological Fund." Ostensibly intended to fight venereal disease, the group's actual purpose was to endorse the play. *Damaged Goods* played without police interference, signaling the beginning of a new era in which PR experts appropriate the authority of science for political ends.[1]

A leaked strategy memo written by the consulting firm of Republican strategist Frank Luntz in 2002 offers a rare peek at how PR continues to shape debate over scientific issues today. In the document, which was part of a briefing book prepared for lobbyists and Republican politicians, Luntz and his employees stated that "The environment is probably the single issue on which Republicans in general—and President Bush in particular—are most vulnerable."[2] They then offered a detailed set of recommendations on language and strategies for Republicans to employ in order to head off this threat.

At one point, they specifically addressed the issue of global warming, writing in bold, underlined type: "The scientific debate remains open." This was not a factual claim, however, but a recommendation for how Republicans should approach the issue in their public statements. "You need to continue to make the lack of scientific certainty a primary issue in the debate," the memo advised, recommending that Republicans "emphasize the importance of 'acting only with *all* the facts in hand.' "[3]

Only after this introductory discussion of strategy did the memo briefly hint at the view of most scientists on the issue. "The scientific debate is closing [against us] but not yet closed," it asserted (brackets in original). "There is still a window of opportunity to challenge the science." In a box labeled "Language That Works," the Luntz memo suggested phrasing Republicans could use to put this strategy into practice: "We must not rush to judgment before all the facts are in. We need to ask more questions. We deserve more answers. And until we learn more, we should not commit America to any international document that handcuffs us either now or into the future."[4] Of course, Luntz and his colleagues were hardly experts on the science of climate change, but they strategically invoked deference to science as a rationale for a policy that was already decided.

The similarity of George W. Bush's scientific and environmental spin tactics to those pioneered by Bernays and modernized by Luntz is undeniable. The President's strategy in framing the debate over global warming, for instance, was remarkably similar to what Luntz recommended. He asserted an allegiance to professional science while playing on the inherent uncertainty of scientific knowledge to misrepresent experts' views.

Bush's spin on scientific issues also extended beyond global warming. When he announced his policy on federal funding of stem cell research in the summer of 2001, the President greatly exaggerated the number of stem cell lines that would be available to researchers. After scientists helped expose the fact that his policy had relied on faulty or misrepresented data, the administration refused to admit Bush's mistake or revisit the issue, claiming that the specifics were not important. It altered, suppressed, or misrepresented scientific and environmental data on several other occasions as well.

The media's record on these issues is mixed. In some cases, they passed on the President's misleading rhetoric without serious challenge. But due in part to public criticism from scientists and the media's generally liberal tilt on environmental issues, reporters were more critical of Bush's spin than they were on many other issues.

In the case of stem cells, press scrutiny led Bush and his aides to compound their initial spin rather than admit error. (The September 11 terrorist attacks soon drew press attention elsewhere.) This strategy of denial and continued evasion would later be expanded and refined in the aftermath of the Iraq war, the next occasion when the press began seriously to challenge the administration.

THE RHETORIC OF UNCERTAINTY

When Bush took office, his position on the issue of global warming was unclear. As a candidate, he had opposed the Kyoto Protocol, a 1997 treaty that would have created caps on the quantity of greenhouse gases that developed countries could emit. However, he also acknowledged that global warming was occurring and appeared to propose mandated reductions of emissions of carbon dioxide, which is thought to contribute to rising temperatures.[5] During an October 2000 debate with Gore, Bush said "global warming needs to be taken very seriously" but added "there's differing opinions" among scientists on the issue. He later asked Gore, "some of the scientists, I believe, Mr. Vice President, haven't they been changing their opinion a little bit on global warming?"[6]

As a result of Bush's hazy position, Treasury Secretary Paul O'Neill and Environmental Protection Agency Administrator Christie Todd Whitman attempted to seize the initiative during the first weeks of the administration, urging action against global warming in private memos to Bush.[7] Whitman also made several public statements about Bush's views on the issue. For instance, on the February 26, 2001 edition of CNN's *Crossfire,* she stated that Bush "has also been very clear that the science is good on global warming."[8] According to O'Neill, however, no one really knew Bush's views on the issue at the time.[9]

The issue was settled by a March 13, 2001 letter from Bush to several U.S. senators who had inquired about his position. In the letter, the President advocated restraint to avoid harming consumers and specifically disavowed mandated reductions in carbon dioxide emissions, citing (among other things) "the incomplete state of scientific knowledge of the causes of, and solutions to, global climate change." Later that month, the administration announced that Bush would not support the Kyoto Protocol.[10]

In May 2001, the White House requested a report from the National Academy of Sciences about the status of research into global warming and its causes.[11] The study, which was released on June 6, stated that "Greenhouse gases are accumulating in Earth's atmosphere as a result of human activities, causing surface air temperatures and subsurface ocean temperatures to rise. Temperatures are, in fact, rising." While noting that "we cannot rule out that some significant part of these changes is also a reflection of natural variability," the overall conclusion of the study was clear: global warming was occurring in large part as a result of human activities.[12]

At this point, the scientific consensus Bush faced was virtually undeniable. The NAS report followed a study by the United Nations Intergovernmental Panel on Climate Change. One of the most exhaustive studies ever on the topic, the IPCC study found that "Concentrations of atmospheric greenhouse gases and their radiative forcing have continued to increase as a result of human activities."[13] The NAS concurred with this finding, stating in its report, "The committee generally agrees with the assessment of human-caused climate change presented in the IPCC Working Group I scientific report."[14] In short, scientists believe global warming is occurring and that human activity has played a significant role in the trend.

There are caveats, of course. Both studies stated that natural variability may play a significant role and that the exact extent of any warming trend or its consequences cannot be precisely determined.[15] These uncertainties reflect the realities of science: because of the imprecision of scientific data and our ability to analyze it, no conclusion is ever completely certain. No matter how much research is conducted, some doubt will always exist. Scientific knowledge relies instead on the consensus view of professional researchers, and there is such a consensus in global warming. As Donald Kennedy, the editor-in-chief of *Science* magazine, stated in a March 2001 editorial, "By now the scientific consensus on global warming is so strong that it leaves little room for the defensive assertions that keep emerging" from industry and "a shrinking coterie of scientific skeptics." Kennedy added, "Consensus as strong as the one that has developed around this topic is rare in science."[16]

Rather than acknowledging this consensus, however, the White House used the uncertainty inherent in science to divert attention from the conclusions of the NAS report that it had originally requested. White House Press Secretary Ari Fleischer struck first, telling the *Washington Post,* "This report shows what is known and certain, and that which is unknown or surmised." He continued, "For instance, it concludes that the Earth is warming. But it is inconclusive on why—whether it's man-made causes or whether it's natural causes."[17]

On June 11, President Bush echoed Fleischer's remarks on the study and his administration's approach to global warming during a speech in the Rose Garden. "[T]he National Academy of Sciences indicate that the increase [in greenhouse gases] is due in large part to human activity," the President correctly noted. After that, however, he focused on what he called the "scientific uncertainties" and "limits of our knowledge" on global warming. "[T]he Academy's report tells us that we do not know how much effect natural fluctuations in climate may have had on warming. We do not know how much our climate could or will change in the future. We do not know how fast change will occur, or even how some of our actions could impact it," Bush said. "[N]o one can say with any certainty what constitutes a dangerous level of warming, and therefore what level must be avoided. The policy challenge is to act in a serious and sensible way, given the limits of our knowledge. While scientific uncertainties remain, we can begin now to address the factors that contribute to climate change."

Bush's statement that "no one can say with any certainty what constitutes a dangerous level of warming" was technically true, but spun away the thrust of the report, which stated that the uncertainty depends on how we define safety or danger. "The question of whether there exists a 'safe' level of concentration of greenhouse gases cannot be answered directly," the NAS report noted, adding, "In general, however, risk increases with increases in both the rate and the magnitude of climate change."[18] With such specifics omitted, Bush could present a less troubling picture.

In short, both Fleischer and Bush were distorting the content of the report, with Fleischer suggesting it was "inconclusive" on the question of why the Earth is warming, and the President claiming that "we do not know" what the impact of natural fluctuations has been. The NAS report actually put the blame much more strongly on human activities, only saying that "we cannot rule out" the role of natural variability in causing "some significant part" of the warming.

On the same day as Bush's speech, the administration released an initial working group report on climate change, which listed a number of actions the U.S. government was taking to address the issue and critiqued the Kyoto treaty (among other things). Like Fleischer and Bush, the working group report focused particular attention on areas of uncertainty in the NAS analysis. After briefly noting its major finding that human activity is playing a major role in global warming, the working group report stated that the authors found "numerous gaps [that] remain in our understanding of climate change" and "critical uncertainties about the science of climate change" before listing a series of areas in which uncertainty exists and proposing action to resolve them.[19] Once again, such gaps in scientific knowledge are a real concern, but the PR-style focus on uncertainty was deceptive.

All of these tactics blurred the differences between specific uncertainty about various aspects of global warming and the consensus of the scientific community that it is real, substantial, and largely driven by human activities.

A number of major media outlets, including Knight Ridder and National Public Radio, relayed the administration's misleading statements to the public with little context comparing them with major scientific findings on the subject.[20] Americans relying on the leader of their country for an accurate description of a serious environmental issue would be sorely disappointed.

It was not the only time that the Bush administration would play the uncertainty card when discussing global warming (though the issue took a less prominent role after the September 11 terrorist attacks). The President's other major action on the issue came in a February 14, 2002 speech, when he announced a climate change initiative intended to slow the growth of greenhouse gas emissions. "We must also act in a serious and responsible way given the scientific uncertainties," Bush said. "While these uncertainties remain, we can begin now to address the human factors that contribute to climate change."[21] Clearly, uncertainty remained a key part of the talking points.

In addition, the Bush administration began to use carefully calibrated language when discussing the issue, frequently substituting the more innocuous-sounding term "climate change" (which does not characterize the nature of the change) for "global warming" after 2001. For instance, the President did not use "global warming" once in his February 2002 speech. The Luntz memo would later provide similar advice. " 'Climate change' is less frightening than 'global warming,' " it said, adding, "While global warming has catastrophic connotations attached to it, climate change suggests a more controllable and less emotional challenge."[22] The way in which the White House repeatedly used the vaguer term was noteworthy.

THE DISAPPEARING STEM CELL LINES

After his June 2001 speech on global warming, Bush would attempt to mislead the public on another scientific issue in even more dramatic fashion. Media buzz began to build in August that the President, who was taking a working vacation at his ranch in Crawford, Texas, would make a much-anticipated decision on federal support for stem cell research.

Stem cells are unspecialized cells that can divide and renew over long periods and have the potential to become many different types of specialized cells. Scientists have speculated that they can be used to develop cures for a number of medical problems, including Alzheimer's disease, Parkinson's disease, and spinal cord injuries. Stem cells can be obtained from a number of human and animal sources, but scientists have devoted extensive effort to investigating the potential uses of stem cells from human embryos, which can self-renew effectively in the laboratory for longer periods and become a larger number of specialized cells than stem cells cultivated from adults.[23]

Bush first tackled the issue during his presidential campaign, when a spokesman stated that the then-Governor opposed "federal funding for stem cell research that involves destroying a living human embryo."[24] Essentially, the future President had pledged not to allow research on embryos obtained from in vitro fertilization.

In the first half of 2001, Bush ordered a review of embryonic stem cell science and solicited opinions on the issue from fellow politicians, aides, and scientists.[25] By July 9, following a meeting with bioethicists Leon Kass and Daniel Callahan, Bush reportedly made the decision to ban federal funding for research on new embryonic stem cell lines but allow funding for work on existing lines created from embryos that had already been destroyed.[26]

However, there was a catch—Bush wanted to know the number of existing lines that would be available for federally funded research. After initially being told by the National Institutes of Health in late July that thirty lines existed, the President requested that NIH search to see whether more were available.[27] In an August 2 meeting, Bush learned that the NIH's Office of Science Policy had found about thirty more lines, resulting in a total of more than sixty.[28] The President later claimed that scientists told him that "there were enough existing stem cell lines to do serious research to determine whether or not embryonic stem cell research could live up to its potential."[29] Bush was ready to go public with his decision.

On the evening of August 9, the President gave a nationally televised address announcing his policy on stem cells. "As a result of private research, more than sixty genetically diverse stem cell lines exist," he said. "I have concluded that we should allow federal funds to be used for research on these existing stem cell lines, where the life and death decision has already been made."

However, this figure quickly came into dispute. As the *New York Times* reported, "Scientists were dubious about [Bush's] assertion that sixty such colonies, or lines, exist, saying reports indicated only about ten, some of which are largely useless. Still others may be off-limits because scientists in other countries may refuse to share them."[30] Responding to these concerns about the number and quality of existing embryonic stem cell lines, Health and Human Services Secretary Tommy Thompson said in a press conference the day after Bush's speech that the more than sixty lines claimed by the President were "diverse," "robust," and "viable for research."[31] Thompson's implication was that criticism was misplaced—if the lines were "robust" and "viable for research," then they should be available for federally funded research immediately.

It would later become clear, however, that neither Bush nor Thompson was telling the truth. In fact, many of the stem cell lines that NIH had told Bush about were only in development and might never become viable for research.[32] At the time, Bush may have simply believed what he had been told by NIH and not known that his address misrepresented the number of viable embryonic stem cell lines available. Over the next few weeks, though, as critics continued to raise questions, the White House employed a bold strategy: rather than looking into the issue and correcting itself, it stuck to its spin at all costs.

Thompson was the leader in this regard. Appearing on NBC's *Meet the Press* three days after the President's address, he insisted that the stem cell lines would be available for research as advertised. NIH, he said, "has called all of these entities" and "re-called them since the President made the decision." In the following days, media reports continued to question the availability of the number of lines Bush had claimed. But there was no way to investigate the White House's story fully without access to the list it was using.

Instead of providing this list to the press and scientific community, the administration responded by stonewalling and attacking its critics. Ari Fleischer said, "The burden of proof is on anyone who doubts" the claim.[33] This was a remarkable statement: rather than responding to criticism with evidence, the White House press secretary argued that political opponents should prove a negative.

On August 27, eighteen days after the President's speech, NIH finally released information on sixty-four stem cell lines, allowing reporters and scientists to evaluate Bush's claim for the first time. The administration trumpeted the occasion. "The knowledge that these sixty-four embryonic stem cell lines exist and will be available for research should inspire our nation's best scientific minds to begin planning for ways they can aggressively take advantage of this historic and unique opportunity," Thompson said in a statement accompanying the information.[34] Again, his language was definitive—the lines "exist" and "will be available for research."

However, it quickly became clear that many of these sixty-four lines were not ready for research and might not ever be. For instance, NIH said there were nineteen stem cell lines at Göteborg University in Sweden. But scientists there told the Associated Press that only three were ready for research and were uncertain whether the other sixteen, which were being processed, would become research-quality lines. Stockholm's Karolinska Institute, which reportedly had five lines, actually did not have any that had been declared ready for research. The University of California, San Francisco, had two lines according to NIH, but only one had been completely analyzed, and financial and patent issues had to be settled before it could be made available for research.[35]

Quite simply, Thompson's statement was incorrect. Within a few days, the press had discovered that while the sixty-four stem cell lines did "exist" in some literal sense, many might not be "available for research" for months or years, if ever. Rather than concede that the President's stem cell address had been misleading, the HHS Secretary simply cited evidence that did not back up the administration's original assertion and pretended that it did so.

This strategy of refusing to concede error continued on September 5, when Thompson boldly told a Senate committee that neither he nor the President had been wrong. "So far, the National

Institutes of Health has identified sixty-four stem cell derivations that meet the President's eligibility criteria," Thompson said. "The President never spoke about or drew any limits on these lines based on where they were in their development. Furthermore, we have consistently said that these lines are at various stages of development. I have spoken to that fact. The NIH has spoken to that fact. And the NIH white paper identifying these derivations makes that fact crystal clear." Someone listening to Thompson would hardly realize that Bush claimed in his national address that the stem cell lines "exist" without specifying that they were in development and might not ever be available for research. Nor would they be aware that the HHS Secretary had definitively said all lines in development "will be available for research."

Despite these obvious contradictions, Thompson acted in his Senate testimony as if those who pointed them out were engaging in mere semantics. "[U]nfortunately, and I believe unfairly," he said, "some are choosing to engage in word games or hear only parts of the story." But under questioning after his prepared testimony, Thompson revealed the accurate number, stating that "We feel right now roughly there are twenty-five, twenty-four, twenty-five fully cell lines established [sic], and there are sixty-four in the various phases, from the proliferation, to the characterization, to the cell line established." [36] In other words, there were not "more than sixty" existing research-quality stem cell lines, but twenty-four or twenty-five.

Thompson's testimony hardly settled the matter, but afterward he seemed to consider the number of available stem cell lines unworthy of further discussion. The next day, he told a *New York Times* reporter, "There are plenty of cells available to do the basic research. Let's get on with it, and stop quibbling about the numbers." [37] After the September 11 attacks took place a few days later, the issue quickly disappeared, letting Bush off the hook.

As of this writing, there are nineteen stem cell lines listed as available for shipping in the NIH human embryonic stem cell registry. This number appears unlikely to increase substantially: a recent letter from NIH to two Congressmen said the "best-case scenario" is that twenty-three lines will become available.[38] There have been no retractions from the Bush administration, however.

We will probably never know, of course, whether Bush was being intentionally deceptive in his initial address on this issue. But as it became clear that most embryonic stem cell lines he cited were not ready for research, the administration mounted an aggressive strategy to avoid admitting that it had not provided accurate information to the public. Thompson and other officials mischaracterized the evidence, attempted to shift the burden of proof onto critics, and tried to revise what Bush had actually said. In the face of overwhelming evidence and unusually strong media scrutiny, the Bush administration simply would not admit error, instead stretching the truth to the breaking point to try to justify its claims.

PREEMPTIVE SPIN

The Bush administration has misrepresented information related to science or environmental policy on several other occasions.

In an April 30, 2001 speech to the annual meeting of the Associated Press in Toronto, Canada, for instance, Vice President Dick Cheney addressed the administration's proposal to allow oil drilling in the Arctic National Wildlife Refuge. "ANWR covers 19 million acres, roughly the size of South Carolina," Cheney stated. "The amount of land affected by oil production would be 2,000 acres, less than one-fifth the size of Dulles Airport. The notion that somehow developing the resources in ANWR requires a vast despoiling of the environment is provably false."

However, the Vice President failed to note that the 2,000-acre figure he cited had been calculated by counting only the amount of space that would be taken up by equipment touching the ground, not the total land area that would be affected by oil exploration and transport. For example, the space "affected" by an aboveground pipeline was measured according to the size of each of the stanchions that hold it up. While ANWR drilling platforms and material might only touch the ground over a total of 2,000 acres, the "amount of land affected" would likely be significantly greater.[39]

In another case, Interior Secretary Gale Norton presented the Senate Energy and Natural Resources Committee with information it had requested about the effects of drilling in ANWR in July 2001. Rather than providing all the relevant data given to her by government scientists at the Fish and Wildlife Service, Norton strategically highlighted certain pieces of information while discarding others.

For instance, she excluded the observation that a herd of more than 130,000 caribou had calved in the area where drilling was proposed to take place for twenty-seven of the last thirty years. Fish and Wildlife also analyzed another caribou herd that historically uses an area for calving where oil development began in 1975. It found that, while the herd grew in size from 5,000 to 27,000 over that period, the herd's birthrate was lower in developed areas, 64 percent versus 83 percent in undeveloped areas. Norton only reported the herd's overall population growth, however, and concluded that the "data do not support the hypothesis that oil fields adversely affect caribou productivity." Finally, she misstated one key fact from Fish and Wildlife's report, telling the Senate that caribou calving has been concentrated *outside* the proposed drilling area in eleven of the last eighteen years rather than inside. (Norton's spokesman told the *Washington Post* that her mistake was due to a typographical error.)[40] Unsurprisingly, each of these omissions and errors cut in the same direction—in favor of Bush's proposal.

A third case of factual distortion concerned the possible existence of a relationship between abortion and breast cancer. As a report from the Democratic staff of the House Committee on Government Reform noted, the National Institutes of Health's National Cancer Institute website originally stated that the question of a connection, while previously unclear, had been largely resolved by the late 1990s, when a large study in the *New England Journal of Medicine* found no such link.[41] However, NCI, the federal government's principal agency for cancer research and training, put a new analysis on its website in November 2002 that exaggerated uncertainty about the issue. "[T]he possible relationship between abortion and breast cancer has been examined in over thirty published studies since 1957," the changed version read. "Some studies have reported statistically significant evidence of an increased risk of breast cancer in women who have had abortions, while others have merely suggested an increased risk. Other studies have found no increase in risk among women who had an interrupted pregnancy."[42] Using a strategy similar to the one it employed on global warming, the administration was playing up uncertainty about an issue on which there was clearly a scientific consensus.

Members of Congress soon discovered the change, however, and after Representative Henry Waxman, the ranking Democrat on the House Committee on Government Reform, sent a letter complaining to Secretary Thompson, NCI held a three-day conference of experts to discuss the link between abortion and breast cancer.

The participants concluded that abortion is not associated with an increase in breast cancer risk. As a result, the website was updated once again to state that participants at the NCI workshop found "having an abortion or miscarriage does not increase a woman's subsequent risk of developing breast cancer." [43] In this case, at least, the administration corrected the record, but only when challenged.

The strategic assertion of uncertainty and misleading presentation of facts on these issues paralleled the White House's spin on global warming and stem cell research, but with a twist. When reading government publications or listening to top officials, the public, the media, and Congress could not trust that they were getting a full picture of the facts. The administration was cooking the books.

FRACTURED FACTS

George W. Bush is hardly the first president to fit the facts to his preferred conclusion. But for anyone concerned about the state of debate over scientific and environmental issues, the reasons for alarm are clear. The President and his aides have misrepresented a range of scientific and environmental issues using subtle public relations techniques that make it difficult to nail them for outright dishonesty. Bush's statements on global warming, for instance, carefully misrepresented a scientific consensus, playing on the nature of scientific knowledge to distort the conclusions reached by major studies on the topic. The White House was caught peddling phony numbers on stem cell research, but refused to admit error. And administration officials sometimes altered or misrepresented scientific and environmental information, allowing them to manipulate debate without appearing to enter the fray.

In the process, the Bush administration demonstrated that its conduct in selling the first tax cut was not an isolated event. On the contrary, such deceptive tactics were part of its presentation of most major policy issues. Not only did the President continue to use PR tactics to misrepresent the facts on a range of topics, but as the stem cell furor demonstrated, even increased scrutiny by the press made little difference. Bush simply turned up the spin, deploying additional methods of deception to avoid admitting he or anyone in his administration had ever said anything untrue.

Scientific and environmental issues would largely fade into the background for both the Bush administration and the media after the September 11, 2001 terrorist attacks. In the fall of 2001 and afterward, the President and his aides would use this national tragedy to go beyond distorting the facts, leveraging the emotion of the attacks to try to prevent their opponents from even engaging in policy debate.

★ 6 ★

UNDERMINING DISSENT AFTER
SEPTEMBER 11

On December 6, 2001, with the country still reeling from the September 11 attacks, Attorney General John Ashcroft was called to testify before the Senate Judiciary Committee on the government's response to the terrorist threat. The USA Patriot Act, which expanded law enforcement's powers to fight terrorism and other crimes, had passed Congress by overwhelming margins after the attacks, and President Bush signed the bill into law in October. By December, however, critics were raising questions about the government's use of these powers and the administration's subsequent proposal to try suspected terrorists in special military tribunals. Democrats, who had largely closed ranks with the President after the attacks, were expected to challenge Ashcroft and the administration.[1]

Before debate could even begin, however, Ashcroft went on the offensive. In his opening statement, he told the committee, "We need honest, reasoned debate and not fear-mongering. To those who pit Americans against immigrants, and citizens against non-citizens; to those who scare peace-loving people with phantoms of lost liberty; my message is this: Your tactics only aid terrorists, for they erode our national unity and diminish our resolve. They give ammunition to America's enemies, and pause to America's friends. They encourage people of good will to remain silent in the face of evil."

This was a stunning statement. The Attorney General of the United States had just accused critics of the government's post–September 11 actions of "aid[ing] terrorists," using vague language that lumped them together with enemies of the nation and implicitly questioned their motives.

Unfortunately, Ashcroft's statement was only one of several instances from the fifteen months after September 11 in which the White House leveraged the attacks to undermine dissent. The President and other officials repeatedly invoked the specter of the attacks to equate support for Bush's policies with support for the war effort. At key moments, they even suggested that critics were unpatriotic or aiding terrorists. And Bush tried to undermine open debate after the attacks by touting his success at "changing the tone"—a phrase which in practice meant that opponents should continue to go along with him and refrain from criticism.

As always, the administration's tactics were based on public relations principles. Just as the White House usually bases its misleading claims on true fact, officials never explicitly stated that their opponents were unpatriotic or committing treason. This allowed the White House to deny such implications when they were raised by critics. However, the President and other White House officials clearly played on the emotional associations of September 11 when they suggested that their opponents should not raise questions about government actions, violating their responsibility as wartime leaders to respect and uphold the right to dissent.

Such tactics did not distort the facts in the same way the President typically did, but they used the methods of PR for the same purpose: preventing honest debate of the issues through strategically chosen language. In this case, by associating its opponents and the arguments they made with terrorists, opposition to the war on terror, or other emotionally charged but unrelated issues, the Bush administration tilted debate away from the substantive matters at hand. This was as calculated and disturbing as its distortion of the facts on issues like the economy and science.

Though these were matters of rhetoric rather than fact, the media still managed to fail in its most elementary duty: informing the public of important news about national politics. In two important cases, a number of reporters failed to accurately document key attacks on dissent by the Bush administration, a passivity that could only have encouraged the White House.

DISSENT AIDS THE ENEMY

One way that President Bush retained the upper hand politically after the attacks was by making an example of those who questioned his policies. In two important controversies, his administration attacked its critics, suggesting they were unpatriotic or helping the enemy.

When Attorney General Ashcroft delivered his statement to the Senate Judiciary Committee declaring that "those who scare peace-loving people with phantoms of lost liberty . . . only aid terrorists," he made no distinctions among critics of the administration. Certainly, some had engaged in exaggerated and unfair attacks on the government's expanded antiterrorism powers. However, Ashcroft's broad language asserted that anyone who claimed that liberties had been lost was incorrect and thereby helped terrorists by scaring "peace-loving people." By smearing critics acting in good faith, the Attorney General's statement served to stifle open debate.

The day after the testimony, Justice Department spokesperson Mindy Tucker lashed out at reporters who had written about Ashcroft's attack on critics. In an email, she wrote that "Ashcroft was very clear that he wanted public debate about the actions of the Justice Department. What he does not think is helpful to the country is misstatements and the spread of misinformation about the actions of the Justice Department." She added that "Anyone who reported this morning that he criticized anyone who opposed him was absolutely wrong and in doing so became a part of the exact problem he was describing." [2] With this bold statement, Tucker both denied the obvious implications of what Ashcroft said and suggested that those who disagreed with her were also aiding terrorists—a cunning bit of doublespeak.

The administration also leveled similar accusations against critics when it came under fire several months later. On May 16, 2002, the White House disclosed that President Bush had received a briefing in August 2001 about the possibility that al Qaeda might hijack airplanes.[3] (It subsequently became clear that this was a reference to the August 6, 2001 President's Daily Brief, which summarized the potential threat from al Qaeda.) Though administration officials stated that there was no specific reference in the briefing to terrorists using planes as weapons, Democrats began to call for further investigation of what Bush knew before September 11.

House Minority Leader Dick Gephardt, D-MO, for example, said that "I think what we have to do now is to find out what the President, what the White House, knew about the events leading up to 9/11, when they knew it and, most importantly, what was done about it at that time." Senate Majority Leader Tom Daschle, D-SD, also asked questions. "Clearly, there is a lot more to be learned before we can come to any final conclusion about all of the facts," he said, "but it clearly raises some very important questions that have to be asked and have to be answered. Why did it take eight months for us to receive this information? And secondly, what specific actions were taken by the White House in response?"[4] There was little question that Democrats were looking to damage the White House politically, but such questions are a part of open and healthy debate about national policy.

The White House responded with a massive counterattack, claiming that Democrats were making unpatriotic accusations that Bush had failed to act on a specific warning of an attack. Vice President Cheney charged on the night of May 16 (reportedly with President Bush's approval) that Democrats "need to be very cautious not to seek political advantage by making incendiary suggestions, as were made by some today, that the White House had advance information that would have prevented the tragic attacks of 9/11." Cheney continued, "Such commentary is thoroughly irresponsible and totally unworthy of national leaders in a time of war."[5] Rather than offering a substantive response, the Vice President had attacked the legitimacy of asking questions and attempted to clamp a lid down on debate.

When asked to define an "incendiary" or "irresponsible" suggestion at a White House briefing the next day, Fleischer said that "anytime anybody suggests or implies to the American people that this President had specific information that could have prevented the attacks on our country on September 11, that crosses the lines." Even First Lady Laura Bush pushed the same spin, telling reporters in Hungary, "it's sad to play upon the emotions of people as if there were something we could have done to stop it, because that's just not the case."[6] Both were attacking a straw man. Though Daschle and Gephardt had suggested that the administration might have been negligent, it was not clear that they or other leading Democrats were insinuating that Bush failed to act on a specific warning of the attacks, and the White House failed to produce any evidence that any leading Democrat had done so.

On the May 19, 2002, edition of *Fox News Sunday*, Cheney was asked who had made the allegations he had denounced. He could only offer Representative Cynthia McKinney, D-GA, who had irresponsibly claimed in April 2002 that Bush failed to act on a specific warning of an attack.[7] However, her statement on May 16, the day that Cheney claimed Democrats had made "incendiary suggestions," was less inflammatory, and McKinney was not a particularly prominent "national leader."[8] It was clear that Cheney had no direct evidence that such comments had been made; his baseless statement was a warning shot (or, as he put it, a "cautionary note") directed at Democrats who were challenging the administration too directly on a very sensitive subject.

Cheney was also asked about his comments in an appearance on NBC's *Meet the Press* the same day. This time he said "I didn't name names" but indicated he was referring to "the rush to the floor of the House and the Senate in front of the cameras saying, 'What did he know and when did he know it?'; people waving newspapers—the one you showed at the outset; the *New York Post* saying, 'Bush Knew.'" While Senator Hillary Clinton, D-NY, did cite the *Post* headline suggestively, Cheney offered no specific evidence that she or any other Democrat had claimed Bush ignored a specific warning of the attacks. (Clinton said she was seeking answers to "questions being asked by my constituents, questions raised by one of our newspapers in New York with the headline 'Bush Knew.' The President knew what? My constituents would like to know the answers to that and many other questions, not to blame the President or any other American, but just to know, to learn from experience, to do all we can today to ensure that a 9/11 never happens again.")[9]

The administration followed up Cheney's speech with a more general effort to silence critics by suggesting their actions were treasonous. White House Communications Director Dan Bartlett was quoted in a May 18 *Washington Post* article saying that the statements by Congressional Democrats "are exactly what our opponents, our enemies, want us to do."[10] This was the most direct administration statement to date equating democratic debate with treason, yet the comment was not picked up by any other major media outlet. An unnamed senior administration official also told the *Post* that the Vice President was worried that "for purposes of politics, that you whip up a frenzy for the kind of hearings that would be very detrimental to the war effort and our ability to protect ourselves."[11] This was the ultimate expression of the administration's efforts to suppress dissent—anonymous attacks on unnamed opponents accusing them of undermining the security of the country.

These tactics were largely successful in stifling questions about the government's pre-9/11 actions for nearly two years after the attacks. They would prove no less powerful in the realm of domestic issues.

THE WAR AT HOME

In the months after September 11, Bush and other White House officials frequently suggested that several domestic issues were matters of national security, a powerful charge with the threat of terrorism looming over the country. During numerous public appearances, members of the administration implied that support for the war required support for Bush's policies on a range of issues, not just foreign and defense policy.

For instance, one of the first partisan debates after September 11 began in October 2001 as Democrats and Republicans argued over the proper size and shape of an economic stimulus package. President Bush responded by tying the nascent war on terror to his domestic priorities. During a visit to a Maryland printing factory on October 24, Bush paid lip service to the spirit of bipartisanship that still prevailed, saying "there is no party that has a lock on patriotism" and that "The Democrats, just like Republicans, want to win this war." However, he was careful to frame the state of the economy as part of the "war" and "homefront security," loaded terms that gave him a tactical advantage by playing to his political strength as commander in chief. "Some might ask why, in the midst of war, I would come to Dixie Printing," he said. "[T]he answer is, because we fight in the war on two fronts. We fight a war at home; and part of the war we fight is to make sure that our economy continues to grow." He added, "I'm here to talk about an important part of the homefront security, and that is our economy," urging the House to pass a stimulus bill he supported and "the Senate to act quickly to make sure that the American people understand that at this part of our homeland defense, our country and the Congress is [sic] united."

By framing economic matters as part of the war and demanding unity, Bush tried to make it appear that support for his economic stimulus plan was inseparable from support for the war on terrorism. In this way, he tilted the playing field unfairly in order to try to ram through his agenda.

A few months later, Bush directly attacked the legitimacy of opposition to his policies during a speech on January 5, 2002, in Ontario, California. "It's time to take the spirit of unity that has been prevalent when it comes to fighting the war and bring it to Washington, DC," he said. "The terrorists not only attacked our freedom, but they also attacked our economy. And we need to respond in unison. We ought not to revert to the old ways that used to dominate Washington, DC. The old ways is [sic]: What's more important, the country or my political party?"

Again, Bush was implicitly defining partisanship as opposition to his policies, suggesting that support for his economic plan was the patriotic response to the 9/11 attacks. He did praise those who cooperated with him in Ontario, saying, "We've made some good progress about working together," but warned that "there are troubling signs that the old way is beginning to creep in to the people's minds in Washington. After all, it's an election year. It's tempting to revert back to the old ways. But America is better than that. We're better than that." This language unfairly framed democratic disagreement as detrimental to the security of the country.

In December 2001 and January 2002, Bush and other administration officials began to redefine his policies in terms of national security, referring to his economic stimulus proposal as the "economic security plan" or "economic security package," an obviously loaded wartime metaphor that would dominate the administration's domestic policy rhetoric for months to come.[12]

"CHANGING THE TONE"

Ironically, only two days before Vice President Cheney first denounced the "incendiary suggestions" coming from unnamed

Democratic leaders, President Bush touted his success at "changing the tone" during a May 14, 2002 Republican National Committee gala in Washington, DC. This phrase originated as a vague claim during the 2000 campaign that Bush would move the nation forward from the partisanship of the Clinton era. As he stated during his speech accepting the Republican nomination for President, "I don't have enemies to fight. I have no stake in the bitter arguments of the last few years. I want to change the tone of Washington to one of civility and respect."[13] After Clinton left the White House and Bush assumed office, however, the new President began to use the relatively innocuous-sounding phrase as an implicit attack on opposition to his policies.

For example, in an April 25, 2001 interview, Bush said, "I've been changing the tone in Washington, and that's very important because Washington can be a very acrimonious and bitter place where people are here . . . to further their own political agendas as opposed to doing what's right for the people."[14] This formulation defined his own agenda as "what's right for the people" and those who criticized him as "acrimonious and bitter." In practice, of course, "changing the tone" is impossible unless one party simply gives in to the other. As Bush defined it, the standard would effectively prohibit vigorous disagreement between the parties—the essence of democratic debate.

Similarly, in a May 2001 speech, Bush said, "Changing the tone of our nation's capital hasn't been easy. . . . When I hear my policies and my nominees attacked in a hostile and partisan way, I simply hear the echoes of an era behind us. I'm not going to take the bait. I'm going to lead this country to a new level of respect."[15] Again, this "new level of respect" was apparently one in which Bush would not be harshly criticized.

With Democrats offering little political opposition in the months after September 11 (partly as a result of Bush's tactics), the President told the RNC gala's attendees that his administration had made "great progress" in changing the tone. "A year ago I said that I would do my part to try to change the tone in Washington, DC," he said, adding, "I believe—and I strongly believe—that we've made great progress." [16] By recycling the phrase in this way, Bush redefined the stunted state of post-9/11 political debate as a norm to which the nation should aspire.

Over the next several months, Bush repeatedly praised GOP candidates from South Carolina to Arizona as people who would work to change the tone, lending a highly partisan cast to his call for civil debate. In two cases, the administration made the implications of the phrase especially clear. During an October 17, 2002 speech in Atlanta, Bush argued for changing the tone by claiming we need to "get rid of all this needless politics," stating that we need to "change the tone in our national capital and our state capital, get rid of all this needless politics, bring people together, achieve big objectives." And during a briefing to the White House press corps the next day, Fleischer explicitly defined "changing the tone" as supporting Bush's budget policies, stating that "changing Washington's big spending ways is an important way to change the tone." [17] The "tone" to which Bush aspired was apparently one in which the opposition gave up and went along with his policies.

TAKING THE WAR ON TERROR
TO THE 2002 CAMPAIGN

These trends culminated in one of Bush's most vitriolic denunciations of his opponents: his claim that Senate Democrats were "not interested in the security of the American people" for opposing his homeland security legislation. For months after the September 11 attacks, Bush had resisted proposals to consolidate the various agencies tasked with homeland security–related duties into one Cabinet-level department. However, in early June 2002, he reversed course and announced a proposal to create just such a department. It initially appeared that the legislation would breeze through Congress, but negotiations soon bogged down in a dispute over collective bargaining rights for department employees.

In speeches rallying public support for his version of the bill, Bush went even further than Ashcroft and Cheney, directly stating that Democrats who disagreed with his position on the issue did not care about national security. On September 5, 2002, Bush said, "I am not going to accept a bill where the Senate micromanages, where the Senate shows they're more interested in special interest[s] in Washington and not interested in the security of the American people." [18] On the same day, he said in South Bend, Indiana, that "there are senators up there [in Washington, DC] who are more concerned about special interests in Washington and not enough concerned about the security of the American people." He then declared that his "message to the Senate is: you need to worry less about special interest[s] in Washington and more about the security of the American people" at a Doug Forrester for Senate event in New Jersey on September 23, 2002. And most egregiously, during a Trenton, New Jersey speech on the same day, Bush said, "I asked Congress to give me the flexibility necessary to be able to deal with the true threats of the 21st century. . . . The House responded, but the Senate is more interested in special interests in Washington and *not interested in the security of the American people* [emphasis ours]." This sort of charge was one of the most loaded that a politician could make in the aftermath of September 11, and it was particularly unfair to use simply because Democrats disagreed with him about a policy issue.

Bush's comments provoked anger in his opponents. Majority Leader Tom Daschle, D-SD, took to the Senate floor to denounce him for politicizing the war on terror. "The President is quoted in the *Washington Post* this morning as saying that the Democratic-controlled Senate is 'not interested in the security of the American people,' " Daschle said on September 25.[19] This quotation was the crux of the dispute.

However, a number of media reports failed to describe Bush's remarks fairly. Several omitted the quote that Daschle had mentioned in which Bush said Senate Democrats were "not interested in the security of the American people." Instead, they incorrectly cited Bush's statement that senators need to "worry . . . more about the security of the American people" as precipitating Daschle's outburst instead. The list of offenders included NBC's Ann Curry and Campbell Brown, CNN's Wolf Blitzer, and the *Washington Times* editorial board.[20] All of these outlets failed to provide citizens with the context they needed to evaluate Daschle's criticism of the President.

FROM SEPTEMBER 11 TO ANOTHER TAX CUT

In late December 2002, Democratic presidential candidates began to step up their criticism of the administration's homeland security efforts, claiming President Bush had not done enough to make America safe. White House Press Secretary Ari Fleischer responded by stating that "Any candidate who suggests that when the enemy attacks, the blame lies with the United States and not with the enemy does so at great peril to their own political future."[21] In this

way, he suggested that criticism of Bush's homeland security policies was an attempt to absolve terrorists from blame for a hypothetical attack—a line of argument intended to shut down debate
about the issue. Fleischer was laying down a marker against any
Democrat who might dare criticize the administration too harshly
in the future.

The administration's attention would soon turn, however, to
another tax cut, which Bush introduced in January 2003. It would
be an important episode in a long sequence of dishonest economic
and budget claims extending through mid-2004. And as he so often
did, Bush would leverage the emotion and power of the terrorist attacks to advance his economic agenda.

NO DEFICIT OF DISHONESTY:
TAX AND BUDGET REDUX

Despite President Bush's popularity after September 11, the economy presented a difficult challenge for the White House. A recession began in March 2001 and persisted through the following November; employment remained stagnant for much of 2002 and 2003; and the surplus the administration inherited quickly gave way to steadily escalating deficits. Bush's response to these problems was the same as it had been throughout his administration: upping the ante of political deception.

As it turned out, his fictitious "trifecta" story justifying federal budget deficits was the opening salvo in a hail of misleading economic claims pushed by the administration for the remainder of Bush's term. To escape blame for mounting deficits in the months after 9/11, promote another tax cut in early 2003, and avoid political fallout for the state of the economy beginning in late 2003, Bush and his team pulled out all the stops. This included distorting tax and budget figures, making a series of tenuous economic claims, trotting out a parade of unrepresentative "tax families," and presenting a series of misleading statistical averages, all of which took liberties with the truth to promote Bush's policies. Some of these assertions were so outrageous that even the President's own economists and other administration officials publicly contradicted them (albeit quietly).

Nonetheless, Bush's tactics continued to receive little attention from the press. Aside from the media's continued lack of interest in the details of fiscal policy and the administration's efforts to avoid scrutiny, the President had an additional factor protecting him: the tense political climate after September 11 apparently made some reporters fearful of criticizing him too harshly. The result was a continued diet of spin and distortions from Bush and his administration.

THE CHICAGO FABLE

During the 2000 campaign, Bush had promised that he would not spend the portion of the federal budget surplus attributable to Social Security, let alone run overall budget deficits. Once in office, he continued to claim that his tax cut—the centerpiece of his campaign platform—would not push the federal budget back into the red. The dramatic reversal in the budget situation beginning in late 2001 therefore posed a major political problem for the administration. Not only had the federal budget sunk into deficit astonishingly quickly, but red ink appeared likely to persist for years to come as a result of Bush's tax cut, a steep decline in tax revenues, and increased government spending, particularly on defense and homeland security.

By August 2001, the President and his aides began listing recession and war as exceptions to his promise that would justify dipping into the Social Security surplus, with economic advisor Lawrence Lindsey claiming that Bush always had the two exceptions in mind.[1]

After the September 11 attacks, which sent tax revenues into a tail-spin at the same time that the government was forced to increase defense and homeland security spending, Bush quickly changed his story and began claiming that he had listed *three* exceptions rather than two—war, recession, and national emergency (the "trifecta"). And instead of using some surplus Social Security funds, Bush claimed that his exceptions justified spending the *entire* Social Security surplus *and* running federal budget deficits.[2]

In an October 3, 2001 appearance with business leaders in New York only a few weeks after the attacks, Bush first stated that he had listed the exceptions in Chicago during the campaign. He repeated this claim thirteen more times over the next nine months and made several other more oblique references to it (see appendix C). Though the details varied, the basic premise of the alleged Chicago appearance was that Bush had made a public statement to an audience or a reporter. As he put it on April 26, 2002: "I want to remind you *what I told the American people,* that if I'm the President—when I was campaigning, if I were to become the President, we would have deficits only in the case of war, a recession or a national emergency. In this case, we got all three [emphasis ours]."[3]

The press's attention was understandably focused elsewhere when Bush first told the story in October 2001, and his next mention of it in January 2002 was elliptical. As a result, the claim did not receive much attention, though the Associated Press and *New York Times* both misdated Bush's alleged statement to 2001 the second time he made it.[4] Beginning in late February 2002, however, Bush began to repeat the story incessantly, and yet the press still paid little attention. Even after the President began the story during an April 26, 2002 press conference by saying "I want to remind you what I told the American people," the media hardly batted an eye.

The "trifecta" was finally exposed by *The New Republic* in late April 2002, more than seven months after Bush first told the story.[5] Despite repeated inquiries from *TNR* and subsequent requests from NBC's *Meet the Press* and the *Washington Post*, the White House press office failed to substantiate Bush's claims.[6] The rest of the press corps seemed not to notice or care. So Bush kept repeating the tale, and most reporters continued to ignore it.

Between May 1 and June 24, 2002, he told the story another eight times—and generated very little attention from the national press.[7] In fact, the *Los Angeles Times* credulously recounted Bush's story in mid-July 2002, weeks after it had been exposed. "In several speeches in recent months," reporter Edwin Chen wrote, "Bush has assiduously sought to inoculate himself against political fallout for presiding over the nation's return to an era of red ink," recounting "an interview that he said he gave to a reporter in Chicago during the 2000 presidential campaign" in which Bush said "he would not deficit spend unless the nation found itself at war, in a national emergency and in a recession."[8] Where had Chen been?

No evidence has ever emerged to prove that Bush made such a statement. The *Washington Post* eventually discovered that Vice President Al Gore had proposed the exceptions back in 1998. Economic advisor Lawrence Lindsey affirmed at the time that Bush would support the idea as well, but the candidate was never quoted to that effect in Chicago or anywhere else.[9]

When Bush finally stopped repeating the story, reportedly at the request of advisors who feared it was beginning to harm his reputation for honesty, it quickly disappeared from the media.[10] Despite the magnitude of the deception, the news pages of the *New York Times* have apparently never reported that the trifecta story was false, nor have CNN news reporters.[11] Unfortunately, this was par for the course in the post-9/11 debate over the economy: the White House spun while the press corps slept.

HIDING THE CRIMSON TIDE

The Bush White House spent most of the period between September 11, 2001, and early 2003 trying to minimize economic issues while pressing its advantage on foreign policy and homeland security. At first, few were inclined to blame the administration for the state of the economy or the federal budget. The decline in both the short- and long-term federal budget outlooks soon began to present a more acute problem, however, especially since Bush had promised that his tax cut wouldn't send the country into the red. As a result, the White House devoted extensive effort to blaming the fiscal decline on the recession and the war on terror, fuzzing up the details and stonewalling when challenged about its assertions. Despite occasional setbacks, this strategy kept deficits from achieving critical mass as a campaign issue all the way through the November 2002 elections.

THE DEFICIT MERRY-GO-ROUND

The public face of the deficit-spinning effort was Mitch Daniels, director of the White House Office of Management and Budget. After Bush's introduction of the trifecta in October 2001, the next major administration statement about deficits was a November 28, 2001 speech by Daniels announcing that the government was in the red and likely to stay there for at least two years. According to the OMB director, three factors led to "a dramatic shift in both our near- and long-term fiscal prospects": the recession, spending on the military and homeland security, and reduced estimates of economic growth. What Daniels left out, however, was the tax cut, which had a moderate short-term impact in 2001–2003 but a major effect on the decline of ten-year financial projections. When asked by a journalist about the omission, Daniels switched to a political argument, stating "one can only say thank goodness for tax cuts" and refusing to admit that the legislation had a negative impact on the budget situation.

The way Daniels parried this question highlights the Bush administration's determination not to concede ground to its critics or the media, even at the price of engaging in overt intellectual dishonesty. The benefits of the strategy are clear: Refusing to acknowledge obvious but politically harmful facts makes it more difficult for the media to present them as truth, reducing reporters to "on the one hand / on the other hand" stories. The Associated Press report on Daniels' speech, for example, framed the impact of the tax cut on long-term budget projections as a matter of partisan dispute, saying Daniels "blamed his prediction [of deficits] on the recession and the war against terrorism," but "Democrats said the real culprit" was Bush's tax cut.[12]

Another White House strategy to avoid blame for the fiscal situation was to ignore long-term projections and focus instead on short-term estimates for which the tax cut was less of a factor. When asked on CNN about the effect of deficits on interest rates in January 2002, for example, Bush economic advisor Lawrence Lindsey pointed to the projected short-term change in the deficit attributable to the tax cut, not its much larger long-term effects. "Remember," he said, "the tax cuts this year amounted to only 15 percent of the change in the deficit."[13] Rather than dealing with the long-term effects of the tax cut, which according to the liberal Center on Budget and Policy Priorities represented 41 percent of the decline in the projected ten-year surplus between January 2001 and January 2002, Lindsey simply used a different time frame.[14]

Bush's first post-9/11 budget, released in February 2002, took these tactics to new extremes. Labeled a "wartime budget" by Daniels, the White House obscured the cost of the President's tax cut and the multi-trillion-dollar decline in the surplus through opaque, highly engineered language.[15] For example, it stated that "In the 1997 [b]udget, rising deficits were forecast totaling $1.4 trillion over a ten year horizon. By the 2002 [b]udget, steadily rising surpluses were projected over a ten year period, totaling $5.6 trillion. Due to the events of last year, the latest projections are in between these wildly divergent estimates."[16] The euphemistic phrase "events of last year" brought to mind the September 11 attacks and subsequent war on terrorism, but the formulation was still technically accurate: the 2001 tax cut, a much bigger part of the decline in the long-term surplus, also took place in the same year.

The budget document also claimed that "if we make the right choices by stimulating growth and controlling spending, deficits will be small and temporary."[17] But the devil was in the details. CBPP demonstrated that the budget understated the true costs of a number of Bush's tax cut proposals and projected unrealistically low levels of government spending, obscuring hundreds of billions of dollars in likely costs.[18] The White House could only arrive at its numbers by ignoring inconvenient facts.

When presenting the administration's proposals to the Senate Budget Committee on February 5, 2002, Daniels bent the truth beyond recognition once again, claiming that the recession was "the reason that our long-term best guesses as to total surpluses have changed." However, a CBPP analysis of Congressional Budget

Office data available at the time found that the tax cut was the single largest factor in the decline.[19]

In July 2002, the administration announced higher deficit estimates. It promised a return to a balanced budget in 2005, however, claiming in its mid-session budget review that "This period in deficit should be brief, because economic fundamentals have stayed strong."[20] Yet its projection was riddled with more of Bush's deceptive budget tricks, including the omission of the costs of a number of proposals the President himself supported.[21] Once again, with more reasonable assumptions, continued deficits appeared likely.

In an illustration of the lengths to which the White House would go to avoid discussing the cost of the tax cut, the White House Office of Management and Budget tried to cover up an obvious factual error in a July 2002 press release announcing the new projections. The document incorrectly claimed that two-thirds of the reduction in the ten-year surplus was due to the recession, with the "costs of security and war" contributing 19 percent and the tax cut "less than 15 percent."[22] Those percentages were short-term figures, however, not ten-year projections as OMB stated. A CBPP analysis of OMB's data at the time showed that the tax cut constituted 38 percent of the reduction in the surplus over the ten-year period.[23]

The administration was clearly aware of this error. Council of Economic Advisors chair Glenn Hubbard conceded during a July 17 Joint Economic Committee hearing that 40 percent sounded "about right" for the ten-year impact of the tax cut on budget projections. However, the White House offered no public correction until July 26, when OMB simply posted a new version of the release on its website with the offending bullet point deleted—and no disclosure that it had been removed. After Paul Krugman wrote a

New York Times column about the matter, Trent Duffy, an OMB spokesperson, sent a letter to the *Times* claiming the "error" had been "retracted weeks ago when noticed." [24] When we reached him by phone, Duffy admitted that this retraction was only provided to reporters who noticed the mistake and contacted the budget office. (OMB eventually added a correction notice to the online version of the release.)

The gambits to deflect blame grew more and more brazen as the red ink continued to flow. In late August 2002, CBO released new figures showing a $5.3 trillion decline in the projected ten-year surplus since January 2001, which prompted Daniels to state that "the recession, the weakened stock market and the war caused the deficit," while omitting the effects of the tax cut. In an analysis of CBO data released a week after Daniels' statement, CBPP found that the tax cut represented 31 percent of the total decline in the ten-year surplus.[25] Once again, the Bush administration was ignoring a politically inconvenient truth.

Bush himself strained credulity even further in defending the tax cut, improbably claiming that it had actually *reduced* the deficit relative to what it would have been otherwise. After a Cabinet meeting on November 13, 2002, the President said, "Make no mistake about it, the tax relief package that we passed—that should be permanent, by the way—has helped the economy, and that the deficit would have been bigger without the tax relief package." [26]

This would mean that the tax cut paid for itself *and* generated additional revenue on top of that. Few mainstream economists think this is plausible. Experts disagree about the extent of the revenue losses attributable to tax cuts, but they are nearly unanimous in their belief that they do not pay for themselves. Every projection, including the one from the White House's Office of Management and

Budget, showed that the tax cut increased the deficit in both the short and long term. Even Duffy, the OMB spokesperson, did not defend Bush's contention, telling the *Washington Post* that the tax cut had produced growth that "certainly softened the recession's impact on revenues" but "by how much and to what degree, it's impossible to know."[27] Yet the *Washington Post* was the only major outlet to address the radical claim in any detail at the time (though the *New York Times* and CNN briefly cast doubt on it).[28] Most of the media simply gave the administration a pass.

Remarkably, Bush's own economists would later undercut his suggestion that tax cuts increased revenue. "Although the economy grows in response to tax reductions (because of higher consumption in the short run and improved incentives in the long run)," they wrote in the 2003 Economic Report of the President, "it is unlikely to grow so much that lost tax revenue is completely recovered by the higher level of economic activity."[29] Even the administration's own economic advisors didn't buy its spin.

THE MISSING INTEREST RATE LINK

In another bid to deflect political fallout, the administration began to imply that there is no connection between deficits and interest rates, a second claim that blatantly contradicted the consensus among economists. OMB first entered the debate on the issue in July 2002 by arguing that "there is no historical correlation between fiscal net position and interest rates," an assertion Daniels repeated during a July 12 briefing.[30]

This claim was accurate, but substantively misleading. As the *Economist* put it, "the formal econometric evidence is inconclusive: plenty of studies find a statistical link between interest rates and deficits; plenty find none." The reason is that "It is hard to disentangle the effect of changes in today's budget deficit from other factors affecting interest rates."[31] As with the debate over the revenue-generating effects of tax cuts, however, nearly every major economist agrees on the theoretical link between deficits and interest rates; the disagreement concerns the strength of the relationship. When liberal economists William Gale and Peter Orszag considered studies that took expectations of future deficits or surpluses into account, they concluded that most found a significant relationship with interest rates.[32] Nonetheless, administration officials tried to suggest that there was no link whatsoever.

Glenn Hubbard, chairman of the CEA at the time, contradicted his own economics textbook, calling the idea that deficits lead to higher interest rates "nonsense" and saying, "As an economist, I don't buy that there's a link between swings in the budget deficit of the size we see in the United States and interest rates. There's just no evidence."[33] During a press briefing in February 2003, Daniels caustically added, "Well, the idea that there is some connection between deficits and interest rates is an article of faith for some people, but I say faith because there is no evidence, zero, and at least at the levels that we are now experiencing, historically very moderate."[34]

The administration itself later undermined these claims. The 2003 Economic Report of the President stated that deficits *do* cause interest rates to rise (though not by very much): "Some calculations . . . imply that interest rates rise by about 3 basis points for every $200 billion in additional government debt." Later, Hubbard's successor Gregory Mankiw would repeatedly endorse this view, saying in a September 15, 2003 speech, for instance, "Of course, the expansionary effects of the tax cuts will be offset to some degree by the effects of the budget deficits that arise from lower revenues. Deficits can raise interest rates and crowd out of investment, although I should note that the magnitude of this effect is much debated in the economics literature."[35] In 2004, Bush himself admitted that "Fiscal policy can determine pressure on interest rates" during a speech in New Hampshire.[36] Once again, without admitting error, the Bush administration was acting as if its previous deceptive statements did not exist.

MORE BUDGET BUNK

In early 2003, Bush rolled out another budget that used the same mix of tactics, attempting to minimize deficits and disguise the severity of the financial situation. His message introducing the budget explicitly ignored the role of his tax cut in the fiscal deterioration, blaming recession and war. The budget later cited defense and homeland security spending increases as "explicit policy decisions [that] also contributed" to the deficit.[37] The 2001 tax cut was conspicuously (but unsurprisingly) absent from the list.

After the budget's release, Daniels returned to Capitol Hill to testify and put on the most ridiculous display of his tenure, refusing to admit the role of the tax cut in the country's fiscal deterioration. When Senator Kent Conrad, D-ND, asked Daniels about the deficit during a Senate Budget Committee hearing on February 5, 2003, the OMB director simply denied the role of the 2001 legislation, claiming that "it simply is not true that any policy, let alone the tax cuts, is responsible for the deficit we're facing today." Conrad incredulously asked, "The tax cuts have no part of the deficits going forward?" Daniels denied he meant this, but when Conrad said "I am talking about the ten years of this budget window. The tax cuts have played a major role in the return to deficits and burgeoning debt," Daniels' reply was "Well, sir, your comment moves me to use a four letter word: bunk," to which he later added, "The only deficit we know about is the deficit we're experiencing right now, perhaps the deficit for next year. Let's be a little humble about what we can and cannot see going forward."[38]

The exchange represented a major reversal for Daniels. In 2001, he admitted that long-term projections were uncertain but claimed that long-term surplus projections were "just as likely to prove low over those ten years as high" when pushing the administration's tax cut.[39] When the projected surplus practically disappeared by February 2002, the administration announced it would only provide five-year estimates of future budgets, which Daniels defended vigorously.[40] And by February 2003, he had been reduced to claiming that "The only deficit we know about is the deficit we're experiencing right now," a stunningly disingenuous refusal to consider obvious facts about projected fiscal imbalances.[41]

TAX CUT II: RETURN OF THE PLAYBOOK

In the first midterm election under President Bush, Republicans captured the Senate and expanded their majority in the House in November 2002, bucking historical trends. Armed with fresh political capital, the President began a push for a $674 billion tax cut in January 2003 using an expanded version of his 2001 playbook, which included a series of misleading averages and claims about benefits to politically popular groups, in this case middle-income families, small business owners, and seniors.

To better promote the plan, Bush ousted economic advisor Lawrence Lindsey and Treasury Secretary Paul O'Neill, who were widely seen as ineffective spokesmen for his policies. A White House official told the *Washington Post* that "They were unable to be effective in carrying the President's message. At the beginning of the administration, that was not as important as it's about to become."[42] Their replacements, Stephen Friedman and John Snow, were reportedly chosen largely for their public relations talents, with Snow saying, "Our job is to make the best possible case for the [President's] proposal, to argue it, to carry the message."[43] In the Bush White House, adherence to the administration's talking points appeared to be valued above all else.

MISLEADING SALES TACTICS

Bush's plan proposed eliminating taxes on stock dividend payments to individuals and accelerating several provisions of the 2001 tax cut, including rate reductions, an increase in the child tax credit, and legislation intended to reduce the so-called "marriage penalty." Rather than present these proposals in a straightforward manner, however, the administration's primary sales tactic was to tout unrepresentative "average" benefits of the plan for a variety of groups.

On the day before Bush's announcement of the proposal, the administration rolled out its first set of figures to counter Democratic criticism that it favored the rich. By releasing its numbers before the plan itself, the administration was able to put them into public circulation before they could be adequately scrutinized. As usual, the media played along. The *New York Times*, for instance, reported that "administration officials produced statistics to show that the tax cuts would benefit millions of middle-income workers," but "Democrats were having none of it, accusing Mr. Bush of proposing tax cuts that would overwhelmingly benefit the nation's wealthiest taxpayers."[44] Who was right? Nobody outside the administration knew yet! But that didn't stop the media from repeating the spin without any context or analysis.

Bush's broadest claim was that "Ninety-two million Americans will keep an average of $1,083 more of their own money," as he put it in his first radio address after announcing the plan.[45] The White House also touted the "average" benefits to seniors, claiming that "13 million elderly taxpayers would receive an average tax cut of $1,384" in its fact sheet. Likewise, Bush said on January 22 that "The average savings for somebody 65 years and older, if we get rid of the double taxation of dividends, will be $936 per year per tax return in America."[46] Finally, the plan was sold as a boon to small businesses, with the President stating that "Twenty-three million small business owners will receive an average tax cut of $2,042 under this plan."[47]

All of these figures were misleading. Like most such statistics from the administration, they represent the sum of all the benefits to taxpayers in the group divided by the number of taxpayers. This type of calculation often exaggerates the benefits for taxpayers in the middle of the income distribution because of the very large tax cuts received by the wealthiest Americans, which pull up the average.

In fact, under Bush's original proposal, the center-left Urban-Brookings Tax Policy Center found that taxpayers in the middle 20 percent of the income distribution would receive an average tax cut of only $227 in 2003 and the next highest quintile of taxpayers would receive only $510.[48] Center on Budget and Policy Priorities analyses of Urban-Brookings data also showed that 79 percent of both seniors and filers with small business income would have received less than the "average" benefits Bush touted for their groups.[49] The administration's averages were atypical and misleading.

Nonetheless, the press often repeated the claims credulously, failing to clarify the meaning of the statistics or offer criticism of the misleading figures. A typical example came from an article in the *Philadelphia Inquirer* that stated, "If Congress passed [Bush's] plan, 92 million taxpayers would get an average tax cut of $1,083, according to White House documents." [50] Such reports gave no help to the public in determining whether those "documents" presented a useful picture of the benefits of the tax cut.

To reinforce the claim of broad benefits, the administration also claimed in its fact sheet on the plan that beneficiaries would include "[e]veryone who pays taxes, especially middle-income Americans, as tax rate reductions passed by Congress in 2001 are made effective immediately." [51] Bush made a similar assertion on January 9, 2003, saying that the 2001 tax cut plan whose provisions would be accelerated "was tax relief for all citizens" and the new tax cut was based on the principle that "All people who pay taxes should get tax relief." In both cases, the administration used sleight of hand to imply that everyone who pays taxes would benefit. However, its plan excluded millions of Americans who pay payroll taxes for Social Security and Medicare, sales and excise taxes, and/or state and local taxes, but have no net federal income tax liability. This echoed the White House's salesmanship of Bush's first tax cut and foreshadowed a number of similar claims it would make later.

Finally, in response to criticism that his tax proposal would expand federal budget deficits, Bush again implied that tax cuts do the opposite, stating that his 2003 plan would generate "higher revenues" for the government. The legislation, he said on January 7, will "lay the groundwork for future growth and future prosperity. That growth will bring the added benefit of higher revenues for the government—revenues that will keep tax rates low, while fulfilling key obligations and protecting programs such as Medicare and Social Security." (He made a similar claim on May 2.)[52] However, as Bush's own economists pointed out, even the additional revenues generated by increased growth from a tax cut are almost always outweighed by revenue losses.

SHUTTING DOWN TAX CUT CRITICS

The administration supplemented its misleading sales pitch for the plan with attempts to silence its critics. Before the plan was even announced, Bush and other officials began to charge Democratic critics with allegedly practicing "class warfare," an *ad hominem* attack intended to preclude any discussion of whether economic policy proposals favor wealthier Americans. During the debate over the 2001 tax cut, Bush and Fleischer had invoked "class warfare" on several occasions, but it played a much larger role in the 2003 sales campaign.

On January 2, 2003, when asked about the benefits of the plan for wealthy Americans, Bush said, "I understand the politics of economic stimulus—that some would like to turn this into class warfare."[53] During a press briefing on January 7 before the announcement of the plan, Fleischer was asked about its distributional benefits and again tried to shut down the discussion. "The President believes that all taxpayers are over-taxed, and we are all in this together. The President does not believe in dividing the American people and playing class warfare," he said.[54] On January 9, Bush derided discussion of distributional benefits for a third time—"You hear the kind of the class warfare of politics"—before saying, "Let me just give you the facts" and launching into his misleading example of the family making $40,000 per year.[55] In an echo of tactics Bush had successfully used during the 2000 campaign and the push for his first tax cut, the catchy phrase served to dismiss criticism without addressing it.

The administration also used the war in Iraq to bully its opponents into going along with the tax cut. During a March 24, 2003 press briefing while the Iraq war was underway, Fleischer said the President "seeks to make sure that the economy can grow and that jobs can be created, so that when our men and women in the military return home, they'll have jobs to come home to." However, full-time military personnel would still have jobs, and reservists have legal protections to ensure they can resume their civilian employment in almost all cases.[56] During the same briefing, he made an even more blatant appeal to patriotism as a reason to support the tax cut: "The stronger the economy, the stronger we are as a country. The stronger we are as a country, the stronger our military." This was disturbingly similar to Bush's use of the war on terror after September 11 to deflect criticism of his domestic agenda.

In the end, Congress passed a compromise $330 billion tax cut bill (which also included $20 billion in aid to states) that Bush signed into law on May 29, 2003. The bill, which was considered a political win for the President, accelerated provisions from the 2001 tax cut and reduced tax rates on dividends and capital gains. The administration's denunciations of "class warfare" and efforts to link the package to patriotic appeals helped to carry the day.

ELECTION SEASON HIJINKS

In mid-2003, the successful invasion of Iraq and the approach of the 2004 presidential election prompted the White House to launch a broader effort to escape responsibility for the deficit and the state of the economy. The administration kicked off its campaign by ratcheting up its attempts to pin blame for the deficits on the war and recession. On May 6, 2003, for example, Bush stated that "we've got a deficit because we went through a recession. . . . Secondly, we've got a deficit because we're at war."[57] He did not mention his tax cuts as a factor, but according to a CBPP analysis of CBO data available at the time it actually accounted for approximately one-third of the decline in the budget situation both over the short term (from fiscal 2003 to fiscal 2004) and in long-term projections.[58] The problem was stubborn—and so was the administration's spin.

The budget situation had deteriorated so much by late 2003 that Bush and other administration officials finally admitted in a few cases that the tax cuts did affect the deficit. However, even when conceding that the tax cuts contributed to the deficit, the administration could not make its point honestly. Instead, they repeatedly misstated the portion of the deficit attributable to the tax cut. Speaking in Kansas City on September 4, 2003, Bush stated, "[T]he tax relief, which is stimulating economic growth, is a part of the deficit. It's about a quarter of the deficit." The President said this again during speeches on September 5 and October 3, and Cheney made the same claim on NBC's *Meet the Press* on September 14.[59] However, the White House's own figures showed at the time that the 2001 and 2003 tax cuts accounted for 31 percent of the 2003 deficit and 72 percent of the projected five-year deficit.[60] (Bush's claim actually referred to the overall change in budget surplus projections from 2001 to 2003 attributable to his tax cuts, a fact Mankiw noted in an online chat.)[61] Even when conceding that the tax cuts had some effect, the administration lowballed it.

These concessions proved to be an aberration, however, as the White House once again refused to admit that the tax cuts had anything to do with the deficit. During two speeches in late September, Cheney blamed the recession and war but didn't mention tax cuts, just as Bush did during his December 15 press conference.[62] Josh Bolten, who replaced Daniels as director of OMB in May 2003, provided a more elaborate version of this defense in December 8, 2003, on CNBC's *Titans with Maria Bartiromo,* when he said, "the deficit situation we face was not created by the tax cuts. I mean, the tax cuts are part of the solution, not part of the problem."

However, the evidence continued to show that Bush's tax cuts played a major role in the short- and long-term deficits faced by the federal government. In January 2004, CBPP found that the tax cut accounted for 35 percent of the $9.3 trillion decline in the projected ten-year surplus from 2002 to 2011, a close second to technical adjustments to revenue predictions (37 percent) that far exceeded increased spending on defense, homeland security, and international affairs, Medicare prescription drug coverage, and other domestic programs.[63]

Even after a Congressional Budget Office analysis released on March 15, 2004, made headlines by showing that the economic slowdown accounted for only 6 percent of the projected $477 billion deficit for fiscal 2004, Bush did not change his spin, saying in a March 25 speech in New Hampshire that "We have a deficit, and we've got a deficit because we were in recession, for starters."[64] As was all too common, the administration simply refused to give the public an accurate picture of the causes for the budget deficit.

READ MY LIPS, NOT MY PLAN

Never content simply to play defense, the administration also went on offense, touting a phony plan to cut the deficit in half that omitted a number of proposals that Bush supported. This game of hide-the-deficit began with the midyear budget review on July 15, 2003. The White House trumpeted claims showing the deficit would be "cut in half" by 2008 to try to minimize the impact of an increased deficit projection of $455 billion for fiscal 2003.[65] However, the plan omitted security and rebuilding costs in Afghanistan and Iraq after September 30, 2003, funding for a defense modernization initiative called the "Future Year Defense Plan," and changes in tax policy required to prevent the alternative minimum tax from affecting millions of middle-income taxpayers. When these and other costs the administration supported were factored in, CBPP found that the deficit would actually *increase* from 2003 to 2008, with a total 2008 deficit of roughly twice what the Bush administration projected.[66]

The day the midsession review was released, Scott McClellan, who had replaced Fleischer as White House press secretary, delivered his talking points during the White House press briefing, telling reporters, "[O]ver the next few years, what you're going to see is that we're going to cut that deficit in half based on the projections that are being outlined later today."[67] President Bush mentioned the claim four times in the following two weeks, including a July 30 press conference.[68]

When CBO released new projections of an increased deficit in August 2003, White House officials, including Bush, McClellan, and Cheney, began to tout the plan more intensely.[69] They did not stop even after Bush's $87 billion request to Congress for operations in Iraq and Afghanistan in September 2003 highlighted the plan's lack of funding for military operations in the two countries.[70] When the facts conflicted with its talking points, the administration's choice was clear.

Meanwhile, Bush and his aides continued to try to put a positive spin on the two major tax cuts passed during his term to counter Democratic proposals to repeal all or part of them. To do so, they often recycled the same tactics used in originally selling the proposals.

For example, Bush repeatedly implied that all Americans got tax cuts, not merely those who pay federal income taxes, as when he said on October 3, 2003, in Madison, Wisconsin, that "We reduced the taxes on everybody who pays taxes—we didn't pick or choose, everybody who pays taxes will get a reduction." That Bush was talking about federal income taxes was once again omitted.

The administration also continued to misrepresent the distributional effects of the tax cuts. During a CNBC appearance with OMB director Bolten in December 2003, Bush economic advisor Stephen Friedman said, "there's a real misimpression that's been spread . . . about the President's tax cuts. A lot of the tax cuts did go toward the lower end."[71] The claim that "A lot of the tax cuts" went to "the lower end" is absurd. When the benefits to lower-income Americans are measured as a portion of the overall cost of the tax cut, they simply do not represent "a lot" of the total.

Similarly, a December 13, 2003 White House fact sheet touted the benefits of the tax cuts using a series of statistical averages that echoed previous administration tactics. As a result of the 2003 tax cut, the White House claimed, "91 million taxpayers received, on average, a tax cut of $1,126. Since the President took office, 109 million taxpayers have received, on average, a tax cut of $1,544. Twenty-three million small business owners received tax cuts averaging $2,209." [72] By then, the administration's unending repetition of these widely debunked figures was beyond farce. [73]

DRAGGING DOWN THE STANDARDS OF ECONOMIC DEBATE

The story about the alleged "trifecta" statement in Chicago may have been the most outrageous economic deception of the Bush presidency since September 11, but as we have seen it is far from the only one. Bush's dishonesty on tax and budget issues has been so relentless that journalists have appeared to become even more uninterested in it as time has gone on, as if misleading claims from the President of the United States about policies affecting millions of people's lives are not matters of importance. Once again, the media's indifference to issues that lack scandal and intrigue served to protect the President from scrutiny. To some, Bush's penchant for misleading the public about tax and budget issues may have seemed to be just another part of the never-ending political game. When the administration made its case for a preemptive war in Iraq, however, the consequences of misleading claims by the White House would become deadly serious.

SELLING THE WAR IN IRAQ

On January 29, 2002, President Bush delivered his State of the Union address before a joint session of Congress and millions of television viewers. After highlighting the nation's recovery from the September 11 attacks and the successful ouster of the Taliban in Afghanistan, he went on to coin the phrase for which the speech quickly became famous:

North Korea is a regime arming with missiles and weapons of mass destruction, while starving its citizens.

Iran aggressively pursues these weapons and exports terror, while an unelected few repress the Iranian people's hope for freedom.

Iraq continues to flaunt its hostility toward America and to support terror. The Iraqi regime has plotted to develop anthrax, and nerve gas, and nuclear weapons for over a decade. This is a regime that has already used poison gas to murder thousands of its own citizens— leaving the bodies of mothers huddled over their dead children. This is a regime that agreed to international inspections—then kicked out the inspectors. This is a regime that has something to hide from the civilized world.

States like these, and their terrorist allies, constitute an axis of evil,
arming to threaten the peace of the world. By seeking weapons of
mass destruction, these regimes pose a grave and growing danger.
They could provide these arms to terrorists, giving them the means to
match their hatred. They could attack our allies or attempt to
blackmail the United States. In any of these cases, the price of
indifference would be catastrophic.

Commentators focused on the phrase "axis of evil," noting its rhetorical connection to the Axis of Nazi Germany, fascist Italy, and imperial Japan during World War II, as well as Ronald Reagan's famous speech labeling the Soviet Union an "evil empire."[1]

In retrospect, however, the suggestion that Iraq's terrorist connections and pursuit of weapons of mass destruction posed a serious danger to the United States was much more important. It would become the core of the administration's justification for military action to overthrow Saddam Hussein's regime.

GETTING INTO IRAQ

Although Iraq had been a concern for the Bush administration from its first days in the White House, the September 11 attacks strengthened its resolve to remove Saddam Hussein from power. In the wake of the terrorist attacks on New York and Washington, DC, Iraq's long history of aggressive actions toward its neighbors and efforts to develop weapons of mass destruction seemed to present an unacceptable risk. The question was how to convince Congress and the American public to put muscle behind the official U.S. policy of "regime change" and support disarming Iraq or removing Saddam from power.

Critics have accused the administration of unduly pressuring intelligence analysts to produce conclusions that would help make its case for war. However, to date, there is little evidence of direct pressure.[2]

Instead, the White House turned to tactics it had used in previous political fights to build public support. Mustering as much damning evidence as possible, the administration executed a carefully crafted public relations campaign centering on Iraq's alleged possession of weapons of mass destruction. Rather than playing up the uncertainty of the data, as it had during debates over scientific and environmental policy, the White House glossed over gaps in intelligence and caveats about sources, frequently presenting worst-case scenarios as fact. Officials also used loaded rhetoric to make suggestions that could not be proven and invoked powerful images, such as a "mushroom cloud," when discussing the threat Iraq posed.

Government officials have a special burden to present intelligence findings responsibly since they often depend upon classified information that cannot be independently confirmed. This includes noting qualifications about the reliability and sources of such information, which by its very nature is rarely definitive. In making the case for military action against Iraq, however, the administration presented ambiguous information as if it were certain and used exaggerated rhetoric to present claims based on patchy evidence. At times, it also implied connections, such as a link between the September 11 attacks and Iraq, which its own evidence did not support. Though the administration was hardly monolithic in its message—Secretary of State Colin Powell tended to be relatively reserved in his claims, for example, while Vice President Dick Cheney tended to be relatively aggressive—the overall pattern is one of sacrificing ambiguity for the sake of selling the war.

Regrettably, a quiescent media allowed the administration to get away with these claims. The perception of Bush as a wartime president promoting a popular war appeared to intimidate the press, which often allowed the White House to enter misleading and false claims into the record without serious challenge. (The Clinton administration, which had made its own share of deceptive claims about Iraq, had prepared the media to believe the worst.) [3] The President relied, in part, on specific intelligence information that the press could not verify, but he and his aides also exaggerated claims that could have been checked with nonclassified sources. By frequently neglecting to do so, the media failed the American public in the prelude to the war.

As a result, the administration's sales campaign was a stunning success. In October 2002, Congress passed a joint resolution by large margins in both the House and the Senate authorizing the President to use force in Iraq if Saddam did not disarm. After an all-out diplomatic effort by the U.S., the United Nations Security Council then passed Resolution 1441 in early November, which sent weapons inspectors back into Iraq and warned of "serious consequences" if Saddam continued to hide prohibited weapons or weapons programs. After several months of Iraqi resistance and limited progress by the inspection teams, the U.S. began arguing that Iraq was not complying with the terms of the resolution and calling for action. Secretary of State Colin Powell's February 2003 speech to the United Nations failed to persuade several members of the Security Council to back a second U.N. resolution authorizing military action against Iraq, but it helped rally support among Americans. The White House then decided to move ahead with military action under the auspices of the first resolution, withdrawing the second from consideration.

By the time military operations began, on March 19, 2003, Bush had convinced most of the nation to go to war. A *Washington Post* / ABC News poll found that nearly two-thirds of those surveyed supported Bush's policies toward Iraq, and 71 percent backed the use of force.[4] Whatever the merits of the larger case for removing Saddam from power, the White House sales campaign was a resounding success.

IRAQ AND SEPTEMBER 11

Iraq has been a major issue in U.S. foreign policy since the 1980s. There was little question that Saddam Hussein was a tyrannical dictator with a history of aggression against other countries, including initiating the Iran-Iraq War of the 1980s (during which the U.S. generally backed Iraq) and invading Kuwait, which sparked the 1991 Gulf War. Saddam had developed chemical weapons before the Gulf War and used them against Iranian soldiers and Kurdish civilians. As part of the agreement ending the war, he promised to destroy his weapons of mass destruction and dismantle his weapons development programs.

U.N. inspectors monitored the regime's compliance with this accord from 1991 to 1998, eventually finding large stocks of chemical weapons, a significant biological weapons program, and a crash program to develop nuclear weapons that had been much more advanced than prewar intelligence suggested. Inspectors destroyed stocks of weapons as well as the raw materials and equipment necessary for their production. Yet Iraq did what it could to thwart the inspectors, refusing to hand over key information and at times blocking access to particular sites. Moreover, Iraq could not account for significant quantities of weapons and weapons-related material;

in most cases, it claimed to have destroyed them but could not provide documentation to the U.N.[5] (These contentions appear to have been borne out by postwar investigations.)[6]

In late 1998, Iraq announced it would no longer cooperate with the inspections program. A few weeks later it backed down, but after it continued to deny inspectors access to several sites, the United States and Great Britain carried out a series of air strikes against the regime. The U.N. inspectors departed just ahead of the bombings and did not return until after the November 2002 U.N. resolution.

Bush took a hard line on Iraq during the 2000 presidential campaign. At a Republican primary debate, he stated that "If I found, in any way, shape, or form, that [Saddam] was developing weapons of mass destruction, I'd take them out." (When questioned by moderator Brit Hume, "Take him out?" Bush replied, "Take out the weapons of mass destruction.")[7]

After taking office, Bush took a more aggressive approach to Iraq than Clinton had. Treasury Secretary Paul O'Neill later described meetings about Iraq held in early 2001 in which officials explored options to undermine Saddam's regime, including the use of force.[8] In addition, during the first few months of his term in office, Bush launched a large number of air strikes to enforce the no-fly zones put in place after the 1991 Gulf War.

The terrorist attacks of September 11 convinced some administration hawks that removing Saddam from power should be an urgent priority. Among them were Defense Secretary Donald Rumsfeld and Deputy Defense Secretary Paul Wolfowitz, two officials who had helped successfully lobby the Clinton administration to make "regime change" the official goal of U.S. foreign policy toward Iraq in 1998.[9]

On September 11, notes taken by aides to Rumsfeld indicate he asked them to "Judge whether good enough to hit S.H. [Saddam Hussein] at same time. Not only UBL [Osama bin Laden, sometimes spelled Usama bin Laden]," despite indications that bin Laden was the perpetrator. The notes indicate the Secretary of Defense wanted the aides to "Go massive. Sweep it all up. Things related and not."[10] According to author Bob Woodward, Rumsfeld asked in a meeting on September 12 if the attacks presented an "opportunity" to attack Iraq.[11] When James Woolsey, former CIA director and member of the Pentagon's advisory Defense Policy Board, suggested later that fall Iraq might be connected to the attacks, the Bush administration flew him to London to investigate.[12]

However, the administration never linked Iraq directly to the September 11 attacks. Although Saddam's government had occasional contact with al Qaeda operatives, no evidence has yet emerged supporting a high level, coordinated relationship between the two.[13]

Nonetheless, many in the administration felt that the possibility that Iraq could pass chemical, biological, or nuclear weapons to terrorists was too dangerous to ignore. Deputy Defense Secretary Paul Wolfowitz, for instance, reportedly suggested the weekend after September 11 that Iraq should be a target in what was emerging as the war on terrorism.[14] Their view eventually prevailed. In late November, President Bush asked Rumsfeld to begin thinking about a war plan to remove Saddam Hussein from power.[15] In a book about his time as a White House speechwriter, David Frum writes that he was instructed to include a rhetorical rationale for war with Iraq in the President's January 2002 State of the Union address, which became Bush's denunciation of the "axis of evil."[16]

The exact time at which the administration decided to confront Iraq is unclear. But evidence suggests that the White House was moving toward war by early 2002. In February, Bush signed a secret order authorizing covert operations to undermine the Iraqi regime.[17] The next month, the President was reportedly confident enough in the decision to casually tell a trio of senators who were meeting with National Security Advisor Condoleezza Rice, "Fuck Saddam. We're taking him out."[18] And later that month, Vice President Cheney told Senate Republicans that the decision to attack had been made— the only question was the timing.[19]

In retrospect, it appears that the decision to act against Saddam preceded the decision about how to sell the war to the public, which was the product of a months-long process that would take place during the summer of 2002.

GATHERING INTELLIGENCE
AND PLANNING THE SPIN

Soon after September 11, the administration began to change the way in which it handled intelligence, especially regarding Iraq. Rumsfeld and Wolfowitz, the top two officials in the Department of Defense, shared a long history of skepticism about the U.S. intelligence community. Wolfowitz and Douglas Feith, Undersecretary of Defense for Policy, were members of a team of outside experts that had analyzed intelligence on Soviet nuclear missiles in the mid-1970s, concluding that CIA analysts were substantially underestimating the threat they posed to the U.S. (much of their analysis later proved to be incorrect).[20] Rumsfeld chaired a similar effort in the late 1990s evaluating the need for a ballistic missile defense program, which also included Wolfowitz.

In October 2001, Rumsfeld, Wolfowitz, and Feith created the Office of Special Plans (OSP), a small group inside the Department of Defense set up to analyze intelligence information independently. The group made a much stronger case than the CIA or the Pentagon's Defense Intelligence Agency that Saddam presented a dire threat.[21] Critics contend that the OSP short-circuited the process for evaluating the reliability of intelligence information, creating "stovepipes" that funneled damaging information about Iraq directly to top officials without adequate screening of its quality.[22]

Another crucial variable was that information about Iraq had become scarce after U.N. weapons inspectors departed in 1998. As CIA Director George Tenet put it after the war, "While we had voluminous reporting, the major judgments reached were based on a narrower band of data."[23] Analysts had to rely more heavily on interpretation of what evidence they had, and as a Pentagon advisor put it, OSP "won the policy debate. . . . They persuaded the President of the need to make a new security policy."[24]

In July 2002, the administration began planning one of its elaborate public relations campaigns, with the goal of convincing Congress to pass a resolution authorizing the President to take military action against Iraq. The rollout was timed to put pressure on Congress as it returned from its August recess and prepared for the November elections. As White House Chief of Staff Andrew Card put it when questioned about the timing of the campaign, "From a marketing point of view, you don't introduce a new product in August."[25]

To coordinate the White House's marketing of this "new product," Card formed a task force known as the White House Iraq Group (WHIG). It included Card; White House political advisor Karl Rove; communications advisors Karen Hughes, Mary Matalin, and James Wilkinson; legislative liaison Nicholas Calio; National Security Advisor Condeleezza Rice and a number of her advisors;

and Lewis Libby, Cheney's chief of staff. The WHIG also included a "strategic communications" task force to help plan speeches and publish white papers.[26]

The administration had several different rationales for action against Iraq. In a postwar interview with *Vanity Fair*'s Sam Tannenhaus, Wolfowitz listed four: weapons of mass destruction, links to terrorism, the possibility of the transfer of WMDs to terrorists, and Saddam's treatment of the Iraqi people. At some point, however, the decision was made to focus on weapons of mass destruction and the threat that Saddam might transfer them to terrorists. Wolfowitz later said, "[F]or reasons that have a lot to do with the U.S. government bureaucracy, we settled on the one issue that everyone could agree on, which was weapons of mass destruction as the core reason."[27]

With this rationale in mind, the WHIG pressed for dramatic material to make its case to the public. The *Washington Post* reported after the war that "the WHIG, according to three officials who followed the white paper's progress, wanted gripping images and stories not available in the hedged and austere language of intelligence." This led to some of the administration's grandest rhetoric invoking mushroom clouds and other disturbing images. An unnamed senior intelligence official told the *Washington Post* that the President's speechwriters took "literary license" in their descriptions of the threat from Iraq.[28]

At roughly the same time, according to former Defense Department intelligence officer and Bush administration critic Karen Kwiatkowski, the Office of Special Plans began circulating internal talking points for use in public statements. These discussed Saddam's prior use of chemical weapons, his relationships with terrorists (including medical treatment received by an al Qaeda member in Baghdad), Iraq's nuclear weapons programs, and the potential for nuclear weapons to be transferred to al Qaeda or other terrorist groups.[29]

The administration's approach to its sales campaign is a classic example of public relations tactics applied to politics. The decision to press for action against Iraq had already been made; the only question was what rationale would provide the greatest sales hook to persuade Congress and the public to back the effort. Instead of presenting intelligence information responsibly, the White House had set up a system to produce compelling marketing messages with minimal concern for their accuracy.

GOING NUCLEAR WITH THE RHETORIC

In early September 2002, the administration launched an all-out marketing blitz. White House sources told the *New York Times* that "the administration was following a meticulously planned strategy to persuade the public, Congress and the allies of the need to confront the threat from Saddam Hussein."[30] On September 8, Cheney gave an extensive interview to NBC's *Meet the Press,* Powell appeared on *Fox News Sunday,* and Rice went on CNN's *Late Edition with Wolf Blitzer.*

The administration's first focus in its marketing campaign was Iraq's nuclear program. The power of nuclear imagery was obvious, and the administration exploited it with references to a "mushroom cloud" and "nuclear blackmail." At the same time, officials exaggerated the evidence indicating that Saddam was pursuing a nuclear weapon.

After inspectors left in 1998, information about Saddam's nuclear program became particularly sketchy. There was little question that the dictator wanted to produce a nuclear weapon (as his pre–Gulf War program had made clear); the issue was whether he could obtain the materials and knowledge necessary to do so. His ability to carry on such a program undetected was also uncertain, since unlike small-scale chemical and biological weapons facilities, which are relatively easy to hide, nuclear weapons facilities require large amounts of equipment, space, and energy that are difficult to disguise.

In 2001, according to former State Department intelligence staffer and Iraq war critic Greg Thielmann, the State Department's intelligence operation gave Secretary Powell a report that, in Thielmann's words, "basically said there is no persuasive evidence that the Iraqi nuclear program is being reconstituted." [31] With only shreds of evidence available, however, multiple interpretations were possible, and an investigation by the *Washington Post* suggested that the administration relied heavily on a worst-case reading of the data.[32]

Despite this ambiguity, the Bush administration illustrated its claims about Iraq's nuclear program with vivid language. A recurring theme was the mushroom cloud that could result from a nuclear blast. On September 8, 2002, Rice stated on CNN's *Late Edition* that "There will always be some uncertainty about how quickly [Saddam] can acquire nuclear weapons, but we don't want the smoking gun to be a mushroom cloud." Bush used a nearly identical phrase in a televised October 7 address to the nation, stating that "Facing clear evidence of peril, we cannot wait for the final proof—the smoking gun—that could come in the form of a mushroom cloud." On November 12, Army General Tommy Franks, the head of U.S. Central Command, said that a failure to confront Saddam could result in "the sight of the first mushroom cloud on one of the major population centers on this planet." [33] Such a powerful image had obvious resonance with the public.

Another evocative piece of rhetoric was the suggestion that if Saddam acquired a nuclear weapon he could engage in "nuclear blackmail," a claim Vice President Cheney introduced in nearly identical speeches to veterans groups on August 26 and 29, 2002.[34] "Armed with an arsenal of these weapons of terror, and seated atop 10 percent of the world's oil reserves," Cheney said in the first speech, "Saddam Hussein could then be expected to seek domination of the entire Middle East, take control of a great portion of the world's energy supplies, directly threaten America's friends throughout the region, and subject the United States or any other nation to nuclear blackmail." In his January 2002 State of the Union speech, President Bush made a slightly softer version of the same claim, stating that, "By seeking weapons of mass destruction, these regimes [Iran, North Korea, and Iraq] pose a grave and growing danger. They could provide these arms to terrorists, giving them the means to match their hatred. They could attack our allies or attempt to blackmail the United States."

Like the image of a mushroom cloud, these references painted a picture of the worst-case scenario without any sort of caveat about the likelihood of such an event. The declassified National Intelligence Estimate of October 2002 did state that "If Baghdad acquires fissile material from abroad it could make a nuclear weapon within several months to a year," a prospect the intelligence community considered unlikely. However, "[w]ithout such material from abroad," it concluded, "Iraq probably would not be able to make a weapon until 2007 to 2009, owing to inexperience in building and operating centrifuge facilities to produce highly enriched uranium and challenges in procuring the necessary equipment and expertise."

This was in part because post–Gulf War sanctions on Iraq had taken a heavy toll on the regime's ability to procure parts for a nuclear weapons program.[35] And although the administration certainly did not know exactly what equipment Saddam had been able to hide or obtain, officials were well aware of the sanctions and other measures being taken to prevent him from acquiring those materials.

The administration continually omitted such qualifiers and context about Saddam's efforts in order to strengthen its sales pitch, particularly when it was asked about claims that were almost surely false. Instead of denying the claim, officials would ominously suggest that the answer was unknown. For example, during a November 8, 2002 appearance on NBC's *Meet the Press,* host Tim Russert asked Cheney, "[Saddam] does not have a nuclear weapon now?" The Vice President replied, "I can't say that. I can say that I know for sure that he's trying to acquire the capability." Bush made a similar claim in a December 31 press conference when he said, "I think it's important to remember that Saddam Hussein was close to having a nuclear weapon. We don't know whether or not he has a nuclear weapon."[36]

Members of the press often failed to include critical information that was available from the public record in their reports about Iraq's nuclear weapons programs. After Cheney's August 26 speech invoking "nuclear blackmail," for example, the *Washington Post* repeated Cheney's remarks without noting either the U.N.'s conclusion from 1998 that the program had been dismantled, or other questions about Iraq's ability to produce such weapons.[37] Not only did the front-page *New York Times* story on Cheney's speech contain almost no context for evaluating claims about Iraq's nuclear program, but the paper also printed excerpts from Cheney's speech inside the front section.[38] The same occurred with Bush's December

31, 2002, remarks; the *Washington Post,* for example, simply transcribed Bush's suggestion that Iraq might have a nuclear weapon without examining whether it was unlikely.[39]

At other times, the administration used old information in deceptive ways, omitting intervening events and contradictory details. In an August 26, 2002 appearance at the Veterans of Foreign Wars convention, Vice President Cheney claimed, "[W]e now know that Saddam has resumed his efforts to acquire nuclear weapons. Among other sources, we've gotten this from the firsthand testimony of defectors—including Saddam's own son-in-law."[40] However, testimony obtained by reporters in 2003 showed that Saddam's son-in-law General Hussein Kamel, the former Iraqi weapons programs head who defected in 1995, actually told U.N. weapons inspectors that "All weapons—biological, chemical, missile, nuclear—were destroyed." This was exactly the opposite of what Cheney was implying.[41]

Moreover, Hussein Kamel and another son-in-law of Saddam's, Colonel Saddam Kamel, were killed in 1996 after returning to Iraq, so neither of them could have been the source for claims about the current state of Iraq's nuclear programs.[42] (The Clinton administration had also played up Hussein Kamel's testimony as evidence of Iraq's illicit weapons programs.)[43] An unnamed Congressional investigator told the *New York Times'* Douglas Jehl and David Sanger in January 2004 that the claim that Saddam was rebuilding his nuclear program was based primarily on a single source who provided intelligence that the Iraqi government was spending money on a physics building.[44]

On another occasion, Bush was deceptive about the source of a claim that Iraq had been close to developing a nuclear weapon. On September 7, 2002, the President stated that "I would remind you that when the inspectors first went into Iraq and were denied—finally denied access, a report came out of the Atomic—the IAEA [International Atomic Energy Agency], that they were six months away from developing a [nuclear] weapon. I don't know what more evidence we need."[45] The IAEA did issue a report in 1998 just after inspectors left Iraq, but it stated that Iraq had been six months away from developing a nuclear weapon in *1991,* not 1998 as Bush implied. Indeed, the IAEA concluded that Iraq's efforts to produce weapons-grade nuclear material had been crippled by the war and the U.N. inspections. It found "no indications that Iraq had achieved its program objective of producing nuclear weapons or that Iraq had produced more than a few grams of weapons-usable nuclear material of any practical significance. Furthermore, there are no indications that there remains in Iraq any physical capability for the production of weapon-usable material of any practical significance."[46]

Rather than simply clarifying the point, however, the White House tried to spin Bush's comment away. When the *Washington Times* pointed out the mistake, spokesman Scott McClellan suggested that the President had been referring to a 1991 IAEA report.[47] However, the agency produced no such report that year. When asked for clarification a few weeks later by the *Washington Post,* the White House claimed that Bush had been "imprecise" and that the source for Bush's claim was U.S. intelligence.[48]

But two days later, in a letter to the editor published in the *Post,* White House Press Secretary Ari Fleischer changed the story again, stating that "It was in fact the International Institute for Strategic Studies that issued the report concluding that Iraq could develop nuclear weapons in as few as six months." However, the IISS report was issued on September 9, 2002—two days *after* Bush had made the original claim. Moreover, the report did not mention a six-month estimate, concluding only that Iraq could "assemble nuclear weapons within months if fissile material from foreign sources were obtained." The administration was once again trying to spin its way out of trouble rather than admitting a mistake and correcting the record.

TALL TALES ABOUT TUBES

On September 8, 2002, the *New York Times* ran a front page story reporting that, "In the last 14 months, Iraq has sought to buy thousands of specially designed aluminum tubes, which American officials believe were intended as components of centrifuges to enrich uranium." A few sentences later, the article noted that "The diameter, thickness and other technical specifications of the aluminum tubes had persuaded American intelligence experts that they were meant for Iraq's nuclear program, officials said, and that the latest attempt to ship the material had taken place in recent months." The *Times* acknowledged that "A key issue is whether the items Iraq tried to buy are uniquely designed for centrifuge use or could have other applications," stating that "Senior administration officials insist that the dimensions, specifications and numbers of the tubes Iraq sought to buy show that they were intended for the nuclear program."[49]

On the surface, this appeared to be very strong evidence that Iraq was attempting to rebuild its nuclear program and manufacture a nuclear weapon, and the tubes quickly became part of the administration's sales pitch for the war. White House officials cited them repeatedly and often without qualification. The same day the *Times* article appeared, Cheney and Rice both referred to the tubes on various talk shows. On *Meet the Press,* Cheney stated that Saddam "has been seeking to acquire, and we have been able to intercept and prevent him from acquiring through this particular channel, the kinds of tubes that are necessary to build a centrifuge." Moments later, he added, "We do know, with absolute certainty, that he is using his procurement system to acquire the equipment he needs in order to enrich uranium to build a nuclear weapon." [50] Rice went even further, telling CNN's Wolf Blitzer that evening that "We do know that [Saddam] is actively pursuing a nuclear weapon" and citing "high-quality aluminum tubes that are only really suited for nuclear weapons programs, centrifuge programs." [51] A few days later, Bush repeated the claim in a speech to the United Nations, stating that "Iraq has made several attempts to buy high-strength aluminum tubes used to enrich uranium for a nuclear weapon." [52]

The administration was overstating the conclusions of its own experts, implying that the tubes were for centrifuges when other explanations were at least as convincing. Once again, George W. Bush's White House was telling a simple story about a complex issue.

CIA analysts had initially concluded that the tubes were intended for a nuclear program. However, other questions emerged when centrifuge experts examined the tubes. Analysts at the Department of Energy's Oak Ridge National Laboratory found that they were poorly suited for uranium enrichment. The tubes were too narrow and long and their walls were too thick to fit into existing centrifuge designs. They could only be used in centrifuges with a great deal of modification. [53]

This evidence suggested that the tubes were intended for artillery rockets, a purpose for which they could be used without modification. Indeed, the tubes fit a known design for an Italian artillery rocket that Iraq could have been copying. [54] As an unnamed expert familiar with the tubes told the *Washington Post,* "It may be technically possible that the tubes could be used to enrich uranium, but you'd have to believe the Iraqis deliberately ordered the wrong stock and intended to spend a great deal of time and money reworking each piece." [55]

Toward the end of September 2002, several other reports reached the conclusion that the tubes were poorly suited for a centrifuge program. On September 23, the Institute for Science and International Security released a report making that point. The British government's dossier on Iraq's prohibited weapons, released on September 24, reached the same conclusion, stating, "There is no definitive intelligence that [the tubes are] destined for a nuclear programme." [56] The declassified portions of the National Intelligence Estimate, released on October 2, stated that "Iraq's aggressive attempts to obtain high-strength aluminum tubes for centrifuge rotors" and other evidence suggested Saddam was "reconstituting a uranium enrichment effort," but it also noted that the Department of Energy and the State Department's intelligence operation were not convinced that the tubes were intended for use as centrifuge rotors.

Yet the administration continued to press the line that the tubes were intended for a centrifuge program, often omitting that the issue was disputed within the government. In his nationally televised address on October 7, 2002, for example, Bush stated that "Iraq has attempted to purchase high-strength aluminum tubes and other equipment needed for gas centrifuges, which are used to enrich uranium for nuclear weapons." [57]

On December 2, White House spokesman Ari Fleischer took the tube spin to the next level. Talking to reporters in a press briefing, he implied that Iraq's insistence that it had purchased the tubes for conventional weaponry was a lie (a theme that the White House was developing in its case for military action). "I will say this is something that the President has said publicly, that Iraq did, in fact, seek to buy these tubes for the purpose of producing, not as Iraq now claims conventional forces, but for the purpose of trying to produce nuclear weapons," Fleischer stated. "And so it's, on the one hand, mildly encouraging that Iraq would now admit to what it's been doing. But on the other hand, a lie is still a lie, because these—they sought to produce these for the purpose of production of nuclear weapons, not conventional." [58]

In January 2003, the International Atomic Energy Agency released its own evaluation of the tubes, concluding that they could be modified for use in centrifuges but were not "directly suitable" for them.[59] The Bush administration responded by attacking the agency; as an unnamed senior administration official told the *New York Times,* "I think the Iraqis are spinning the IAEA. The majority of the intelligence community has the same view as before." [60] Most of the time, however, officials simply ignored the IAEA report. In his 2003 State of the Union address, Bush claimed that "Our intelligence sources tell us that [Saddam] has attempted to purchase high-strength aluminum tubes suitable for nuclear weapons production."

In February 2003, Colin Powell noted in his speech to the United Nations that "There is controversy about what these tubes are for" but downplayed the dispute. He stated that "Most U.S. experts think they are intended to serve as rotors in centrifuges used to enrich uranium. Other experts, and the Iraqis themselves, argue that they are really to produce the rocket bodies for a conventional weapon, a multiple rocket launcher." One of his slides, however, was much less equivocal, captioning a picture of one tube, "Aluminum Tube for Uranium Enrichment."

Powell's presentation ignored additional contradictory evidence obtained from inspections in Iraq that strongly suggested the tubes were intended for rockets. As the *Washington Post* reported in the summer of 2003, while Iraq had asked for different tube specifications in different orders, its orders did not show a clear progression to higher tolerances, as might be expected in a centrifuge program. (The requests might have been due to a mishap with one of the rockets, after which Baghdad apparently asked for more precise specifications.) Weapons inspectors had also observed that the tubes were needed for rocket production at a factory north of Baghdad.[61] Even Powell's mild equivocations glossed over the real debate about the tubes and misrepresented the state of U.S. knowledge.

In addition, Powell claimed during his speech to the U.N. that "The high tolerance aluminum tubes are only part of the story. We also have intelligence from multiple sources that Iraq is attempting to acquire magnets and high-speed balancing machines; both items can be used in a gas centrifuge program to enrich uranium." He continued with the assertion that "In 1999 and 2000, Iraqi officials negotiated with firms in Romania, India, Russia and Slovenia for the purchase of a magnet production plant. Iraq wanted the plant to produce magnets weighing 20 to 30 grams. That's the same weight as the magnets used in Iraq's gas centrifuge program before the Gulf War. This incident linked with the tubes is another indicator of Iraq's attempt to reconstitute its nuclear weapons program."

Yet under close scrutiny this claim fell apart as well. The declassified October 2002 National Intelligence Estimate had noted that the State Department's Bureau of Intelligence and Research called the case of the magnet production line "ambiguous" and stated that the magnets' "a suitability for centrifuge programs remains unknown." The IAEA's Mohamed El Baradei told the U.N. Security Council on March 7, 2003, that the weight of the magnets themselves "was not enough; you don't have a centrifuge magnet because it's 20 grams." [62]

As it had in previous political battles over science, the administration simply dismissed facts that contradicted its message.

NIGER, AFRICA, AND YELLOWCAKE

In the late summer or early fall of 2002, the White House Iraq Group produced an internal report on the nuclear threat as part of its communications planning effort. The *Washington Post,* which obtained a draft of the paper, noted that it contained the first known instance of the administration's claim that Iraq had attempted to obtain uranium from Africa. [63]

The initial mention of the claim outside the White House came in the declassified National Intelligence Estimate of October 2002, which asserted in its "key judgements" that "Iraq also began vigorously trying to procure uranium ore and yellowcake [refined natural uranium]; acquiring either would shorten the time Baghdad needs to produce nuclear weapons." It continued:

> *A foreign government service reported that as of early 2001, Niger planned to send several tons of "pure uranium" (probably yellowcake) to Iraq. As of early 2001, Niger and Iraq reportedly were still working out arrangements for this deal, which could be for up to 500 tons of yellowcake. We do not know the status of this arrangement.*
>
> *Reports indicate Iraq has also sought uranium ore from Somalia and possibly the Democratic Republic of Congo.*
>
> *We cannot confirm whether Iraq succeeded in acquiring uranium ore and/or yellowcake from these sources. Reports suggest Iraq is shifting from domestic mining and milling of uranium to foreign acquisition.*

However, administration officials should have been aware that the Niger claim was based on forged documents. In late 2001, the Italian intelligence service had passed along a report to the CIA about a 1999 visit to Niger by the Iraqi ambassador to the Vatican. The report suggested that the ambassador's trip had included an attempt to broker a deal to buy yellowcake. Though CIA analysts apparently had reservations about the quality of the information, the report was passed to Vice President Cheney, among others.[64] In February 2002, the CIA asked Joseph Wilson, former ambassador to Gabon and a former advisor to the National Security Council under Clinton, to travel to Niger to verify the authenticity of the claim. Wilson flew to Niger and discovered no evidence to support the story.[65]

There were also broader questions about Iraq's attempt to procure uranium from elsewhere in Africa. The Niger claim seemed to have died with Wilson's return, but British officials released an intelligence dossier on September 24, 2002, stating that "there is intelligence that Iraq has sought the supply of significant quantities of uranium from Africa."[66] Though the precise source for the claim remains unclear, John Scarlett, chairman of the British Joint Intelligence Committee that had been charged with drafting the dossier, noted in an internal memo that the evidence for the claim was in the possession of a foreign intelligence service rather than the British themselves.[67]

One month later, in October 2002, the administration received evidence that appeared to confirm the Iraq-Niger deal. The documents had been obtained by an Italian newspaper, which had investigated them and determined that they did not demonstrate a sale had taken place. The Pentagon, however, apparently believed in the authenticity of the documents, though the CIA appears to have been ambivalent. (Tenet eventually persuaded the White House to cut the claim from the speech that Bush gave on October 7.)[68]

Despite all these questions about the veracity of the information, President Bush's 2003 State of the Union address connected the alleged Niger deal with the aluminum tubes to make the case that Saddam was attempting to produce a nuclear weapon. In what would later become his most controversial prewar statement, Bush claimed, "The British government has learned that Saddam Hussein recently sought significant quantities of uranium from Africa. Our intelligence sources tell us that he has attempted to purchase high-strength aluminum tubes suitable for nuclear weapons production. Saddam Hussein has not credibly explained these activities. He clearly has much to hide."

Though Bush's statement was technically true, the administration clearly had reason to doubt it. Yet by stringing it together with the tubes claim, the President gave the impression Iraq was close enough to acquiring a nuclear weapon that military action was justified. As a source familiar with the findings of the Foreign Intelligence Advisory Board, which conducted a review of prewar intelligence, told the *Washington Post* in December 2003, there was "no deliberate effort to fabricate" evidence about Saddam's nuclear ambitions. Instead, the White House simply ignored caveats from the intelligence community about the information because it wanted "to grab onto something affirmative," according to the source.[69]

The administration continued to press its case based on the uranium claim, using it to suggest that Iraq had lied in its December 2002 declaration to the U.N. about the country's nuclear programs. In a January 23, 2003 op-ed in the *New York Times,* Rice stated that, among other things, "the declaration fails to account for or explain Iraq's efforts to get uranium from abroad."[70]

In February 2003, Colin Powell suggested in his speech to the United Nations that Iraq was rebuilding its nuclear program, though he did not include the claim that Saddam had attempted to acquire uranium ore from Niger. Jacques Baute, who headed up the IAEA inspection team in Iraq, later asked to see what evidence the administration had to support that contention.[71]

Among the pieces of evidence that the administration produced were the documents on the yellowcake sale that had been passed to the administration in October 2002. However, Baute did some initial research which suggested the documents had been forged. He reportedly contacted the American diplomatic mission in Vienna to ask if the administration had any evidence to support the authenticity of the documents and was told that neither the Americans nor the British would provide additional evidence. On March 7, 2003, El Baradei told the U.N. Security Council that the documents were fakes—but by then, twelve days before bombings began, the issue was moot.[72]

THE CHEMICAL AND BIOLOGICAL THREAT

The administration's claims about Saddam's chemical and biological weapons were as overstated as those about his alleged nuclear arsenal. The White House cited pre–Gulf War uses and programs as if they were more recent; gave the impression that all of Saddam's old weapons stocks remained potent; exaggerated the credibility of information about Iraq's reconstruction of its programs; and, as it had with Saddam's nuclear program, presented the worst-case scenario as if it were fact. And in a new twist, the administration began to suggest that the absence of evidence that Iraq had destroyed old chemical and biological weapons was definitive proof that they still existed.

There was no question that Saddam Hussein had developed chemical and biological weapons before 1991. However, the Gulf War, subsequent U.N. inspections, and U.S. bombings in 1998 had destroyed many of these weapons and the facilities used to make them. Iraq had also unilaterally destroyed some weapons.[73] Powell himself seemed satisfied with Iraq's disarmament when he stated in February 2001 that Iraq "has not developed any significant capability with respect to weapons of mass destruction."[74]

Questions remained, though: inspectors could not account for significant quantities of weapons and precursors used to make biological weapons, and defectors provided contradictory evidence. In addition, because Iraq's chemical weapons, with the exception of mustard gas, would have degraded significantly over time, stockpiles produced before the Gulf War and subsequent inspection regime would likely present little threat. (No evidence exists that Iraq was able to preserve the longevity of its chemical weapons by adding a stabilizer to its pre–Gulf War chemical stocks.)[75] There were similar questions about the viability of stocks of biological weapons that Iraq might have been able to conceal from U.N. inspectors, though they were more likely than chemical weapons to remain viable.[76] In terms of the threat Saddam posed to the world, the most important question was whether he had been able to rekindle his weapons programs and produce new stocks of biological and chemical weapons.

As with Iraq's nuclear program, the administration had lost a significant source of information on its chemical and biological programs when the U.N. weapons inspectors left in 1998. Evidence about subsequent activities was sketchy. A classified September 2002 report from the Defense Intelligence Agency made the problem clear, stating that "There is no reliable information on whether Iraq is producing and stockpiling chemical weapons, or where Iraq has—or will—establish its chemical warfare agent production facilities."[77] A second DIA report produced in November reached essentially the same conclusions.[78] Even the declassified NIE produced in October noted that "We lack specific information on many key aspects of Iraq's WMD programs."

Yet members of the administration repeatedly cited these programs as if the evidence was definitive, glossing over the very real questions about whether Saddam had chemical and biological weapons and had reactivated his programs to develop more. Cheney claimed in an August 26, 2002 speech to the Veterans of Foreign Wars that "there is no doubt that Saddam Hussein now has weapons of mass destruction" and added in a September 8 interview on *Meet the Press* that the U.S. had seen him "increase his capacity to produce and deliver" biological and chemical weapons. On September 26, Bush claimed that "The Iraqi regime possesses biological and chemical weapons."[79] This pattern continued in the President's October 7, 2002 address and afterward, culminating in his March 17, 2003 speech giving Saddam forty-eight hours to leave Iraq. "Intelligence gathered by this and other governments leaves no doubt," he said, "that the Iraq regime continues to possess and conceal some of the most lethal weapons ever devised."

U.N. Security Council Resolution 687, which ended the Gulf War, had placed the burden upon Iraq to prove that its weapons of mass destruction had been destroyed. (Resolution 1441 reaffirmed this obligation.) Iraq had clearly fallen short of this mandate. When U.N. inspectors left Iraq in 1998, they had been unable to ascertain what had happened to significant stocks of chemical and biological weapons and had failed to account for a number of munitions that could be used to deliver chemical or biological weapons, such as artillery shells. Iraq contended that the material had been destroyed, either by coalition bombs during the Gulf War or by the regime shortly afterward (though questions remained about these claims). As Hans Blix, executive chairman of the U.N. inspections program, told the U.N. Security Council on February 14, 2003, "To take an example, a document, which Iraq provided, suggested to us that some 1,000 tons of chemical agent were 'unaccounted for.' One must not jump to the conclusion that they exist."

However, the administration made a number of suggestions that weapons which had not been accounted for still existed. It also extrapolated a series of worst-case scenarios about the maximum amount of biological and chemical weapons he could produce from raw materials the inspectors had not found. For example, in his January 2003 State of the Union address, Bush claimed:

> *The United Nations concluded in 1999 that Saddam Hussein had biological weapons sufficient to produce over 25,000 liters of anthrax—enough doses to kill several million people. He hadn't accounted for that material. He's given no evidence that he has destroyed it.*
>
> *The United Nations concluded that Saddam Hussein had materials sufficient to produce more than 38,000 liters of botulinum toxin— enough to subject millions of people to death by respiratory failure. He hadn't accounted for that material. He's given no evidence that he has destroyed it.*
>
> *Our intelligence officials estimate that Saddam Hussein had the materials to produce as much as 500 tons of sarin, mustard and VX nerve agent. In such quantities, these chemical agents could*

also kill untold thousands. He's not accounted for these materials. He has given no evidence that he has destroyed them.

In each of these statements, Bush glossed over questions about what had actually happened to Iraq's stockpiles and ignored the fact that botulinum, sarin, and VX—three potent types of biological and chemical weapons—would almost certainly have degraded significantly since they were produced.[80] (Statements by other members of the administration highlighted this: Powell said in his February 2003 speech to the U.N. that "UNSCOM estimates that Saddam Hussein *could have* produced 25,000 liters [of anthrax]" [emphasis ours].) Even if Saddam did have the necessary chemical or biological materials, though, there were significant questions about his ability to process them into actual weapons. Yet Bush, stringing his claims together with the suggestion that such weapons could kill "several million people" and "untold thousands," implied that Saddam actually had them, a fact that remained unverified.

On February 6, Ari Fleischer, suggesting that inspections were not working, portrayed another worst-case scenario as fact, telling reporters that "We're not interested in the tip of the iceberg that Saddam Hussein may show above water. We're interested in the iceberg that remains below water that can sink the lives of *tens of millions of people* [emphasis added]."[81]

Once again, the press often failed to include information available in the public record that cast doubt on the administration's claims. The *San Francisco Chronicle,* for example, reported that Bush listed "thousands of liters of anthrax, botulinum toxin, and other biological weapons" held by Saddam "along with tons of sarin, mustard, and VX nerve agents that could kill millions of people" without explaining to readers that Bush was referring to claims about the amount of weapons that *could* have been produced from chemical and biological stockpiles that *might* have still existed. The *Chronicle* also omitted the fact that any weapons Saddam had retained would almost certainly have lost their potency.[82]

At other times, the administration presented claims about Iraq's older weapons in deceptive ways. In his nationally televised October 7, 2002 speech, for example, Bush stated that "We know that the regime has produced thousands of tons of chemical agents, including mustard gas, sarin nerve gas, VX nerve gas." This assertion was clearly based on Iraq's pre–Gulf War production. By failing to note that this was a pre–Gulf War figure, Bush's statement that "the regime has produced" such weapons implied that Iraq still had those weapons and was currently producing more.

Secretary of State Colin Powell made similar claims about Iraq's VX program before the United Nations in his February 2003 speech, stating that "It took years for Iraq to finally admit that it had produced four tons of the deadly nerve agent VX. A single drop of VX on the skin will kill in minutes. . . . UNSCOM also gained forensic evidence that Iraq had produced VX and put it into weapons for delivery, yet to this day Iraq denies that it had ever weaponized VX. And on January 27, UNMOVIC [which replaced UNSCOM in running the inspection program] told this Council that it has information that conflicts with the Iraqi account of its VX program." Powell clearly implied that Iraq still had potent VX that it could use, failing to note once again that any of the VX being discussed would have degraded over time.

Many in the press went along with Powell's claims, presenting them to readers with little qualification. For instance, reporters often failed to explain the source of his figures about the amount of biological and chemical weapons agents Iraq might possess. The

Atlanta Constitution-Journal told readers that Powell had "said Iraq has stockpiled 100 to 500 tons of chemical weapons agents"—omitting the fact that these estimates were based on gaps in the UN's accounting.[83]

Perhaps the most disingenuous implications about Iraq's biological weapons came from Vice President Cheney, who insinuated during a September 8, 2002 interview on *Meet the Press* that Iraq might have been involved in the 2001 anthrax attacks. "Who did the anthrax attack last fall, Tim? We don't know," Cheney said. Host Tim Russert asked, "Could it have been Saddam?" Cheney replied, "I don't know. I don't know who did it. I'm not here today to speculate on or to suggest that he did. My point is that it's the nature of terrorist attacks of these unconventional warfare methods, that it's very hard sometimes to identify who's responsible."

Secretary Powell's February 2003 speech to the U.N. also included a number of assertions about biological and chemical weapons that were based on disputed, circumstantial evidence. For example, he presented satellite photographs showing an ammunition storage site at Taji, which he suggested might be hiding chemical or biological munitions. He claimed that the satellite photos showed a "decontamination vehicle," which demonstrated that chemical and/or biological weapons were being stored at the site. Yet Greg Thielmann, a former State Department intelligence official and administration critic, told CBS News that "My understanding is that these particular vehicles were simply fire trucks. You cannot really describe [them] as being a unique signature."[84]

Showing a second photo of the site, Powell stated, "It's been cleaned up. And it was done on the 22nd of December as the U.N. inspection team is arriving, and you can see the inspection vehicles arriving in the lower picture on the right. The bunkers are clean when the inspectors get there. They found nothing." The picture had actually been taken weeks before the inspectors arrived.[85]

DELIVERY SYSTEMS

The administration also made exaggerated claims when it came to Iraq's ability to use weapons of mass destruction against the United States. On September 26, 2002, Bush gave a speech in the White House Rose Garden. "The danger to our country is grave," he said. "The danger to our country is growing. The Iraqi regime possesses biological and chemical weapons. The Iraqi regime is building the facilities necessary to make more biological and chemical weapons. And according to the British government, the Iraqi regime could launch a biological or chemical attack in as little as 45 minutes after the order was given." The clear implication was that Iraq could use the weapons against U.S. interests at any moment. (Bush made the same claim in his radio address that week.)[86]

The 45-minute figure had originated in a dossier produced by the United Kingdom and released on September 24, 2002. However, a later investigation revealed that the only source for the claim was an Iraqi military officer. Moreover, the Iraqi source was referring to battlefield weapons, a much narrower claim than the U.K. made. The CIA reportedly did not find the information credible and excluded it from its intelligence estimates.[87]

Other claims about Iraq's ability to deploy its chemical and biological weapons were equally suspect. Powell suggested during his speech to the U.N. that Iraq had constructed unmanned aerial vehicles (UAVs) and spray tanks that could be used "to disperse lethal biological agents widely, indiscriminately . . . into the air." He showed a video of one such vehicle spraying "2,000 liters of simulated anthrax." "UAVs outfitted with spray tanks constitute an ideal method for launching a terrorist attack using biological weapons," he said. "Iraq admitted to producing four spray tanks. But to this day, it has provided no credible evidence that they were destroyed, evidence that was required by the international community."

The U.N. inspectors' reports, however, stated that the video had been shot before the Gulf War and that the plane Powell showed had been destroyed. In addition, contrary to Powell's contention, the U.N. also noted that three of the four spray tanks had been destroyed in the 1990s.[88] The declassified October 2002 National Intelligence Estimate included the caveat that "The Director, Intelligence, Surveillance and Reconnaissance, U.S. Air Force, does not agree that Iraq is developing UAVs *primarily* intended to be delivery platforms for chemical and biological warfare agents. The small size of Iraq's new UAV strongly suggests a primary role of reconnaissance, although CBW [chemical and biological weapons] delivery is an inherent capability [emphasis in original]."

Powell was not the only administration official to make overstated claims about UAVs. President Bush cited them in his October 7, 2002 speech, claiming that "Iraq has a growing fleet of manned and unmanned aerial vehicles that could be used to disperse chemical or biological weapons across broad areas. We're concerned that Iraq is exploring ways of using these UAVS for missions targeting the United States." Yet the declassified NIE of October 2002 noted that "Baghdad's UAVs could threaten Iraq's neighbors, U.S. forces in the Persian Gulf, *and if brought close to, or into, the United States, the U.S. Homeland* [emphasis in original]." Bush was clearly exaggerating the threat for rhetorical effect.

Likewise, Cheney and Tenet reportedly told Congress that Iraq's UAVs could be used to target the United States. Florida Senator Bill Nelson, a Democrat who voted in favor of the October 2002 resolution authorizing military action in Iraq, stated after the war that "I was told not only that [Saddam had weapons of mass destruction] and that he had the means to deliver them through unmanned aerial vehicles, but that he had the capability of transporting those UAVs outside of Iraq and threatening the homeland here in America, specifically by putting them on ships off the eastern seaboard."[89]

During his February 2003 presentation to the United Nations, Powell also suggested that Iraq retained several Scud-type missiles, which Iraq had outfitted before the Gulf War to carry biological and chemical weapons. "While inspectors destroyed most of the prohibited ballistic missiles," Powell said, "numerous intelligence reports over the past decade, from sources inside Iraq, indicate that Saddam Hussein retains a covert force of up to a few dozen Scud-variant ballistic missiles." In September 2002, Powell made a similar claim, and Rice had stated on the same day that "We know that there are unaccounted-for Scud and other ballistic missiles in Iraq."[90]

The declassified October 2002 NIE drew a similar conclusion, stating that "Gaps in Iraqi accounting to UNSCOM suggest that Saddam retains a covert force of up to a few dozen Scud-variant SRBMs [short-range ballistic missiles] with ranges of 650 to 900 km."

However, the UN inspectors claimed to have destroyed or otherwise accounted for all but two of these missiles.[91] (Powell was reportedly aware of this fact, but made his claim based on other information suggesting more Scuds were still in circulation.)[92] Thielmann, the State Department intelligence official, told CBS, "I wondered what [Powell] was talking about. We did not have evidence that the Iraqis had those missiles, pure and simple."[93] (Reports during the war that Iraq had fired Scud missiles turned out to be false. Nor were any located by Special Forces soldiers sent into Iraq in mid-March 2003 to find them, according to a former high-level intelligence official interviewed by journalist Seymour Hersh.)[94] As it had with other aspects of Iraq's weapons programs, the administration had misrepresented evidence and misinformed the public to strengthen its case for war.

THE MISSING LINK: AL QAEDA AND IRAQ

One of the most controversial and inflammatory tactics used by the Bush administration to sell the war was the suggestion that Iraq was somehow tied to al Qaeda. Secretary of Defense Donald Rumsfeld reportedly asked the CIA ten separate times for evidence of such a link between September 2001 and May 2002.[95] Yet the evidence connecting the two was thin. The administration was able to document some meetings between Iraqi intelligence officials and members of al Qaeda, but there was no proof of a long-term, high-level connection.

Instead of simply noting the evidence in its possession, the administration used deliberately vague and misleading language to stretch the facts beyond what they could prove. Officials obscured the distinction between Iraq's ties to al Qaeda specifically and its ties to terrorism in general, cited bits of evidence in extremely misleading ways, and repeatedly mentioned the September 11 attacks during discussions of Iraq despite no clear links connecting the two.

In late 2001, the administration received a tip from the Czech intelligence service that Mohamed Atta, the lead September 11 hijacker, had met with an Iraqi intelligence operative in April.[96] The report turned out to have been based on a statement by a student working for the Czech intelligence service who recognized Atta when post–September 11 news reports carried his picture. The Czech Republic's interior minister cited the meeting publicly in November 2001, and the next month, Cheney stated on *Meet the Press* that it had been "pretty well confirmed."[97]

From there, however, the story began to unravel. In an article published in May 2002, *Newsweek*'s Michael Isikoff reported that the FBI could not produce any records that Atta, who had been living in Virginia at the time, had left or reentered the U.S. in April 2001.[98] After the Isikoff report appeared, an unnamed senior Bush administration official told the *New York Times* that FBI and CIA analysts had concluded the meeting did not occur.[99]

Some Czech officials stood by the report, but the *New York Times* reported in October 2002 that Czech president Vaclav Havel had told the White House that there was no evidence confirming the meeting. Havel later denied that he had contacted the White House but stated that there was no evidence demonstrating that the meeting took place.[100] (A classified Department of Defense memo leaked in November 2003 noted that although the CIA could confirm two trips to Prague by Atta at other times, neither the CIA nor the FBI could confirm details of the alleged April 2001 meeting).[101] The evidence was shaky and hardly constituted definitive proof of a connection between Iraq and al Qaeda.

Yet Cheney cited the alleged meeting as if it constituted a smoking gun. On September 8, 2002, he minimized the debate over whether the meeting occurred, stating on *Meet the Press* that "we spent time looking at that relationship between Iraq on the one hand and the al Qaeda organization on the other. And there has been reporting that suggests that there have been a number of contacts over the years. We've seen in connection with the hijackers, of course, Mohamed Atta, who was the lead hijacker, did apparently travel to Prague on a number of occasions. And on at least one occasion, we have reporting that places him in Prague with a senior Iraqi intelligence official a few months before the attack on the World Trade Center. The debates about, you know, was he there or wasn't he there, again, it's the intelligence business." When pressed by host Tim Russert, Cheney said, "It's credible. But, you know, I think a way to put it would be it's unconfirmed at this point." Viewers were left to wonder why the Vice President of the United States was citing unconfirmed evidence on national television to justify war.

AL QAEDA "WITHIN" IRAQ

Some of the administration's most specious claims concerned the alleged presence of al Qaeda operatives within Iraq and their ties to Saddam's government.

This case was laid out in detail by Secretary of State Colin Powell in his February 2003 speech to the United Nations. After noting that Saddam had ties to terrorist organizations other than al Qaeda, Powell asserted that "Iraq today harbors a deadly terrorist network headed by Abu Musab al-Zarqawi, an associate and collaborator of Osama bin Laden and his al Qaeda lieutenants." Outlining Zarqawi's activities in Iraq, he stated that "When our coalition ousted the Taliban, the Zarqawi network helped establish another poison and explosive training center camp, and this camp is located in northeastern Iraq."

After that seemingly devastating assertion, Powell noted an important caveat—Ansar al-Islam operated in an area of Iraq that Saddam did not control: "Those helping to run this camp are Zarqawi lieutenants operating in northern Kurdish areas *outside Saddam Hussein's controlled Iraq* [emphasis ours]. But Baghdad has an agent in the most senior levels of the radical organization, Ansar al-Islam, that controls this corner of Iraq. In 2000, this agent offered al Qaeda safe haven in the region. After we swept al Qaeda from Afghanistan, some of those members accepted this safe haven. They remain there today."

Powell ignored another significant caveat about Zarqawi's connection to Saddam Hussein: The U.S. government was unsure what the Iraqi "agent" inside Ansar was doing. "He may be spying on the Ansar group," an unnamed senior government official told the *Washington Post* the day after Powell's speech. "He may be a liaison with Baghdad. Saddam Hussein likes to keep an eye on such groups."[102]

Although Ansar was an al Qaeda offshoot and clearly linked to the group, intelligence officials had already concluded that Zarqawi's own ties to al Qaeda were thin. For starters, he was hardly a "very senior al Qaeda leader," as Bush asserted on February 13.[103] According to sources familiar with the intelligence, he was loosely affiliated with the group but was largely concerned with running his own independent network.[104] Finally, Zarqawi's sojourn in Baghdad, while likely implying tolerance of his presence by Saddam, was hardly conclusive proof of collaboration with the Iraqi leader.

After trumpeting the Zarqawi connection, Powell's speech continued with the assertion that "We are not surprised that Iraq is harboring Zarqawi and his subordinates. This understanding builds on decades-long experience with respect to ties between Iraq and al Qaeda." Powell stated that "an al Qaeda source" had told the U.S. that Saddam and bin Laden had reached a nonaggression pact in the mid-1990s. He cited high-level meetings from the period, when bin Laden and al Qaeda were based in Sudan. However, as the *Washington Post* reported, the classified version of the National Intelligence Estimate of October 2002 indicated that those contacts did not precipitate a lasting relationship between Saddam and al Qaeda.[105]

Powell concluded his description of Iraq's potential ties to al Qaeda with a particularly chilling story. Sourcing his information to a "senior al Qaeda terrorist [who] was responsible for one of al Qaeda's training camps in Afghanistan," the Secretary of State told the U.N. that al Qaeda successfully requested training in WMDs from Iraq. "The support that this detainee describes included Iraq offering chemical or biological weapons training for two al Qaeda associates beginning in December 2000," Powell stated. "He says that a militant known as Abdallah al-Iraqi had been sent to Iraq several times between 1997 and 2000 for help in acquiring poisons and gases. Abdallah al-Iraqi characterized the relationship he forged with Iraqi officials as successful."

According to experts who had seen the classified version of the National Intelligence Estimate of October 2002, that information had not been confirmed.[106] Bush, however, presented the claim as fact in his January 2003 State of the Union address, stating, "We've learned that Iraq has trained al Qaeda members in bomb-making and poisons and deadly gases."

When the available facts demonstrating a link between Iraq and al Qaeda fell short, the administration often resorted to vague rhetoric to fill in the cracks. One strategy was to refuse to give an accurate accounting of the state of information about such a link. On September 8, 2002, when Wolf Blitzer asked Rice on CNN's *Late Edition* "is there any hard evidence directly linking the Iraqi government to al Qaeda and the 9/11 terror attacks against the United States?" Rice replied that "There is certainly evidence that al Qaeda people have been in Iraq. There is certainly evidence that Saddam Hussein cavorts with terrorists," before stating that "I think that if you asked, do we know that he had a role in 9/11, no, we do not know that he had a role in 9/11. But I think that this is the test that sets a bar that is far too high."

A second strategy was to connect Iraq and al Qaeda conceptually rather than with specific evidence, a classic example of a technique borrowed from public relations. In a press conference on September 25, when asked "do you believe that Saddam Hussein is a bigger threat to the United States than al Qaeda?" Bush replied, in part, "the danger is, is that they work in concert. The danger is, is that al Qaeda becomes an extension of Saddam's madness and his hatred and his capacity to extend weapons of mass destruction around the world. . . . The war on terror, you can't distinguish between al Qaeda and Saddam when you talk about the war on terror. And so it's a comparison I can't make because I can't distinguish between the two, because they're both equally as bad, and equally as evil, and equally as destructive."

In his televised address on October 7, 2002, President Bush made an equally slippery rhetorical connection between them:

> We know that Iraq and the al Qaeda terrorist network share a common enemy—the United States of America. We know that Iraq and al Qaeda have had high-level contacts that go back a decade. Some al Qaeda leaders who fled Afghanistan went to Iraq. These include one very senior al Qaeda leader who received medical treatment in Baghdad this year, and who has been associated with planning for chemical and biological attacks. We've learned that Iraq has trained al Qaeda members in bomb-making and poisons and deadly gases. And we know that after September the 11th, Saddam Hussein's regime gleefully celebrated the terrorist attacks on America.

The statement bracketed assertions about operational contacts between Iraq and al Qaeda with broad rhetoric suggesting that their shared dislike for the U.S. meant that they were somehow allied. More important, it muddled the blame for September 11, suggesting that the Iraqi government was somehow connected to the attacks, because it "gleefully celebrated" them.

Colin Powell used the same vague rhetoric in his February 2003 speech to the U.N. At the conclusion of his presentation summarizing evidence linking Iraq and al Qaeda (much of which was questionable), Powell stated that "Terrorism has been a tool used by Saddam for decades. Saddam was a supporter of terrorism long before these terrorist networks had a name. And this support continues. The nexus of poisons and terror is new. The nexus of Iraq and terror is old. The combination is lethal. With this track record, Iraqi denials of supporting terrorism take the place alongside the other Iraqi denials of weapons of mass destruction. It is all a web of lies." By conflating Saddam's general support for terrorism with specific links to al Qaeda, Powell implied the existence of a high-level, operational relationship between Iraq and the group that went far beyond what his presentation had proved.

Despite Powell's assertions, the administration's own intelligence was far from certain about the "nexus" of Iraq, weapons of mass destruction, and al Qaeda. The declassified October 2002 National Intelligence Estimate stated that there was "low confidence" about "Whether in desperation Saddam would share chemical or biological weapons with al Qaeda." In fact, the NIE suggested that "Baghdad for now appears to be drawing a line short of conducting terrorist attacks with conventional or CBW [chemical and biological weapons] against the United States, fearing that exposure of Iraqi involvement would provide Washington a stronger cause for making war."

The administration exaggerated its own evidence, suggested that geographic proximity implied a high-level relationship between Iraq and al Qaeda, and used carefully ambiguous language to suggest that Saddam was in league with the group—and the press and public largely believed it. A February 2003 *Time*/CNN poll found that 76 percent of those surveyed believed that Iraq was giving assistance to al Qaeda.[107]

CLOSING THE SALE

The combination of all of these claims was extremely effective in making the administration's case. The White House saturated the airwaves with dire warnings about Saddam's weapons programs, his ties to al Qaeda, and the possibility that Iraq could use those weapons or pass them to terrorists. To build this case, the administration heavily spun its own evidence for maximum rhetorical impact. By presenting ambiguous information as fact again and again and filling in the gaps with vague but dramatic rhetoric, the impact of the limited evidence was greatly magnified.

The Bush White House violated the trust of the American people in the prewar debate. It would spend much of the period after the war trying to deflect blame by spinning away its previous claims.

REVISING THE RECORD ON IRAQ

On May 1, 2003, with the Iraq conflict seeming firmly in hand, the White House organized the photo opportunity of a lifetime. President Bush flew from an airbase outside San Diego to the nearby aircraft carrier USS *Abraham Lincoln*—not in a helicopter, as other presidents had done when they had visited warships, but in an SB-3 Viking jet with "George W. Bush, Commander-in-Chief" stenciled below the cockpit window. After a tailhook landing on the carrier deck carried live by the cable news networks, the President emerged from the plane wearing a military flight suit and spent several minutes greeting the crew of the carrier.

Bush's speech, three hours later, was just as rousing. Appearing under a banner that read "Mission Accomplished," the President gave a powerful address carried live by the broadcast networks. "Major combat operations in Iraq have ended," he told the crowd of soldiers. "In the battle of Iraq, the United States and our allies have prevailed."

No other event so vividly illustrates the administration's sophisticated image creation and communications apparatus. White House officials had carefully designed the landing and speech for maximum visual impact. Scott Sforza, a former television producer working in the White House Office of Communications, led a team that coordinated the visual details of the speech, ranging from choosing the time of day for the best light to placing colorfully dressed members of the *Lincoln*'s crew behind Bush.[1] Even after the ship made better time than expected and ended up only thirty miles offshore, well within helicopter range, Bush chose to fly in on a jet. And during the speech, officers slowed the ship and turned it so that the cameras would not capture the land in the background.[2]

Later that summer, however, as casualties continued to mount in Iraq, the event became a liability for the White House. The triumphant implications of the speech and the "Mission Accomplished" banner behind the President had set expectations for the postwar period extremely high. Critics suggested that the appearance was emblematic of everything wrong with the Bush administration's policies in Iraq. In response, the White House reverted to its tried and true methods of spinning to deflect criticism.

On July 1, 2003, Press Secretary Ari Fleischer told reporters, "Certainly in early May when the President said major combat operations have ended, major combat operations had ended. The President didn't say all combat operations have ended. He used a very specific word with a very specific meaning when he said major, leaving wide open that knowledge—and he said it to the American people, and he said it remains dangerous—that combat operations of various levels will, of course, continue."[3] This was a new (and extremely fine) parsing of the President's words—and a preview of the administration's strategy to come.

The White House also altered its own website to deemphasize the victorious tone of Bush's address. The President's speech was originally posted online under the headline "President Bush Announces Combat Operations in Iraq Have Ended." Shortly after *Washington Post* reporter Dana Milbank took note of the headline in an August 19 article, however, the White House added the word "major," so that by August 26 it read "President Bush Announces Major Combat Operations in Iraq Have Ended."[4]

In the fall of 2003, with White House critics gaining traction, the administration continued to try to distance itself from the "Mission Accomplished" banner that had hung so prominently behind the President during his May address. White House communications director Dan Bartlett told *U.S. News & World Report* that "[t]he President said exactly the opposite: The mission continues." Bartlett also claimed that the captain of the *Lincoln* had hung the banner to thank the crew for their mission, and attacked the media: "On TV, they never play the [audio] of the president, they just show the image with the banner."[5] Bartlett's statement stood in direct contradiction to his earlier comment that "If Americans can have an instant understanding of what the president is talking about by seeing sixty seconds of television, you accomplish your goals as communicators."[6] Apparently that only applies to messages the White House still wants to emphasize.

Echoing Bartlett's story, Bush told reporters on October 28 that "The 'Mission Accomplished' sign, of course, was put up by the members of the USS *Abraham Lincoln,* saying that their mission was accomplished. I know it was attributed somehow to some ingenious advance man from my staff—they weren't that ingenious, by the way."[7]

As reporters dug into this story, however, they found that the White House had been closely involved in producing the banner. Press Secretary Scott McClellan carefully parsed Bush's words later that day, noting that the banner "was suggested by those on the ship. They asked us to do the production of the banner and we did. They're the ones who put it up." [8]

Yet when the *New York Times* followed up with the White House and officers of the *Lincoln,* no one could confirm who had come up with the idea. According to Lieutenant Commander John Daniels, spokesman for the *Lincoln,* "The White House said, 'Is there anything we can do for you?' Somebody at that meeting [with the White House advance team] said, 'You know, it would sure look good if we could have a banner that said 'Mission Accomplished.' " Asked precisely who had made the suggestion, Daniels said, "No one really remembers." [9]

The media proved to be far less complacent after the Iraq invasion than it had been before the war began. When American forces failed to find weapons of mass destruction, the press became far more critical, culminating in the miniscandal over President's Bush's citation of an alleged Iraqi attempt to obtain uranium in Africa. Unfortunately, the reporters were so hungry for a story (and perhaps eager to make up for the appearance of having been too soft on Bush before the war) that at times they misreported the facts.

As press coverage become more skeptical, the President deployed the most aggressive spin campaign of his term. Bush's appearance on the USS *Lincoln* and the administration's subsequent claims about it illustrate how the tactics that the White House had perfected during its tenure were brought to bear on its postwar image problems. The appearance itself was masterfully crafted, creating a powerful association between Bush, the military, and the end of Saddam's regime. As the situation in Iraq soured, however, the administration backtracked and spun rather than admitting error, distancing itself from its prewar claims with selective representations and careful parsings of its previous statements. The White

House was trying to erase inconvenient history, just as it had on its website.

THE MISSING WEAPONS OF
MASS DESTRUCTION

In the months before the war, the Bush administration had been unequivocal that Saddam Hussein possessed biological and chemical weapons. Yet as U.S. troops advanced in Iraq and no weapons were found, the White House felt mounting pressure to explain the discrepancy. Members of the administration variously suggested that Saddam might have destroyed some or all of the weapons just before the invasion, hidden them inside Iraq, or smuggled them out of the country.[10]

An unnamed government official, addressing charges that the administration had misled the public, told ABC News that "We were not lying. But it was just a matter of emphasis." [11] As more time passed and stockpiles of weapons failed to emerge, however, the White House began to make misleading claims suggesting that the absence of weapons of mass destruction did not contradict its prewar assertions.

FROM WEAPONS TO WEAPONS "PROGRAMS"

In late April 2003, the administration began to suggest that Saddam's weapons *programs* justified the invasion of Iraq, rather than the possession of actual weapons of mass destruction. Before the war, the White House had nearly always paired discussions of Iraq's weapons programs with the suggestion that the regime possessed prohibited weapons. As Bush had put it on September 26,

2002, "The Iraqi regime possesses biological and chemical weapons. The Iraqi regime is building the facilities necessary to make more biological and chemical weapons." [12]

Yet when U.S. forces failed to find actual weapons of mass destruction in Iraq, members of the administration began to suggest that Iraq's weapons programs had provided the rationale for the use of force. In an April 25, 2003 interview, Bush stated, "I think there's going to be skepticism until people find out there was, in fact, a weapons of mass destruction program" and added a few moments later that Saddam Hussein "had a weapons of mass destruction program. We know he had a weapons of mass destruction program." [13]

Though at times the President and others continued to refer to weapons themselves (as Bush did on May 2), the administration began a concerted effort to shift attention from weapons to weapons programs.[14] For example, responding to a question on May 6 about possible evidence of a biological weapons lab, Bush repeated "weapons program" four times in three sentences, stating, "I'm not surprised if we begin to uncover the weapons program of Saddam Hussein—because he had a weapons program. I will leave the details of your question to the experts, but one thing we know is that he had a weapons program. We also know he spent years trying to hide the weapons program." [15]

On June 9, when asked "Is U.S. credibility on the line over weapons of mass destruction in Iraq?" the President replied, "I'm not exactly sure what that means. Iraq had a weapons program. Intelligence throughout the decade showed they had a weapons program. I am absolutely convinced with time we'll find out they did have a weapons program." [16]

Bush's careful use of "weapons program(s)" rather than simply "weapons" represented a rhetorical sleight-of-hand designed to deflect attention from the failure to find actual weapons. The subtle shift of emphasis in these statements was the first indication of the White House's strategy to distance itself from its prewar claims.[17] Rather than admit that its statements about WMDs appeared to be wrong, the President simply began ignoring them.

"WE FOUND THE WEAPONS OF MASS DESTRUCTION"

In mid-April 2003, government officials discovered a pair of trailers that appeared similar to mobile biological weapons production facilities that Colin Powell had cited in his prewar address to the United Nations. No traces of weapons themselves were found, but a team of military experts concluded that the trailers could have been used to produce such weapons, though they acknowledged potential nonmilitary applications.[18]

Other experts who examined the evidence later, including analysts at the State Department's Bureau of Intelligence and Research (INR), expressed serious doubts that the trailers were weapons labs.[19] When fifteen experts from the CIA, Defense Intelligence Agency, and INR gathered in June to analyze the evidence, only one agreed with the conclusion that they were most likely biological weapons labs.[20]

The evidence was mixed at best, but the administration suggested that its analysis was conclusive, omitting caveats just as it had on a number of issues before the war. On May 22, 2003, Fleischer told reporters, "we now have assessed that there are two biological mobile trucks that could have no use other than for the production of biological weapons. These are prohibited items. Iraq said they didn't have them. They've been caught red-handed, they have them for the purpose of producing weapons."[21]

On May 29, Bush blatantly misrepresented the find, telling Polish television that "We found the weapons of mass destruction. We found biological laboratories. You remember when Colin Powell stood up in front of the world, and he said, Iraq has got laboratories, mobile labs to build biological weapons. They're illegal. They're against the United Nations resolutions, and we've so far discovered two. And we'll find more weapons as time goes on. But for those who say we haven't found the banned manufacturing devices or banned weapons, they're wrong, we found them." [22]

This was an outright falsehood. Not only was Bush overstating the nature of the evidence about the trailers, but he was also collapsing one of the administration's biggest prewar claims—that Saddam had biological and chemical weapons—to fit what had been found. Bush was changing the definition of "weapons" in an attempt to short-circuit criticism.

As for the trailers themselves, Vice President Cheney continued to cite them as evidence of weapons programs.[23] When confronted in January 2004 with the discrepancy between Cheney's statements and the facts, an unnamed White House official flippantly retorted, "We'll have to get Cheney the new memo. As soon as we write it." [24] CIA Director George Tenet later testified that he had corrected Cheney privately.[25]

The President's false claim that weapons of mass destruction had been found would seem to be major news, but none of the broadcast networks carried a story about it. On cable, several reporters repeated or aired Bush's assertion without directly challenging it. CNN's John King, for example, introduced video of Bush making the claim by saying that "you hear in some European capitals rumblings that there have been no major finds of weapons of mass destruction in Iraq, some saying this is proving that George

Bush's war was illegitimate. The President, in an interview with Polish television, forcefully disputes that. He says those weapons are being found."[26]

Most print reports were no better. For instance, the *New York Times* failed to cover the quote in its news pages, although a staff editorial mentioned it.[27] The Associated Press reported Bush's claim, adding that "In an interview with Polish television, Bush provided no details, but he followed his statement with comments about the labs. It was not clear whether he was equating the labs with weapons."[28]

The *Washington Post* ran a front-page story analyzing Bush's claim, but the only other critical report, which ran in a number of Knight Ridder newspapers, framed the President's false claim as a "he said / she said" debate, quoting Bush before noting that "CIA officials on Wednesday said U.S. troops in Iraq found two mobile laboratories that analysts believed were intended to make biological weapons, but they said the labs contained no evidence the Iraqis had actually produced such weapons."[29] The press had once again failed to adequately cover a major story of deception by the President (due in part, no doubt, to the fact that Bush had made the claim to the Polish media rather than the American press).

EQUATING WEAPONS AND WEAPONS PROGRAMS, PART II

Throughout the summer of 2003, the administration continued to suggest that weapons programs were equivalent to weapons, culminating in a display by Press Secretary Ari Fleischer that almost defies parody. On June 10, after Bush had repeatedly emphasized "weapons programs" in remarks to the media, Fleischer claimed that "[W]hen the President talked about weapons programs, he includes weapons of mass destruction in that." When a reporter asked, "So he means by weapons, weapons programs, he means weapons, themselves?" The Press Secretary replied, "That's correct." A few moments later, the reporter followed up, asking, "So he uses [the terms] interchangeably?" Fleischer again affirmed his statement: "That's correct. He did yesterday." [30]

Obviously, the terms do not mean the same thing. Rather than admitting this, however, Fleischer extended the administration's spin to its absurd conclusion.

Other members of the administration were also careful to emphasize weapons programs and capabilities over weapons themselves. Powell, who had affirmed the existence of WMD in his prewar presentation to the U.N., stated in an interview on National Public Radio's *All Things Considered* on June 27, 2003, that "Our concern was that Iraq was keeping in place this *capability,* waiting for the day when they were free of sanctions and could go about putting all of their *programs* back in place. This particularly applies to the nuclear *program.* What I said in February when I spoke to the UN, was that they had the brainpower, they had the plans, and they were working on acquiring the *capability* . . . there was no doubt in my mind Saddam Hussein still had the intention of developing such a *capability* [emphasis ours]." [31]

Cheney stated on September 14 that one of the reasons for the invasion was "to wrap up all the WMD *capability* [Saddam] had possessed or developed." [32] In an October 8 speech, National Security Advisor Condoleezza Rice stated that "[Saddam] continued to harbor *ambitions* to threaten the world with weapons of mass destruction, and to hide his illegal weapons *programs* [emphasis ours]." [33]

This campaign to redefine the reasons for war reached its

apex in December 2003 when Bush took up Fleischer's claim that weapons programs were equivalent to weapons. In a nationally televised interview, ABC's Diane Sawyer pressed the President about the administration's prewar claims that Iraq possessed weapons of mass destruction, asking him about the distinction between "stated as a hard fact, that there were weapons of mass destruction" and "the possibility that [Saddam] could move to acquire those weapons still."

Explicitly conflating weapons and weapons programs, Bush replied, "So what's the difference?" The President added, "If [Saddam] were to acquire weapons, he would be the danger. That's what I'm trying to explain to you. A gathering threat, after 9/11, is a threat that needed to be dealt with." [34] Before a prime-time television audience, Bush had dismissed the premise of Sawyer's question as if it were unimportant. In doing so, he took the administration's efforts to obscure the distinction between weapons programs and weapons themselves to a new extreme.

DISTORTING THE INSPECTIONS

The President's claim that "we found the weapons of mass destruction" was hardly the only instance of an outright falsehood used to justify the war in Iraq after the fact. On July 14, 2003, Bush told reporters, "The larger point is, and the fundamental question is, did Saddam Hussein have a weapons program? And the answer is, absolutely. And we gave him a chance to allow the inspectors in, and he wouldn't let them in. And, therefore, after a reasonable request, we decided to remove him from power." [35]

This was simply an invention. A United Nations inspection team had been in Iraq from late November 2002 through March 18,

2003 (when Bush gave an ultimatum to Saddam and the team exited for its own safety). Though the Baathist regime had often impeded the inspectors' work, Bush's implication that inspectors had not been allowed into Iraq was plainly untrue.

When questioned about Bush's statement at a press briefing the next day, however, White House spokesman Scott McClellan suggested that "What he was referring to was the fact that Saddam Hussein was not complying with 1441, that he continued his past pattern and refused to comply with Resolution 1441 of the United Nations Security Council, which was his final opportunity to comply. And the fact that he was trying to thwart the inspectors every step of the way, and keep them from doing their job. So that's what he's referring to in that statement." This, of course, was hardly what Bush had said; McClellan was being no more honest than the President had been.

Bush repeated this trick on January 27, 2004, during an informal press conference with Polish President Aleksander Kwasniewski. Asked about differences between prewar intelligence and what had been found since the invasion, he answered, in part, "[W]e went to the United Nations, of course, and got an overwhelming resolution—1441—unanimous resolution, that said to Saddam, you must disclose and destroy your weapons programs, which obviously meant the world felt he had such programs. He chose defiance. It was his choice to make, and he did not let us in."

Though Bush's statement may have been a reference to the lack of full cooperation by Saddam, the phrasing "he did not let us in" implied that inspectors had not been allowed into the country or had been refused access to suspicious facilities. However, inspectors had been on the ground in the country for four months before the war began in March 2003 and had inspected a number of suspected weapons sites despite Iraqi resistance to some of the inspections. Even though Bush had made a similar claim before, no one in the White House press corps followed up on the President's statement, and the American news media did not even note the discrepancy between Bush's statement and the facts until nearly a week afterward, when a single article appeared in the *Washington Post*.[36]

MISREPRESENTING THE KAY REPORT

On October 2, 2003, David Kay, the head of the Iraq Survey Group tasked with gathering evidence of Iraq's weapons of mass destruction programs, gave a preliminary report to Congress. It undermined key assertions that the administration had made before the war about the regime's weapons stockpiles and programs. Yet the White House repeatedly suggested that the report vindicated its prewar claims, selectively citing evidence to suggest broad conclusions directly at odds with Kay's testimony.

In appearances before members of the House and Senate intelligence committees elaborating on the report, Kay described evidence suggesting that Iraq had continued research on WMD programs after U.N. weapons inspectors left in late 1998. However, he carefully qualified his statements, noting that "We have not yet found stocks of weapons, but we are not yet at the point where we can say definitively either that such weapons stocks do not exist or that they existed before the war and our task is to find where they have gone."[37] Later in his testimony, he stated that "Multiple sources with varied access and reliability have told ISG [Iraq Survey Group] that Iraq did not have a large, ongoing, centrally controlled CW [chemical weapons] program after 1991" and that "Our efforts to collect and exploit intelligence on Iraq's chemical weapons program have thus far yielded little reliable information on post-1991 CW stocks and CW agent production." In short, evidence of large-scale chemical and biological weapons programs was thin.

Kay also reported several important discoveries of conventional weapons programs, in particular an ambitious program to develop a long-range missile that he contended "would have, if OIF [Operation Iraqi Freedom] had not occurred, dramatically breached U.N. restrictions placed on Iraq after the 1991 Gulf War."

During a press conference the day after Kay's testimony, Bush tried to suggest that the report supported his prewar claims, saying that "[Kay's] report summarized the regime's efforts this way, and I quote from the report: 'Iraq's WMD programs spanned more than two decades, involved thousands of people, billions of dollars, and was elaborately shielded by security and deception operations that continued even beyond the end of Operation Iraqi Freedom.' That is what the report said. Specifically, Dr. Kay's team found, and I quote, 'dozens of WMD-related program activities and significant amounts of equipment that Iraq concealed from the United Nations during inspections that began in late 2002.'" [38]

In response to a question, Bush claimed Kay had stated that "Iraq's weapons of mass destruction program spanned more than two decades," and that "In other words, [Kay was] saying Saddam Hussein was a threat, a serious danger." Cheney quoted the same passage on October 10, suggesting that information from the report "provide[s] a compelling case for the use of force against Saddam Hussein." [39] Bush and Cheney's quotations were technically accurate, but they were carefully selected to give a misleading impression of the overall thrust of Kay's testimony. [40]

The President also cited the Kay report to suggest that the evidence of WMD programs that had been uncovered demonstrated

"Saddam Hussein was in material breach of 1441, which would have been [a] *causus belli* [legal justification for war]. In other words, he had a weapons program, he's disguised a weapons program, he had ambitions," as he put in it an October 28, 2003 Rose Garden press conference.

This was technically true; David Kay did find evidence of WMD programs, and he testified that Saddam's conventional long-range missile programs eventually would have constituted a material breach of the U.N. resolution. However, Bush combined these two facts to leave his audience with the impression that Kay had uncovered substantial weapons of mass destruction programs when the opposite was true. On December 16, Bush made a similar claim during his prime-time interview with Sawyer, suggesting "what David Kay did discover was they had a weapons program" and that "it's more extensive than missiles. Had that knowledge been examined by the United Nations or had David Kay's report been placed in front of the United Nations, he, Saddam Hussein, would have been in material breach of 1441, which meant it was a *causus belli*."

In late January 2004, Kay, who had just resigned as head of the Iraq Survey Group, gave an interview to the *New York Times* describing what it had found to date. "I'm personally convinced that there were not large stockpiles of newly produced weapons of mass destruction," he told the *Times,* continuing, "We don't find the people, the documents, or the physical plants that you would expect to find if the production was going on." Kay also told the *Times* that Iraq had continued research on biological weapons including ricin, but that "they didn't have large-scale production under way." [41] Kay echoed these statements during testimony to the Senate Armed Services Committee on January 28.

The White House responded by continuing to spin. In a February 8 interview on NBC's *Meet the Press,* Bush told interviewer Tim Russert, "David Kay did report to the American people that Saddam had the capacity to make weapons. Saddam Hussein was dangerous with weapons. Saddam Hussein was dangerous with the ability to make weapons. He was a dangerous man in the dangerous part of the world." [42] While technically true—Kay did tell Congress that Saddam "could have produced small amounts" of chemical and biological weapons—Bush was distorting the thrust of Kay's conclusions.

Likewise, answering questions about Kay's resignation on January 26, Attorney General John Ashcroft suggested that Saddam's "evil chemistry and evil biology" justified the war.[43] This statement was a perfect summation of the administration's postwar rhetoric: vague, emotionally loaded language that obscured specific prewar claims.

URANIUM FALLOUT

The White House also aggressively spun another aspect of Iraq's weapons of mass destruction program: Saddam's alleged attempts to acquire material to build a nuclear weapon, which had been a centerpiece of Bush's case for war. As casualties in Iraq increased and the media's honeymoon with the commander in chief ended, Bush's claim in the January 2003 State of the Union that "The British government has learned that Saddam Hussein recently sought significant quantities of uranium from Africa" came under heavy fire. Although the administration repeatedly changed its story in an attempt to spin its way out of trouble, the press often misrepresented what Bush had actually said, revealing itself once again as a hapless watchdog.

Few had questioned Bush's claim in the period following the State of the Union. One reason was that the British intelligence dossier on Iraq released publicly in September 2002 stated that "there is intelligence that Iraq has sought the supply of significant quantities of uranium from Africa." Only a few days before the war began, however, the IAEA had conclusively demonstrated that the documents backing up this intelligence that the U.S. possessed were obvious forgeries—so obvious, in fact, that intelligence officials probably should have spotted them immediately.[44] (As of this writing, the British government continues to stand behind its claim, which was apparently based on different sources from those of the U.S. government.)[45]

On May 6, 2003, however, less than a week after the President's speech aboard the USS *Lincoln, New York Times* columnist Nicholas Kristof leaked word of a February 2002 trip to Africa by former ambassador Joseph Wilson, who had found nothing to support the contention that Iraq had attempted to purchase uranium from Niger (though Kristof did not identify Wilson by name).[46] The revelations in Kristof's column sparked a media feeding frenzy. Yet instead of setting the record straight, the Bush administration misrepresented the State of the Union claim in several different ways.

At first, the White House appeared to suggest that it had been based on the forged Niger documents. After Wilson outed himself in a July 6, 2003 *New York Times* op-ed as the unnamed envoy, saying it was "highly doubtful that any such transaction had ever taken place," Fleischer told the press that the President's statement about Iraq's attempts to obtain uranium had been based on the Niger allegations and that they "did, indeed, turn out to be incorrect."[47]

Yet the next day, July 8, the administration changed its line. Michael N. Anton, spokesman for the National Security Council, claimed, "The documents alleging a transaction between Iraq and Niger were not the sole basis for the line in the President's State of the Union speech that referred to recent Iraqi attempts to acquire uranium from Africa."[48]

On July 11, CIA Director George Tenet took responsibility for the claim, saying in a written statement that "the President had every reason to believe that the text presented to him was sound. These sixteen words should never have been included in the text written for the President."

The uncharacteristic admissions of error from Fleischer and Tenet intensified the media furor. On July 13, 2003, the *Washington Post* revealed that Tenet had asked to have the Niger claim removed from Bush's televised address in October 2002.[49] That day, with the story refusing to die, the administration changed its tune about the validity of the claim once again. Rumsfeld stated on NBC's *Meet the Press* that "It turns out that it's technically correct what the President said, that the U.K. did say that and still says that."

The Defense Secretary also defended the claim on ABC's *This Week,* stating that "they were technically correct, that the reporting that the British had said that. The British today still believe they're accurate," and "it's not clear that, it's not known, for example, that it was inaccurate. In fact, people think it was technically accurate." On *Fox News Sunday,* Rice claimed that "the statement that [the President] made was indeed accurate. The British government did say that."

The next strategy was to plead ignorance. On July 18, the White House released declassified portions of the October 2002 National Intelligence Estimate, which suggested that Saddam had attempted to obtain the material from Niger, Somalia, and "possibly" the Congo. Yet the declassified portions showed that the State

Department's Bureau of Intelligence and Research (INR) had added a footnote stating that "the claims of Iraqi pursuit of natural uranium in Africa are, in INR's assessment, highly dubious."

An unnamed senior administration official, however, told the *Washington Post* that Bush and Rice "did not read footnotes in a 90-page document [the length of the classified version]."[50] And on July 20, Deputy National Security Adviser Stephen Hadley, who had been in charge of approving national security information in both Bush's October 2002 speech in Cincinnati and the January 2003 State of the Union, said that Rice had not known that the Niger claim had been removed from the October speech.[51]

Finally, on July 30, the President acknowledged that the claim was inaccurate and took responsibility for it. In a Rose Garden press conference, a reporter asked, "why is Dr. Condoleezza Rice not being held accountable for the statement that your own White House has acknowledged was a mistake in your State of the Union address regarding Iraq's attempts to purchase uranium? And also, do you take personal responsibility for that inaccuracy?" Bush responded, "I take personal responsibility for everything I say, of course. Absolutely."[52]

The White House's continually changing story about the uranium claim was fresh meat for a press corps usually starved by the Bush administration's unrelenting adherence to its official message. Even though this was one of the few cases in which the media extensively covered the White House spin, reporters often failed to fairly evaluate the administration's claims. Rather than focusing on the Bush administration's continued evasions, journalists took the internal White House conflict as de facto evidence that the President's claim was wrong.

Indeed, the storyline that Bush's State of the Union claim was false formed early and was repeated throughout the summer. The Niger documents were clearly forgeries, but the British intelligence had not been disproved, and the U.K. stood by its claims. Nevertheless, CBS reporter David Martin referred to "President Bush's false claim about Iraqi weapons; he made it despite a CIA warning the intelligence was bad" on July 10, ignoring the British sourcing and status of that evidence.[53] The next day, ABC *World News Tonight* anchor Peter Jennings referred to Bush's "false claims" and reporter Martha Raddatz called it "false information."[54] Even worse, several commentators, such as Kristof and the *Washington Post*'s Harold Meyerson, claimed that Bush had referred directly to Niger in his speech, rather than Africa.[55]

In short, the media, so frequently toothless, was just as incompetent when it did try to hold the White House accountable, leaving the public with a confused impression of the facts and administration officials with an easy retort when called on their deceptions.

NUCLEAR SPIN GENERATOR

As the alleged Iraqi attempt to obtain uranium from abroad was largely discredited in the public eye, the administration turned to other aspects of Iraq's nuclear program to validate its prewar claims.

During a September 14, 2003 interview on *Meet the Press,* Vice President Cheney stated that "We believed, the [intelligence] community believed, that [Saddam] had a workable design for a [nuclear] bomb. And we know he had 500 tons of uranium. It is there today at Tuwaitha, under seal of the International Atomic Energy Agency. All those facts are basically not in dispute. And since we got in there, we found—we had a gentleman come forward, for example, with full designs for a process centrifuge system to enrich uranium and the key parts that you'd need to build such a system."

However, the uranium Cheney referred to was the waste product of a nuclear reactor and it could not be used for bombs without being refined, a capability that postwar inspectors found Iraq did not possess.[56] Mahdi Obeidi, the Iraqi scientist who came forward with the centrifuge plans, had actually told U.S. authorities that Iraq's nuclear program had not been resumed after 1991 (a fact largely borne out by David Kay's October 2003 report to Congress).[57]

In the same *Meet the Press* interview, Cheney also stated that "this week, the Committee of the British Parliament, which just spent 90 days investigating all of this, revalidated their British claim that Saddam was, in fact, trying to acquire uranium in Africa. What was in the State of the Union speech and what was in the original British white papers." However, the British Parliament's Intelligence and Security Committee had noted only that the Africa claim was being reinvestigated and that the claim was "reasonable."[58] Just as he had done before the war, Cheney was overstating the strength of the available evidence.

EXAGGERATING LINKS TO AL QAEDA

The question of whether and to what extent Iraq had connections to al Qaeda was crucial to the public debate over taking military action. Before the war, the administration argued that such a connection existed based on an episodic set of contacts that had largely petered out by the late 1990s, along with suggestions that the presence of al Qaeda members in Iraq demonstrated the existence of a working relationship. However, the White House lacked conclusive proof that Saddam had an operational relationship with the international terrorist network. Instead, it papered over the gaps in the evidence with strong rhetoric implying a much more significant connection.

Secretary of State Colin Powell admitted the weakness of this evidence in a remarkable statement in January 2004: "My presentation on the 5th of February [2003] when I talked to this issue made it clear that we had seen some links and connections to terrorist organizations over time, and I focused on one particular case, Zarqawi, and I think that was a pretty solid case. There is not—you know, I have not seen smoking-gun, concrete evidence about the connection, but I think *the possibility of such connections* did exist and it was prudent to consider them at the time that we did [our emphasis]."[59]

In the wake of the war, little new evidence emerged of direct, high-level Iraqi support for Osama bin Laden or al Qaeda. A memo recovered from the headquarters of the Mukhabarat, a branch of Iraq's intelligence operations, described a messenger from bin Laden who stayed in the country for about two weeks in 1998 as a guest of the government, but there is no indication that the visit resulted in any sort of lasting relationship.[60]

Administration officials also suggested that Iraqi intelligence officer Farouk Hijazi met with members of al Qaeda and possibly bin Laden himself when the organization was based in Sudan in the mid-1990s, and again in Afghanistan in 1998. (Hijazi, who was captured by American forces during the war, reportedly acknowledged the 1994 meeting in Sudan but denies that the alleged Afghanistan meeting took place.)[61] There is little doubt that Iraq had occasional contact with members of al Qaeda; however, as of this writing, there is no evidence of a sustained, high-level relationship.

Nonetheless, even after the war, members of the administration continued to exaggerate the evidence of such a relationship. Using the same strategy it had employed so successfully in its prewar sales campaign, the White House implied an operational connection between Iraq and al Qaeda without ever demonstrating that such a connection existed. And once again, because these claims were so ambiguous, they continued to receive little scrutiny from the press.

FUZZY AL QAEDA CONNECTIONS

Aboard the USS *Abraham Lincoln* on May 1, 2003, Bush continued the administration's prewar strategy of linking Iraq to Al Qaeda. He stated, "The battle of Iraq is one victory in a war on terror that began on September the 11, 2001—and still goes on." A few moments later, he claimed that "The liberation of Iraq is a crucial advance in the campaign against terror. We've removed an ally of al Qaeda, and cut off a source of terrorist funding. And this much is certain: No terrorist network will gain weapons of mass destruction from the Iraqi regime, because the regime is no more."

Bush's speech clearly linked Iraq to al Qaeda by suggesting that the country was "an ally" of the terrorist group, then immediately stating that Iraq had "been a source of terrorist funding," a phrase that refers to Saddam's statements promising payments to the families of Palestinian suicide bombers.[62] Likewise, Bush vaguely claimed on July 1 that Iraq had "harbored and supported terrorists" and, on October 9, that it "sponsored terrorist groups."[63] Such statements blurred the distinction between Saddam's support for other terrorist groups and his murky connections to al Qaeda.

On October 10, Cheney brought this point together with another key bit of administration spin: the implication that Iraq had harbored al Qaeda terrorists before the war. "If Saddam Hussein were in power today," the Vice President told the Heritage Foundation in a speech, "there would still be active terror camps in Iraq, the regime would be allowing terrorist leaders into the country, and this ally of terrorists would still have a hidden biological weapons program capable of producing deadly agents on short notice."[64]

Cheney's reference to "terror camps in Iraq" was a veiled reference to Ansar al-Islam, the al Qaeda offshoot that operated in an area of northern Iraq which had been outside Saddam's control since the end of the 1991 Gulf War. Little new evidence of ties between Ansar and Iraq emerged after the war. Deputy Secretary of Defense Paul Wolfowitz claimed there were unspecified "links" between the two in testimony before the Senate Armed Services Committee on September 9, 2003, stating that both Saddam and Ansar al-Islam "went to very great lengths to bury and hide the links that they had with one another. So you have to recognize, we'll probably see only the tip of the iceberg, but we certainly see links."

Rather than explain this muddled evidence, the administration repeatedly cited the fact that Ansar had technically operated within Iraq's borders to imply that Saddam had intentionally harbored al Qaeda before the U.S. invasion. Bush claimed in a White House speech on July 1, 2003, that "among these terrorists [now attacking American forces] are members of Ansar al-Islam, which operated in Iraq before the war and is now active in the Sunni heartland of the country" and made a nearly identical assertion during a December 16 interview on ABC.[65]

Rice and Cheney made similar unqualified claims, as did Rumsfeld, who made the connection in three separate interviews on November 2, 2003.[66] These misleading statements avoided the obviously relevant fact that Ansar operated in areas outside of Saddam's control.

THE MISSING 9/11 LINK

During his September 14, 2003 *Meet the Press* interview, Cheney explicitly and irresponsibly raised the possibility that Saddam was involved in the September 11 attacks, without sufficient evidence. When host Tim Russert asked, "69 percent [of people surveyed] said he [Saddam] was involved in the September 11 attacks. Are you surprised by that?" Cheney answered, "No. I think it's not surprising that people make the connection." Russert pressed on: "But is there a connection?" Cheney was vague: "We don't know."

The Vice President continued by restating the administration's prewar talking points about Saddam's connections to al Qaeda: "We learned more and more that there was a relationship between Iraq and al Qaeda that stretched back through most of the decade of the '90s, that it involved training, for example, on BW [biological weapons] and CW [chemical weapons], that al Qaeda sent personnel to Baghdad to get trained on the systems that are involved. The Iraqis provided bomb-making expertise and advice to the al Qaeda organization."

He went on to state that "With respect to 9/11, of course, we've had the story that's been public out there. The Czechs alleged that Mohamed Atta, the lead attacker, met in Prague with a senior Iraqi intelligence official five months before the attack, but we've never been able to develop any more of that yet either in terms of confirming it or discrediting it. We just don't know." (An October 27, 2003 memo from Undersecretary of Defense for Policy Douglas Feith that was leaked to the conservative *Weekly Standard* cast even more doubt on the meeting, stating that "CIA and FBI cannot confirm Atta met with the IIS [Iraqi Intelligence Service]," though it noted that "Czech Interior Minister Stanislav Gross continues to stand by his information.")[67]

This was astounding: the Vice President of the United States was speculating about intelligence on national television, raising the possibility that Iraq had a direct connection to the September 11 attacks without sufficient proof and misrepresenting the debate over his sole piece of evidence.

The media actually paid attention this time around, prompting officials to disavow Cheney's statement, though they asserted that links existed between Saddam and al Qaeda.[68]

Nonetheless, Cheney made a similar claim about Atta's alleged visit to Prague during a January 9, 2004 interview with the *Rocky Mountain News*. Asked about a connection between Iraq and al Qaeda, Cheney again said that "We did have reporting that was public, that came out shortly after the 9/11 attack, provided by the Czech government, suggesting there had been a meeting in Prague between Mohamed Atta, the lead hijacker, and a man named al-Ani [Ahmed Khalil Ibrahim Samir al-Ani], who was an Iraqi intelligence official in Prague, at the embassy there, in April of '01, prior to the 9/11 attacks. It has never been—we've never been able to collect any more information on that."[69] The Bush administration seemed unable to stop repeating its deceptive talking points, even after they had been widely discredited.

CONVENIENT GEOGRAPHY AND THE "CENTRAL FRONT"

The administration's spin on Ansar al-Islam echoed a broader strategy of connecting Iraq to the September 11 attacks simply by virtue of its location in the Middle East. In a July 30, 2003 interview on PBS, Rice asserted, "What we knew going into the war was that this man [Saddam Hussein] was a threat. . . . He was sitting astride one of the most volatile regions in the world, a region out of which the ideologies of hatred had come that led people to slam airplanes into buildings in New York and Washington."[70]

Cheney made a similar linkage between Saddam and the September 11 attacks in a September 14, 2003 appearance on NBC's *Meet the Press,* claiming that "If we're successful in Iraq . . . we will have struck a major blow right at the heart of the base, if you will, the geographic base of the terrorists who have had us under assault now for many years, but most especially on 9/11."

Suggestions that Iraq's geography somehow implied a connection to al Qaeda culminated in claims by the White House that Iraq had become "the central front" in the war on terrorism, a response to critics who alleged that Iraq had distracted the country from pursuing the terrorist group.

Certainly, some of the irregular forces attacking U.S. and coalition troops had ties to international terrorist organizations. However, many of those attackers had entered Iraq only after coalition forces had invaded; others, especially Ansar al-Islam, had technically been inside the country before the war but had operated in areas outside Saddam's control; and many of the insurgents were Baath Party loyalists or other Iraqis with no clear ties to terrorism. Yet the administration once again spun a technically true claim to imply a conclusion far beyond the mere facts, in this case suggesting that the presence of some guerillas with ties to terrorist groups in post-Saddam Iraq justified its previous statements tying the dictator's regime to the war on terrorism.

President Bush debuted the line in a televised speech to the nation on September 7, 2003: "Two years ago, I told the Congress and the country that the war on terror would be a lengthy war, a different kind of war, fought on many fronts in many places. Iraq is now the central front." He continued moments later by stating that "we are taking direct action against the terrorists in the Iraqi theater, which is the surest way to prevent future attacks on the coalition forces and the Iraqi people."

Still later, Bush tied the campaign against insurgents in Iraq to September 11 and international terrorism: "And for America, there will be no going back to the era before September 11, 2001—to false comfort in a dangerous world. We have learned that terrorist attacks are not caused by the use of strength; they are invited by the perception of weakness. And the surest way to avoid attacks on our own people is to engage the enemy where he lives and plans. We are fighting that enemy in Iraq and Afghanistan today so that we do not meet him again on our own streets, in our own cities." (He made a nearly identical statement at a speech in Fort Stewart, Georgia, on September 12.)[71] Bush's vague language again collapsed the distinctions between terrorists in general and al Qaeda specifically, and tied Iraq to the emotionally charged threat of terrorist attacks on American soil.

Then, in a September 23, 2003 address to the United Nations, the line evolved. Bush stated that "Our international coalition in Iraq is meeting its responsibilities. We are conducting precision raids against terrorists and holdouts of the former regime. These killers are at war with the Iraqi people. They have made Iraq the central front in the war on terror, and they will be defeated." By linking two separate groups, international terrorists and others attacking U.S. troops, Bush was able to suggest that the entire Iraq effort had become a fight against terrorism.

Finally, the administration continued its efforts to tie Iraq rhetorically to the attacks of September 11 and the popular campaign in Afghanistan. Cheney, in particular, frequently repeated these vague claims. On December 23, 2003, he told a crowd assembled at McChord Air Force Base in Tacoma, Washington, that "as President Bush decided that very first night after 9/11, we also have to go after terror-sponsoring states, and that those who provide safe harbor and sanctuary for terrorists to launch attacks against the United States will be deemed just as guilty as the terrorists themselves for the attacks that have been launched. That's why we went into Afghanistan. That's why we went into Iraq."[72] The careful linking of 9/11 and Afghanistan with Iraq implies that targeting "terrorists [who] launch attacks against the United States"—al Qaeda—had been the rationale for invading Iraq, while leaving an escape clause with the phrase "terror-sponsoring states."

Cheney also attempted to make it appear that the U.S. had invaded Iraq to stop a direct threat to America's security. As he put it on February 8, 2004, "[Saddam] will never again brutalize his people, never again support dangerous terrorists, and never again threaten the United States of America."[73] (He made nearly identical claims twice on January 27.[74]) Saddam was allegedly connected to a planned assassination of Bush's father, President George H. W. Bush, after he left office, and he certainly threatened U.S. *interests* in the Middle East, but Cheney's statement suggested much more.[75]

Bush was even more explicit. At a fund-raiser in Dallas on March 8, 2004, he said, "We saw war and grief arrive on a quiet September morning. So we pursued the terrorist enemy across the world. We've captured or killed many of the key leaders of the al Qaeda network. And the rest of them will learn, there is no cave or hole deep enough to hide from American justice. We confronted the dangers of state-sponsored terror and the spread of weapons of mass destruction. So we ended two of the most violent and dangerous regimes on Earth."[76] By collapsing the distinction between the Afghanistan and Iraq campaigns and tying both back to September 11 with vague rhetoric, Bush was rewriting the administration's justification for going to war in Iraq.

REVISING HISTORY

Bush's appearance on the USS *Abraham Lincoln* in May 2003 demonstrated the White House communications team's masterful image creation skills. As the situation in Iraq continued to produce U.S. casualties on a nearly daily basis, however, the administration relied on its unprecedented ability to spin its way out of trouble.

When troops failed to find the stockpiles of weapons the White House had accused Saddam Hussein of hiding, the administration simply moved the metaphorical goalposts, suggesting that it had always talked about weapons programs rather than weapons themselves. When confronted with Bush's questionable claim in the 2003 State of the Union that Iraq had attempted to obtain uranium from Africa, it repeatedly changed its story in an attempt to dodge the controversy. And when investigations in Iraq failed to produce intelligence tying Saddam Hussein's regime to al Qaeda, Bush and his aides fell back on their prewar strategy of linking the two with strategically ambiguous rhetoric.

Even as the White House did its best to rewrite the history of its prewar claims and give the public misleading impressions of evidence found after the war, it went on the offensive against its critics. In June 2003, members of the administration began suggesting that criticism of its previous statements amounted to "revisionist history."

On *Face the Nation* on June 8, Rice dismissed critics as engaging in "a bit [of] revisionist history." In a speech on June 16, Bush repeated the charge, claiming "there are some who would like to rewrite history—revisionist historians is what I like to call them. Saddam Hussein was a threat to America and the free world in '91, in '98, in 2003."[77] And in a June 17 press briefing, Fleischer made it clear that the charge was an attack on critics, stating that Bush had referred to "revisionist historians who are seeming to make the case that Saddam Hussein likely did not have, or did not have weapons of mass destruction prior to the war," adding "[the President] looks at it and describes as revisionist history those who now seem to cast doubt on the accuracy of the intelligence information that stated that Saddam Hussein had weapons of mass destruction prior to the war."

The irony of calling critics "revisionist historians" in the midst of a months-long campaign to rewrite prewar claims appeared to be lost on the White House.

CAMPAIGN 2004:
SPIN-RELATED PROGRAM ACTIVITIES

On January 20, 2004, President Bush gave his State of the Union address laying out his agenda for the upcoming campaign. In it, he offered a tough defense of the war in Iraq, which had become increasingly controversial:

> *After the chaos and carnage of September the 11th, it is not enough to serve our enemies with legal papers. The terrorists and their supporters declared war on the United States, and war is what they got. Some in this chamber, and in our country, did not support the liberation of Iraq. Objections to war often come from principled motives. But let us be candid about the consequences of leaving Saddam Hussein in power. We're seeking all the facts. Already, the Kay report [on findings about Iraq's weapons of mass destruction] identified dozens of weapons of mass destruction–related program activities and significant amounts of equipment that Iraq concealed from the United Nations. Had we failed to act, the dictator's weapons of mass destruction programs would continue to this day.*

As he had in the months before, Bush implicitly linked Iraq to the September 11 attacks using vague but potent rhetoric that the media would not call into question. But the President's use of the phrase "weapons of mass destruction–related program activities" was more noteworthy. It represented a new stage in the administration's attempts to obscure prewar claims about Iraq's weapons of mass destruction. In his 2003 State of the Union address, for example, Bush had asserted, "Year after year, Saddam Hussein has gone to elaborate lengths, spent enormous sums, taken great risks to build and keep weapons of mass destruction." In 2004, however, claims about Saddam's weapons themselves disappeared entirely, replaced by the awkward and confusing "weapons of mass destruction–related program activities."

Aside from mocking the phrase itself, the media failed to ask tough questions about the meaning of "weapons of mass destruction–related program activities" (a phrase that came from Iraq Survey Group head David Kay's October 2, 2003 testimony to Congress). In the eleven days following the speech, no one in the press corps requested a definition of the term from the White House. When Kay was questioned about it at a Congressional hearing after the State of the Union, he noted that the term included work on precursors for chemical weapons and research on "the lethality of [chemical and biological] agents." Asked how many countries in the world were engaging in "weapons of mass destruction–related program activities" under that standard, he stated, "probably fifty countries." Not a single major media outlet picked up on these revelations.[1]

The 2004 State of the Union also continued Bush's economic spin. The President touted another version of his deficit reduction "plan," saying Congress needed to "focus on priorities, cut wasteful spending, and be wise with the people's money. By doing so, we can cut the deficit in half over the next five years." He and other administration officials continued to talk about this plan for weeks without releasing any details, generating a great deal of coverage before reporters had a chance to scrutinize it.[2]

When the administration finally unveiled its budget in February 2004, it became clear that the supposed plan to trim the deficit closely resembled the deceptive July 2003 version. According to the liberal Center on Budget and Policy Priorities, it excluded funding for the likely costs of the alternative minimum tax relief after 2005 and funding for operations in Iraq and Afghanistan after September 30, 2004. It also did not provide full funding for the "Future Year Defense Plan" supported by the Bush administration. Once again, with such costs included, the deficit would not decline by anywhere near 50 percent over the five-year period.[3]

However, this conclusion received far less attention from the press than the White House's claim to have a deficit reduction plan, which Bush and other officials mentioned over and over on the day the budget was released.[4] The President once again got away with a misleading claim by doing little more than repeating it endlessly.

In short, the 2004 State of the Union served as a signaled that the Bush administration's spin campaigns on Iraq and tax and budget issues would continue through the November election. And with three years of policy deception behind them, the spin was as much about distorting the President's record as it was about misleading the public about its new proposals.

In early March, however, the campaign unexpectedly swung into gear when Bush and Senator John Kerry of Massachusetts, the presumptive Democratic nominee, began slugging it out.

The first stages of the general election provide a window into the way Bush has changed the presidency and presidential campaigning. Kerry appeared to be following in Bush's footsteps during the opening stages of the campaign, matching the President in an early and aggressive war of distortions and half-truths.

In addition, the media continued to fail to effectively counter the candidates' spin. Despite the press's intensive coverage of stories about scandal and political process, such as Bush's service in the Air National Guard in 1972–1973 and the claims made by former counterterrorism official Richard Clarke, it has continued to display relatively little interest in dishonesty about public policy issues, an area in which Bush has continued to excel and Kerry has already displayed substantial talents.

THE DUELING WAR ROOMS

As the general election campaign got off to a very early start in March and April, it quickly became clear that the pace of the spin war had accelerated. Rather than raising money and gradually laying out an agenda, the normal spring activities in recent presidential elections, the candidates moved into a rapid-fire slugfest. In speeches, media appearances, emails to reporters, Internet videos, and television ads, the candidates attacked and counterattacked with a speed and ferocity that put the famed 1992 Clinton campaign "war room" to shame. As one high-ranking Bush campaign official put it, "It's not just rapid response. It's rapid response six times a day." [5]

Both campaigns were built for high-speed media warfare. Bush's headquarters set up a cluster of TiVo digital video recorders that continuously monitored the media for statements from Kerry. Each morning at 4:30 A.M., a group of staffers began sorting through overnight developments and preparing responses to the other side's latest statements, which could be incorporated into speeches that day by Bush and other Republicans.[6]

Like Bush, Kerry's team of rapid response experts was set up to respond to the President within minutes and quickly integrate new lines of attack into the Senator's speeches. The campaign catalogued its responses to all of Bush's attacks on an Internet weblog called the D-Bunker and offered "pre-sponses" intended to preempt anticipated criticism.[7]

In this unprecedented campaign environment, the pace of the debate often swamped the ability or willingness of reporters to check the facts.

AN AVALANCHE OF EARLY CAMPAIGN SPIN

Voters got a preview of the general election campaign to come on February 12 when Kerry scored victories in the Virginia and Tennessee primaries, making him the likely nominee. President Bush's campaign issued its first direct attack on the Senator that day in the form of an Internet video. The campaigns' attacks on each other escalated after Kerry's March 2 victories in the Super Tuesday primaries drove his last major opponent, North Carolina Senator John Edwards, from the race. Bush addressed Kerry by name for the first time on March 4, extremely early for a sitting president to engage his opponent.[8]

Bush's salvos were part of a ninety-day media strategy planned by the campaign and presidential advisor Karl Rove, with the goal of defining Kerry as "indecisive and lacking conviction" before people begin paying less attention to politics in early June. Bush media advisor Mark McKinnon said, "It's easiest to define somebody when they're ill-defined, and John Kerry's ill-defined."[9] The spin war had accelerated to the point that "defining" someone months before an election was a strategic necessity.

DEFENSE, INTELLIGENCE, AND PATRIOTISM

The first major dispute between the campaigns took place in February, when Bush's campaign joined the Republican National Committee in attacking Kerry's record on national security, beginning with campaign manager Ken Mehlman's comments on February 9 that "we question the judgments of [Kerry's] votes to consistently cut defense and intelligence funding." [10] When Senator Saxby Chambliss, a Georgia Republican, attacked Kerry in a conference call organized by the Bush campaign on February 21, he responded in a letter to President Bush stating that "I will not sit back and allow my patriotism to be challenged."

But Chambliss had not challenged Kerry's patriotism. He had claimed that Kerry has "a 32-year history of voting to cut defense programs and cut defense systems." [11] (Kerry was actually elected to the Senate in 1984, so Chambliss's claim of a "32-year history of voting" was exaggerated by more than ten years.) The Kerry campaign had engaged in similar tactics after a January 29, 2004 speech by Republican National Committee chairman Ed Gillespie criticizing the Senator's record on defense, which prompted campaign manager Mary Beth Cahill to write an email to supporters claiming that Gillespie had "made another desperate attack on the patriotism of John Kerry." [12]

However, though Bush's campaign did not question Kerry's patriotism, some of its charges were deceptive. In a response to Kerry's February 21 letter, Bush-Cheney '04 chairman Marc Racicot stated, "Senator Chambliss addressed your Senate record of voting against the weapons systems that are winning the war on terror." He then accused Kerry of trying to "cut intelligence spending by $1.5 billion for the five years prior to 2001," noted a "1996 proposal to cut defense spending by $6.5 billion," and suggested Kerry had supported "canceling or cutting funding for the B-2 Stealth Bomber, the B-1B, the F-15, the F-16, the M1 Abrams, the Patriot Missile, the AH-64 Apache Helicopter, the Tomahawk Cruise Missile, and the Aegis Air-Defense Cruiser." [13]

Although Kerry did vote against or oppose a number of major weapons systems, including the B-2 bomber, some of the charges about him were exaggerated. [14] Even though Racicot made a reference to Kerry's "votes as a senator," his claim that Kerry supported "canceling or cutting funding" for a number of weapons systems was backed up by an article about Kerry's first run for the Senate in 1984, not the Senator's voting record. [15]

Vice President Dick Cheney also attacked Kerry for supposedly voting against the Apache helicopter, Bradley Fighting Vehicle, and Tomahawk cruise missile. [16] Kerry had actually voted against two huge defense appropriations bills from 1990 and 1995 that included hundreds of individual items (although he did support a 50 percent cut in spending on the Tomahawk in a 1984 campaign memo). [17] By this absurd logic, Kerry and every other member of Congress who has ever opposed a defense appropriations bill for any reason have voted against practically every weapons system in use today.

Reporters who covered these charges usually failed to fact-check them. The Associated Press repeated Racicot's charge that Kerry "[voted] against the weapons systems that are winning the war on terror" without context. [18] Similarly, weeks after the exaggerations of Kerry's Senate voting record had been exposed, the *Los Angeles Times* quoted Cheney's misrepresentation with no context and New York *Newsday* simply reprinted the charge, writing that "Cheney said Kerry had voted against many weapons systems used by today's military, including the Apache helicopter, the Tomahawk cruise missile and the Bradley Fighting Vehicle." [19]

Racicot's allegation about Kerry's proposed cuts to intelligence, which Bush claimed on March 8 proved the Senator "was willing to gut the intelligence services," was equally disingenuous.[20] In 1995, Kerry did propose cutting $300 million per year for five years from the intelligence budget. But Bush's strong language obscured the fact that Kerry's proposed cut in that year's intelligence budget amounted to roughly 1 percent of total spending.[21] Moreover, the legislation coincided with revelations that the National Reconnaissance Office (NRO), which builds and operates the nation's spy satellites, had secretly accumulated between $1 and $1.7 billion in unspent funds. Kerry's proposal never made it to the Senate floor, but a similar measure cutting $1 billion from the intelligence budget in response to the disclosures about NRO was overwhelmingly approved the same day Kerry introduced his bill.[22]

KERRY'S MISLEADING COUNTERATTACKS

Kerry quickly reeled off a string of misleading counterattacks against Bush. On February 26, 2004, he claimed that Bush had created a deficit that was the "largest in history." This was accurate when measured in absolute dollars, but when measured as a portion of the economy and adjusted for inflation (a more accurate measure), the projected deficit for fiscal year 2004 represented only 4.5 percent of GDP, smaller than deficits under Reagan or George H. W. Bush and far smaller than those during World War II.[23]

On February 27, Kerry's campaign released an Internet ad claiming that, under Bush, there have been "200,000 veterans cut off from health system."[24] The figure actually refered to a Veterans Administration estimate of the number of veterans who would voluntarily stop using the VA prescription drug benefit plan if Bush's proposal to increase fees were to be implemented, something that had not taken place (and, as of this writing, still has not).[25] Kerry had also previously claimed that Bush reduced funding for the VA, including at a February 15 debate when he said Bush "cut the VA budget." However, although Bush may have cut funding for various VA programs, Kerry wrongly suggested that the department's overall budget had been cut. It actually increased substantially each year Bush has been in office.[26]

Kerry's February 27 ad also included a graphic with the words "2.9 Million Jobs Lost" under Bush. However, this figure referred to the net decline in *private sector* jobs according to Bureau of Labor Statistics data available in February 2004; the total net decline in jobs under Bush was actually substantially less, 2.2 million according to BLS. The difference was the result of increased government employment, a caveat Kerry and his campaign often failed to note.[27]

Even after new economic data released in early April reduced job losses under Bush to 1.8 million overall and 2.6 million in the private sector, the Senator trotted out the 3 million jobs canard again during a conference call with college reporters.[28]

Kerry and other Democrats pushed these bogus statistics so often that a huge number of media outlets repeated the 3 million jobs claim without clarification, and others, including the Associated Press, Fox News, National Public Radio, the *Sacramento Bee,* Cox News Service, and the *Baltimore Sun,* reported it as fact.[29] In a classic illustration of how the media's obsession with presenting both sides stands in the way of factual clarity, the Portland *Orego-nian* wrote, "While Democrats point to a loss of about 3 million jobs during the Bush administration, [Bush advisor Karl] Rove argued that a more accurate accounting would be 2 million," offering readers no clue as to whose view was correct.[30]

MISQUOTATIONS GALORE

Another dispute erupted in early March as the campaigns mischaracterized each other's statements.

In an interview with the *New York Times* published on March 6, Kerry stated that "The final victory in the war on terror depends on a victory in the war of ideas, much more than the war on the battlefield." He continued, "And the war—not the war, I don't want to use that terminology. The engagement of economies, the economic transformation, the transformation to modernity of a whole bunch of countries that have been avoiding the future."[31]

Bush and Cheney seized on the phrase "I don't want to use that terminology"—which in context clearly referred to "the war of ideas"—to suggest that Kerry opposed calling the campaign against terrorism a "war" (Kerry had repeatedly used the phrase "war on terror" during the campaign, including during the *New York Times* interview). On March 11, for example, Bush stated at a campaign fund-raiser that "my opponent indicated that he's not comfortable using the word 'war' to describe the struggle we're in. He said, 'I don't want to use that terminology.' "[32] Cheney also made the sound bite a staple of his stump speech, such as when he told a crowd on March 23 that "Senator Kerry has questioned whether the war on terror is really a war at all. Recently he said, quote: 'I don't want to use that terminology.' "[33]

In at least two cases, the media reported Cheney's mistaken claim as if it were fact. Paraphrasing the Vice President's remarks at a fund-raiser, a March 8 Associated Press article stated that "Democrat John Kerry, Bush's likely opponent in November, has said he doubted the need for war." The Louisville *Courier-Journal* also approvingly quoted Cheney calling Kerry "uncomfortable with the idea we are at war" and cited his quotation of Kerry without pointing out that it was misleading.[34]

The Kerry campaign fought back with a March 15 press release offering two highly misleading claims about Bush's record in a list of allegedly false statements from the White House. The first stated that the administration had claimed "There was 'no doubt' Iraq had 'reconstituted' nuclear weapons and other weapons of mass destruction."[35] But while the administration exaggerated the certainty of intelligence findings about Iraq's WMD programs, the use of the phrase "no doubt" by Bush and Cheney referenced the regime's possession of weapons of mass destruction generally, not nuclear weapons specifically.[36]

During a March 16, 2003 interview on NBC's *Meet the Press,* Cheney did say "we believe [Saddam] has, in fact, reconstituted nuclear weapons," but it appears that he simply misspoke, because the Vice President also said four separate times in the interview that Saddam was pursuing nuclear weapons, not that he already had them (nor did any others in the administration ever make the definitive claim that Iraq had such weapons).[37] In addition to using both quotes deceptively, Kerry's campaign strung them together as if they came from the same interview or speech, when they were actually parts of completely different statements.

The Kerry release also stated that the administration had claimed "Iraq was an 'imminent' or 'uniquely urgent' threat to the

U.S." Though Bush administration officials often framed their claims about the threat from Iraq in hyperbolic language, they never directly claimed that Iraq was an "imminent threat," a concept that refers to an enemy that is poised to attack. In three isolated cases, White House officials gave affirmative answers to reporters' questions asking if Bush believed Iraq posed an imminent threat, but in none of those cases did they bring it up or say the phrase.[38] Much more frequently, Bush and other members of the administration argued that Iraq was an enemy for which the concept of "imminent threat" was insufficient. In the 2003 State of the Union address, for instance, Bush said, "Some have said we must not act until the threat is imminent. Since when have terrorists and tyrants announced their intentions, politely putting us on notice before they strike?"

TAX AND SPEND

In March, the campaigns also began flailing at each other over economic issues, launching a series of deceptive claims about their opponents' policies and records.

First, Kerry's campaign, echoing some of Bush's tactics, started playing fast and loose with the numbers as it promoted a so-called "Bush tax." Kerry said in Chicago on March 10 that, "If you add up the true costs of this President's economic policies, you get a Bush Tax of higher property taxes, higher fees, higher health care costs— at the same time middle class incomes are going down. . . . This Bush Tax can take $3500 or more from the pockets of America's middle class."[39]

However, Kerry's figure was based on a calculation combining changes in income, college tuition, health care costs, gasoline costs, and state and local taxes. The statistics he used represented averages for the entire U.S. population. Actual figures vary widely for individual families, many of whom, for example, are not currently paying college tuition for their child at a four-year public college (which Kerry used to represent the price of tuition). Moreover, it is hardly clear that Bush is responsible for all of these costs, many of which are largely (or entirely) the result of factors beyond his control. Yet Kerry's campaign pretended the sum of the alleged "Bush Tax" was meaningful. This tactic aped the manipulative statistics that the President had used to sell his tax cuts.

Meanwhile, the Bush campaign launched an ad called "100 Days" on March 11 that sought to portray Kerry as a tax-and-spend liberal, stating, "John Kerry's plan: To pay for new government spending, raise taxes by at least $900 billion." A later Bush press release also described Kerry as having a "plan to raise taxes by at least $900 billion his first 100 days," an outright fiction.[40] Kerry had not endorsed a tax hike of that size; the number was calculated by making assumptions about how the cost of his health care proposal and other spending plans compared with the revenue his tax proposals would generate.[41] While Kerry—like Bush—was offering a deficit reduction plan that did not add up (a February 2004 analysis by the *Washington Post* found his proposals would cost at least $165 billion more from 2005 to 2008 than the revenues his tax plan would generate), this hardly amounted to endorsing a huge tax increase.[42]

The Kerry campaign quickly swung into action when it learned of the ad's release on March 11. Within hours, the Senator asked his team to prepare a rebuttal ad and denounced the Republican ad to reporters. After the release of Bush's ad, the Kerry team wrote the script of their response in thirty minutes, gave it to reporters, and produced the ad overnight, finishing at 5 A.M. the next morning. As

Kerry spokesperson Stephanie Cutter told the *Washington Post*'s Howard Kurtz, "Why let them have the news cycle?"[43]

The Bush campaign later recalculated the amount of the alleged difference between Kerry's spending plans and his revenue proposals to suggest the Democrat had a "trillion-dollar tax gap." While the Kerry campaign did admit that its numbers didn't quite add up, it denied that the Senator favored such a tax increase and said that more specifics would be forthcoming.[44]

Bush and his campaign soon turned the contention into a doubly misleading talking point, making unsupported claims about Kerry's plans to raise taxes. As Bush put it at a March 25 fund-raiser, "There's a gap between Senator Kerry's spending promises and Senator Kerry's promise to lower the deficit—it's called a tax gap. Given Senator Kerry's record for supporting tax increases, it's pretty clear how he's going to fill the tax gap. He's going to tax all of you."[45]

Bush had come full circle: In 2001 and 2003 he had falsely implied that he *cut* taxes for everyone. Now he was speculating that Kerry would *raise* them for everyone.

MORE DEFENSE VOTES, MORE SPIN

A few days after the first Bush-Kerry ad war over the alleged $900 billion "tax gap," the Bush campaign discovered that Kerry planned to give a speech on national defense in West Virginia on March 16. In response, they produced an ad within twenty-four hours to air in the state.[46] It was finished at 1 A.M. the night before Kerry's appearance. At 10:45 A.M. campaign manager Ken Mehlman held a conference call for reporters to discuss the ad, thirty minutes *before* Kerry's speech began.[47]

As Bush campaign press secretary Terry Holt said, "If John

Kerry is going to give a series of speeches on veterans' issues, the right time for us to act is while he is giving those speeches, not two days afterward." He added, "It's extremely important to do it in the same news cycle so his words don't go unchallenged. He went from playing offense to playing defense in the space of minutes." [48]

The ad accused Kerry of voting against "body armor for troops in combat," "higher combat pay," and "better health care for reservists and their families," implying he had cast separate votes specifically opposing each of the items in question. [49] As with his supposed votes against weapon systems, however, these accusations were all based on Kerry's October 2003 vote against an $87 billion supplemental appropriations bill to fund military operations in Iraq and Afghanistan. [50]

Once again, many in the press were taken in by campaign spin. For instance, Mike Glover of the Associated Press gave the assertions from the original West Virginia ad the gloss of fact in a March 17 article that suggested Kerry cast specific votes against the items in question. "Citing the Massachusetts senator's votes against pay increases for military personnel, military housing, body armor, armored Humvees and health care benefits for reservists," he wrote, "[Bush-Cheney spokesman Scott] Schmidt said, 'Almost everything he claimed to support in his speech he has voted against when it counted on the Senate floor.' " [51] By treating Schmidt's spin as fact, the AP served as a wire service for campaign dishonesty.

OUTSOURCING AND TAX INCREASES

Bush's campaign also distorted Kerry's record to support allegations that "he's voted over 350 times for higher taxes on the American people," as the President put it on March 20. [52] Others were more direct, with Mehlman and Commerce Secretary Don Evans claiming that the 350 votes were all in favor of tax increases.[53]

Yet when pressed on the issue, a Bush campaign official told FactCheck.org that "these are votes for higher taxes, *not necessarily tax increases,* meaning it includes votes against tax cuts [our emphasis]." The documentation Bush's campaign provided lists the following votes as counting toward the total: "Votes for tax increases," "Votes against tax cuts," "Votes to reduce the size of a tax cut," "Votes against repealing tax hikes," "Votes against making tax cuts permanent," and "Votes for watered-down, Democrat 'tax cut' substitutes."[54] Even votes *for* tax cuts counted if they weren't big enough! Vice President Cheney also began making ridiculous calculations using the figure, saying, "Add it all up, and it turns out John Kerry has voted in the Senate at least 350 times for higher taxes. That averages to one vote for higher taxes every three weeks for almost two decades."[55]

Using the same tenuous methodology, the Bush-Cheney campaign began to claim that Kerry supported higher gas taxes eleven times (many of which were actually votes opposing reductions in the gas tax) while touting his long-rescinded support for a $0.50 gas tax increase in 1994.[56] The campaign even offered a "Kerry gas tax calculator" on its website to allow visitors to calculate what Kerry's alleged proposal would cost them.

When challenged about the fact that Kerry's support for a gas tax increase was ten years old on MSNBC's *Hardball* on April 2, Bush campaign advisor Tucker Eskew wove both attacks together, stating, "[I]f he didn't have 350 other times that he has been in favor of higher taxes it would stand out, it would be something separate. Instead, it's part of a pattern."

Not long after, Kerry shot back with an ad that misconstrued

Bush administration comments about the practice of outsourcing service jobs to foreign countries. The ad, which ran in early April, claimed that "George Bush says sending jobs overseas 'makes sense' for America" and that his "top economic advisors say 'moving American jobs to low-cost countries' is a plus for the U.S." [57]

Bush never stated that moving jobs overseas "makes sense." The 2004 Economic Report of the President actually said that it "makes more sense" for firms to import a cheaper good or service from abroad when costs are lower overseas and that "[t]he basic economic forces behind" outsourcing services and importing goods "are the same." Kerry's ad misquoted the phrase "makes more sense" and falsely portrayed it as an explicit endorsement of outsourcing. In addition, Bush's economic advisors did not endorse "moving American jobs to low-cost countries." The quote is a reporter's paraphrase of comments by Treasury Secretary John Snow.[58] Instead, Snow and Council of Economic Advisors Chairman Gregory Mankiw had simply stated their support for the overall economic benefits of free trade.[59]

THE NEXT ADMINISTRATION

When Kerry claimed in March 2004 that he had the support of several foreign leaders in his campaign for president, Bush responded by saying, "If you're going to make an accusation in the course of a presidential campaign, you ought to back it up with facts." [60] Unfortunately, the early stages of the general election campaign showed no sign that either candidate would honor this maxim.

What would a second Bush term be like? Would John Kerry adopt the President's style of policy deception once he was in office?

As of this writing, we can't say. But Bush shows no signs of changing his approach. And the 2000 campaign demonstrated how the type of PR-driven spin Kerry has used could be the opening act to a deeply dishonest administration. Given recent trends in American politics, Bush's misleading tactics could very well become the norm.

honesty as politics as usual. But there is nothing normal about these tactics.

Bush has gone well beyond the stereotypical "spin" of emphasizing one side of an issue while downplaying another. Instead, he has built his sales campaigns around blatantly misleading factual claims and insinuations. However, because those claims usually rest on some slender foundation of truth, Bush and his aides have frequently avoided scrutiny of their tactics by the press.

This pattern of deception originated with Bush's first run for the presidency and is woven through his time in office. The administration led off with a disingenuous sales campaign for its first tax cut; distorted a series of scientific and environmental issues; leveraged the September 11 attacks to squelch opposition to its policies; conducted an extensive effort to avoid blame for budget deficits and promote a second tax cut; successfully executed a misleading PR campaign to rally support for a confrontation with Iraq; and spun heavily in the invasion's aftermath to try to justify its pre-war claims. As of this writing, Bush's reelection campaign has demonstrated that he will not relent before Election Day.

Bush's approach represents a new and destructive way of doing business in the White House. His arsenal of dishonest public relations tactics is not a principally defensive tool for fending off criticism or scandal, as it was for Clinton, though Bush has certainly used it that way when under attack. Nor is it employed primarily on foreign policy issues as it was under Reagan, although Bush has applied it to debates about the Iraq war and the war on terror.

Instead, Bush has made dishonest PR tactics his standard method for marketing policies to the press and public. Whether on offense or defense, whether the issue is foreign or domestic, the answer is almost always the same—more deceptive spin. For all of his

★ CONCLUSION ★

THE ROAD WE'RE ON
AND HOW TO CHANGE COURSE

Regardless of whether he serves another term in the White House, George W. Bush has inflicted a great deal of damage on the American political system. He may not be the most dishonest president ever elected, but the sophistication of his spin about policy issues and the consistency with which he has misled the public has set a new standard. Nearly every president has been dishonest at some point during his term, and Bush is hardly the first to use public relations techniques. But none of his predecessors engaged in such a nonstop barrage of PR-driven policy deception. In less than four years, Bush has redefined the way in which presidents sell their policies to the public.

The President has accomplished this by taking advantage of the "permanent campaign" of polling, image management, and spin techniques pioneered by Bill Clinton and Ronald Reagan. He has also added something far more destructive to the mix: a willingness to engage in day-to-day dishonesty on nearly every major issue he has addressed. At this point in the Bush presidency, many have come to see the combination of public relations tools and policy dis-

personal and scandal-related dishonesty, Clinton did not promote his policies in such a continually misleading fashion, nor did Reagan use them as systematically or consistently.

Although Bush and his aides have uttered outright falsehoods at times, his presidency does not stand out in this regard—nearly all presidents have dissembled on occasion. Instead, George W. Bush's administration has broken new ground with its penchant for technically true but misleading factual claims, accurate statistics that are substantively misleading, and strategically ambiguous language. Few of these may be blatant lies, but they're just as dishonest.

The President has gotten away with these tactics in large part because of the failings of the press corps, which he has charmed, intimidated, and bamboozled. From the 2000 campaign through the war in Iraq, Bush was protected by the prevailing image of him as a fundamentally honest man. This was buttressed after September 11 by the media's reluctance to challenge a popular wartime president. Even after the Iraq war, the press rarely treated the White House's statements with more than passing skepticism.

More importantly, though, Bush has exploited the failings of the political media more extensively than any modern president. Expectations of balance and objectivity often make reporters reluctant to note the implications of the President's strategically ambiguous language or call him on his frequent distortions of the facts. And when reporters do address these tactics, they usually report that someone is *saying* that Bush is dishonest, a "he said / she said" style of coverage that lends the administration's claims the air of possible truth. In short, though journalists are eager to highlight political conflict or personal scandal, they have generally failed to fact-check the everyday dishonesty that this White House has made standard operating procedure.

Some might question whether the media has really been so easy on Bush, perhaps pointing to the intense scrutiny of alleged gaps in his service record in the Air National Guard or the attention given to claims of negligence in the war on terror made by former administration official Richard Clarke. Rather than proving how hard the press has been on Bush, however, these examples illustrate how coverage of dishonesty in the media tends to swing between two extremes: passive restraint (the norm from 2001–2003) or wild feeding frenzies (coverage of Bush's military record, his sales of Harken Energy Stock while serving on the company's board, Clarke's allegations, and a few other isolated cases).

As this book goes to press, journalists have begun to scrutinize coverage of the debate leading up to war in Iraq, especially the media's credulous repetition of misleading evidence from the Bush administration and its allies.[1] While this rare episode of self-criticism is welcome, it's not likely to go far enough. Nor is it a substitute for real-time coverage of deception from our nation's leaders. Only when journalists separate truth from fiction in the present tense will they truly fulfill their responsibilities.

Their failure to do so has had serious consequences. The White House has been able to disseminate misleading claims to the public about nearly all of its proposals, making it difficult for citizens to understand and participate in the political debates that affect their lives. If average Americans are poorly informed by politicians and the press about the likely effects of a major tax cut proposal, the number of embryonic stem cell lines available for research, or the evidence justifying an invasion of Iraq, they can't realistically make informed judgments.

By treating politics as little more than a sales challenge, George W. Bush is undermining the vigorous debate that is necessary for a healthy democracy. Just as Madison Avenue markets products using shaky claims and emotional appeals, Bush and his aides have tried to win support for their policy agenda without letting Americans get a fair look at the details. But we must insist on more from our leaders—promoting a tax cut should be different from selling sneakers or soft drinks.

THE NEW POLITICAL ARMS RACE

Some citizens might hope that things will get better when Bush leaves office. But the problem is unlikely to disappear regardless of who occupies the White House. Bush's presidency has changed the rules of the game, accelerating a larger trend toward PR-driven deception. By altering the incentives for other politicians and political organizations, Bush has fueled an ongoing arms race in which both sides employ ever more sophisticated tactics to manipulate the public and the press.

The current leader in this respect among Democrats is Senator John Kerry. His presidential campaign traded half-truths with Bush's team on an hour-by-hour basis during the early stages of the 2004 general election. It seems that PR tactics and strategic dishonesty have become a necessity for those who wish to succeed at the highest levels of American politics.

The same thing is true for interest groups, particularly those attempting to beat Bush at his own game. Several new liberal organizations are at the cutting edge of this trend.

John Podesta, a former Clinton administration official who now heads a liberal think tank called the Center for American Progress, has argued that liberals need to counter conservatives' superior communication tactics. "The question I'm asked most often is, 'When are we getting our eight words?' " he told the *New York Times Magazine* in October 2003. Conservatives "have their eight words in a bumper sticker: 'Less government. Lower taxes. Less welfare.' And so on. Where's our eight-word bumper sticker?"[2]

Of course, Democrats and interest groups have ruthlessly employed PR tactics in the past, such as the successful effort by the Clinton White House and Congressional Democrats to demonize former House Speaker Newt Gingrich. They have continued to do so sporadically and relatively ineffectively during Bush's time in office. Until recently, however, the liberal establishment lagged behind conservatives in its efforts to build an institutional communications apparatus to churn out party-line deception, attacks on opponents, and bumper sticker slogans.

The Center for American Progress represents a new effort by liberals to build that institutional capacity. The largest and most important liberal organization to be founded in the last decade, CAP is at the leading edge of Democratic efforts to seize the initiative in the media wars. The organization lists four major objectives on its website, two of which specifically focus on communication: "responding effectively and rapidly to conservative proposals and rhetoric with a thoughtful critique and clear alternatives" and "communicating progressive messages to the American public."[3] With a budget of more than $10 million per year and an experienced team of political operatives, CAP has the muscle to accomplish its mission, putting out a daily stream of heavily spun attacks on conservatives that are picked up and repeated by a growing cadre of liberal pundits.[4]

In the most prominent example from its short history, CAP distorted the evidence about the administration's public statements before the war in Iraq, claiming the Bush White House said Iraq was an "imminent threat." To back up its claim, CAP wrote in its Progress Report online newsletter on January 29, 2004, that "almost exactly a year ago, it was [White House Press Secretary Scott] Mc-Clellan who said the reason NATO should go along with the administration's Iraq war plan was because 'this is about imminent threat.' " The clear implication was that McClellan had made this statement in the context of a discussion of the threat Iraq posed to the United States.

However, a transcript of McClellan's comments, which were made during a February 10, 2003 White House press briefing, shows that he was saying that if a war started, Iraq would pose an imminent threat to its neighbor Turkey. McClellan argued that, if that were the case, other NATO members should therefore defend Turkey against this threat under their NATO charter obligations.[5] CAP linked to the press briefing transcript in its newsletter, but the organization somehow failed to mention that McClellan was talking about a hypothetical imminent threat against Turkey, not the U.S. The way CAP twisted a technically true fact into a substantively misleading claim mirrors some of the worst spin from the Bush White House.

The deception was quite successful. The out-of-context quote suckered NBC *Meet the Press* host Tim Russert, *New Republic* writer Noam Scheiber, and WashingtonPost.com columnist Dan Froomkin, all of whom were later forced to correct the record.[6]

In another case, CAP claimed in its March 9, 2004 newsletter that the Bush administration cut counterterrorism funding before September 11 "while giving gifts to the Taliban" government of Afghanistan. Though it quoted one article stating that the package consisted of "$43 million in drought aid," CAP also approvingly quoted a New York *Newsday* editorial calling the May 2001 aid an "outright gift" without providing further details, implying the aid was provided in cash or given directly to the Taliban.[7] In fact, the package of food aid and food security programs for starving Afghans was administered by the United Nations and nongovernmental organizations, not the Taliban.[8]

With its frequently updated website, top-notch communications staff, and slippery style of analysis, CAP has quickly fulfilled Podesta's goal of getting a liberal message into the press. They have also shown that in the modern world of politics, media savviness seems to have become a synonym for a willingness to deceive.

THE FRAMEWORKS AND ROCKRIDGE INSTITUTES

In late 2003, two groups looking to improve liberals' ability to win the communications war stepped onto the national scene. The FrameWorks Institute and the Rockridge Institute both argued that liberals were losing the battle of ideas because they were ineffective at framing debates to their advantage.

Rockridge, for instance, states that it is working to "Reframe the terms of political debate to make a progressive moral vision more persuasive and influential."[9] U.C. Berkeley linguistics professor George Lakoff, one of the founders of Rockridge, said his organization was launched because "conservatives, especially conservative think tanks, have framed virtually every issue from their perspective.

They have put a huge amount of money into creating the language for their worldview and getting it out there. Progressives have done virtually nothing." The organization is intended to change that equation, Lakoff explained: "Rockridge's job is to reframe public debate, to create balance from a progressive perspective," he said. "It's one thing to analyze language and thought, it's another thing to create it. That's what we're about." [10] In this way, Lakoff carefully justified Rockridge's tactics as necessary to "create balance."

A similar organization called the FrameWorks Institute seeks to help nonprofit groups communicate their messages about social problems. It does not specifically promote liberal policy positions, but the FrameWorks approach mirrors Rockridge. Explaining its philosophy, the group states, "Strategic frame analysis is an approach to communications research and practice that pays attention to the public's deeply held worldviews and widely held assumptions . . . strategic frame analysis taps into decades of research on how people think and communicate." [11] This approach harkens back to the early days of PR, when practitioners hoped to use the emerging social sciences to manipulate public perceptions.

Both groups were founded recently (FrameWorks in 1999 and Rockridge in 2000) and are just beginning to have an impact on politics and the media. [12] Their existence and guiding principles speak to goals of contemporary political groups and the incentives to which they respond. Neither one seeks to improve the substance of liberal ideas or better refute the arguments of conservatives. Instead, their mission is to help liberals win the debate by manipulating it.

CHANGES TO CHEER

Despite these ominous developments, there are a number of promising trends that can help counter deception from our leaders. Because much of this dishonesty is being driven by perverse incentives in the political system, change seems unlikely to come from within. Instead, we must look to the press, the one institution that can effectively hold politicians accountable for deception, to shake things up.

There are a number of standard fixes that have been proposed by media critics over the years, ranging from devoting greater attention to policy to moving away from such a heavy reliance on narrative storylines.[13] Some of these ideas are worthwhile, but they seem unlikely to take hold anytime soon. Instead of simply scolding journalists, we should look to the most positive trends in recent press coverage of dishonesty to see whether they can help reform the system.

OBJECTIVITY RECONSIDERED

Some of the most troubling and least appreciated problems with the media stem from the artificial constraints imposed by the standard of objectivity. The ideal can help to lift the news above rank partisanship and ideology, but it has created serious problems with the way the press deals with political dishonesty, which the Bush administration has used to its advantage.

Most important, news reporters often fail to sort out competing factual claims. This has contributed to the rise of pundits, who provide the context that "objective" reporters cannot, interpreting the news from broader or more ideological perspectives. This group, which consists in large part of ex-political operatives, often contributes little besides partisan spin to our national dialogue. The result is the worst of all possible worlds: Reporters who are trained in gathering and interpreting facts hesitate to take sides in factual disputes, while pundits trained in political warfare dissemble and twist the truth with abandon.

Though there will always be a role for both journalists and pundits in our national political debate, America lacks a middle ground of reporters who uphold professional standards of accuracy but call politicians to account for misleading statements. Rather than transcribing deceptive assertions for fear of appearing unfair or nonobjective, we need a press corps that is willing to clarify complex issues for readers, weigh in on the merits of factual claims, and hold politicians accountable.

The major media institution that comes closest to this in its coverage of the Bush administration is the *Washington Post*, whose reporting we have drawn on heavily in this book. The *Post* has frequently offered fair but skeptical coverage of the White House that measures administration statements against the facts. At times, it has fallen prey to the pathologies of the media, hyping minor scandals, playing into preexisting narratives about politicians, or taking cheap shots at the President. But its coverage of Bush's dishonesty stands as the best example of a publication that remains fair without being bound by artificial notions of balance and objectivity.

It's perhaps not surprising that one of the *Washington Post*'s White House reporters, Dana Milbank, came to the paper from the *New Republic*, a center-left magazine of political opinion. *TNR* has been particularly critical of President Bush and has engaged in its fair share of partisan sniping. Unlike most liberal outlets, however, it has published a significant number of intensively researched critiques of the President's deceptions, particularly on economic matters. As an opinion magazine that is immune to charges of bias, *TNR* can criticize Bush administration dishonesty much more forcefully than news reporters. Its work stands as proof that journalists operating outside of norms of objectivity can still be effective critics of political deceit.

The same can be said for what is perhaps the nation's leading conservative media outlet, Fox News Channel. Despite Fox's claim to be "fair and balanced," it's obvious even to many conservatives that the channel approaches the news from a right-leaning perspective. And although pundit-driven shows like *The O'Reilly Factor* and *Fox & Friends* illustrate some of the worst pathologies of modern political commentary, the channel's news reporting is often better at critiquing liberal deception than its competitors. It was Fox, for instance, that demonstrated that the Bush administration did not make the direct claim that Iraq was an "imminent threat." *Fox Special Report with Brit Hume* and *Fox News Sunday* highlighted the fact that many liberal politicians and media outlets were mischaracterizing the administration's words.[14]

The possibilities offered by a less objective approach to the news are exemplified by one of the world's oldest and most respected publications, the *Economist*. Widely praised as the world's best weekly newsmagazine, the *Economist* approaches the news from a largely pro-business, libertarian point of view, regularly presenting news stories from a clear perspective (even gently mocking its subjects in photo captions) while operating within the standards of professional journalism. As a result, the magazine is more provocative—and more analytical—than American competitors like *Newsweek* and *Time*.

THE BENEFITS OF "INFOTAINMENT"

Another style of journalism that some commentators believe is worrisome could actually help broaden the range of perspectives available in the media: shows that blend entertainment and politics. At their worst, these programs cheapen political debate by focusing on trivia and gossip at the expense of serious issues. However, they can also be a welcome corrective to stale, formulaic news media that often seem incapable of escaping their own pathologies and breaking down the spin that permeates our political culture.

Comedy Central's *The Daily Show* is the leading example of this type of show. It is one of the few programs on television that regularly skewers the press for its focus on process rather than substance. *The Daily Show* also frequently highlights deceptive claims from politicians and their adherence to PR-driven talking points, as when it showed clips of Bush administration officials' repetition of the same phrases and claims in response to former counterterrorism official Richard Clarke.

In addition, the entertainment format frees *The Daily Show* from the "gotcha" questions and overheated rhetoric that mar political talk shows. As a result, host Jon Stewart's interviews with leading political figures are some of the best on TV. Stewart generally sticks to substantive issues; allows politicians to speak without regular interruption; asks challenging questions about the prevalence of deception in our political system; and refuses to let misleading assertions go by without comment. (Similarly, CBS *Late Show* host David Letterman's interview with Bush was one of the most challenging and unusual of the 2000 campaign season.)[15]

Much to the chagrin of some critics, the influence of such shows is increasing. A February 2004 study by the Pew Research Center found that 21 percent of Americans under thirty regularly get campaign news from comedy programs such as *Saturday Night Live* and *The Daily Show*. Pew lamented that this segment of the electorate is particularly poorly informed about the candidates and issues, especially compared with those who get information from the Internet.[16]

Certainly, "infotainment" cannot provide all of the information that citizens need or replace a professional media. However, rather than decrying the rise of entertainment values in the news, journalists and media critics would be well advised to think about why *The Daily Show* is so popular with young people, a group that has grown up in an age of toothless journalism and sophisticated professional spin.

THE POWER OF "BLOGS"

Weblogs represent another way to help change incentives for politicians and the media. These perspective-driven websites (also known simply as "blogs") offer short posts and essays, usually from a clearly articulated personal viewpoint. The low cost of producing a blog (usually little more than the author's time and a few dollars for a domain name and server space) means that the medium is accessible to nearly anyone with a computer.

Over time, a community of bloggers has developed that avoids some of the worst excesses and failures of traditional political debate and media coverage. The online medium allows authors to link to the articles they write about so readers can check their assertions directly against their sources and make independent judgments about the facts in question. In addition, the top political bloggers tend to be better than the traditional media at admitting error, correcting factual mistakes, and engaging the substance of their opponent's arguments.

Together, political blogs have helped to create a culture of fact-checking that has served as a check on inaccuracy in the mainstream media. With bloggers sounding the alarm and spreading the word, deceptions have been exposed, myths explained, and falsehoods debunked in near-real time, helping prevent journalists and politicians from misleading the public. Blogs now regularly wring corrections from major media outlets. The format is also starting to have an effect on the mainstream press. Such outlets including the *Washington Post* and ABC News have begun to experiment with blogs as an alternative means to deliver news to the public.

This process can also help to bring citizens into public debate. With politicians incessantly repeating talking points, pushing misleading factual claims, and bombarding the airwaves with emotional catchphrases, it is not surprising that citizens are disengaged. The Internet can help to create a culture of participation in which members of the public make their voices heard and debate the merits of their positions with others. This process can promote democratic citizenship and channel the wisdom of the public, bringing a diversity of ideas and perspectives to bear on the issues and widening the bounds of political conversation.

Certainly, the Internet is no panacea. Myths can spread rapidly online; debate can degenerate into vitriol and ignorance; and many citizens cannot or will not participate. Nor will blogs ever replace the reporting performed by professional journalists. They can help to hold media organizations and politicians accountable, however, and improve the prevailing political culture.

THE KAREN RYAN INCIDENT

An incident from early 2004 demonstrates the current state of affairs and how the media can help pull America back from the brink.

After Bush signed controversial legislation in December 2003 adding a prescription drug benefit to Medicare, the Department of Health and Human Services launched a multimillion-dollar government-funded campaign to promote the new law. The department sent a ten minute "video news release" to local news stations that included footage of Bush signing the law, a statement by HHS Secretary Tommy Thompson, and two 90-second segments designed to look like news reports. These segments were aired fifty-three times on forty television stations across the country without disclosure that they came from the government. (Local news stations routinely air such packages from corporations or nonprofits unaltered.) [17]

The English language segment in the package was clearly intended to appear as though it had been prepared by a journalist. (The government also included a similar segment in Spanish.) [18] The administration provided suggested scripts for news anchors, which told them to say "Reporter Karen Ryan helps sort through the details" about the new Medicare law. Then, during the phony news segment itself, the unseen narrator, speaking as though she were a reporter, appeared to knock down questions about the legislation: "The new law, say officials, will simply offer people with Medicare more ways to make their health coverage more affordable." The segment concluded with the signoff, "In Washington, I'm Karen Ryan reporting," omitting any disclosure that would alert viewers that it was funded or distributed by the U.S. government. In fact, though HHS identified Ryan as a "freelance journalist," she was a PR professional subcontracted by an ad agency to create the spot, not a member of the news media.[19]

When the media began raising questions about the use of a fake news segment, a spokesman for HHS betrayed no doubt that the administration sees such practices as acceptable. "The use of video news releases is a common, routine practice in government and the private sector," Kevin W. Keane said, adding, "Anyone who has questions about this practice needs to do some research on modern public information tools."[20] Another HHS spokesman, Bill Pierce, later claimed, "There is no way this can be deceptive," saying, "If [local newscasts] run the whole package, that's their choice."[21] In a different interview, Pierce cited the Clinton administration's use of the same style of video news release (including at least one case where the narrator claimed to be "reporting") and suggested "All we have done is promote our point of view. Everything that's in the video is true; none of the facts are incorrect."[22] With these statements, Keane and Pierce threw down the gauntlet to those who question the use of misleading corporate-style PR tactics in politics.

Luckily, the chutzpah of the administration's tactics sparked widespread outrage after the *New York Times* exposed the video's existence.[23] *Columbia Journalism Review*'s Campaign Desk blog (where one of us works) played a crucial role in investigating the story, compiling a list of newscasts that aired the video, locating Ryan for an interview, and revealing CNN's role in distributing the segment to local newscasts.[24] The combined effect of attention from Campaign Desk and other bloggers helped to keep the mainstream media focused on the story, which led to even more coverage.

In the end, though HHS refused to back down, the results were largely positive. A number of local newscasts were publicly shamed for their use of video news releases; Ryan eventually admitted that she was "reading a script" and stated that she would no longer use the term "reporting" in her video news release work; and CNN, which had distributed the video to local stations, changed its policies so that video news releases would be distributed to local news stations separately from actual news footage.[25] The Public Relations Society of America, an influential industry group, also issued new guidelines to its members, telling them not to use the word "reporting" in video news releases if the person speaking is not a journalist.[26] And in May, the General Accounting Office, the investigative arm of Congress, issued a report finding that the phony news segments violated restrictions against "using appropriated funds for publicity or propaganda purposes."[27]

THE FUTURE OF DEMOCRACY

The harm George W. Bush has done to our political system is profound and will almost certainly last far beyond his time in office. Bush has tamed the media and spun the public with unprecedented sophistication. His success in doing so is strengthening the perception that politicians cannot disarm in the spin war without conceding defeat. At this point, we must consider the possibility that future presidents, whether Democrat or Republican, will use Bush's tactics as their starting point and apply the vast power and influence of the White House to mislead the American people still further.

This would be a disaster for our democracy. If policy dishonesty becomes the norm for future presidents and other politicians, we lose any hope of having a reasonable, fact-based political discourse.

When citizens cannot understand the issues or the positions of their leaders, real democratic accountability is impossible.

We must therefore create new incentives that make political success dependent upon fair and open debate. Given the problems of the mainstream professional media, our best chance is to encourage news outlets that offer responsible coverage of dishonesty outside the framework of "objectivity"; political blogs that fact-check the media, politicians, and each other; and entertainment programs that satirize mainstream political debate. This is where we will find the energetic culture, engaged analysis, and sharply critical points of view that our political press so desperately needs to expose the Karen Ryans of the future and stop presidents who would conduct themselves like George W. Bush.

There are no easy answers, but for citizens concerned with the future of American political debate, the only long-term solution is to be skeptical, oppose dishonesty in all its forms, and support those who hold political figures accountable. Spin will never disappear, but an informed and active citizenry can still prevent the worst excesses of PR-driven deception from corrupting our democracy.

O'NEILL UNVEILS THE BUDGET

After leaving office, Treasury Secretary Paul O'Neill provided 19,000 documents that crossed his desk while serving in the Bush administration to author Ron Suskind, who drew on them for his book *The Price of Loyalty*. Suskind has since released a number of these documents into the public domain on his website (www .ronsuskind.com). Two of them illustrate the message discipline the administration tries to enforce. In the first, which is reprinted below, Assistant Secretary of the Treasury for Public Affairs Michele Davis advises O'Neill on a February 28, 2001 press conference unveiling the President's first budget.

MEMO

To: Secretary O'Neill
From: Michele
Date: Tuesday 2/27/01
Re: Tomorrow's Press Conference Unveiling the Budget

You and Mitch Daniels are scheduled to unveil the President's budget at a press conference in the OEOB at 10:15 tomorrow morning. This event, more than anything you've participated in to date, requires that you be monotonously

<u>on-message.</u> In addition to the media attending, this event is simulcast to the White House press corp that is traveling with the President in Pennsylvania.

Daniels will speak first, and he will present the overall themes of controlling the growth in spending and paying off all the debt available for retirement. He will leave most of the tax cut discussion to you.

Your role is to 1) repeat the message that we will pay off all the debt available to pay off and 2) state clearly that we must cut taxes because we take more from people than we need to fund these new priorities, and if we don't give it back to the people who paid it, we'll end up wasting it in Washington.

Key background information: The public prefers spending on things like health care and education over cutting taxes. It's crucial that your remarks make clear that there is no trade off here—that we will boost education spending and set aside Social Security and Medicare surpluses to address the future of those programs, and still we will have an enormous surplus. This isn't an "either/or" question.

Roll-out events like this are the clearest examples of when staying on message is absolutely crucial. Any deviation during the unveiling of the budget will change the way coverage plays out from tomorrow forward. For example, you do not want to discuss potential Social Security reform ideas. Your remarks should be very focussed and your answers during the Q and A should only repeat your remarks.

1. We have funded America's priorities of education and national defense.
2. We have walled off Social Security and Medicare funds where they can only be used to modernize those programs.
3. We will pay off all the debt available to be retired.
4. That still leaves an enormous surplus. We need structural tax reform, because the tax system is taking more from working people than Washington needs to pay for America's priorities.
5. If we don't let taxpayers keep more of what they earn, those tax surpluses will be spent expanding government beyond our needs. Spending grew 8% last year—that's a recipe for waste.
6. We all know government is full of duplication—there are places we need to consolidate programs and spend the taxpayers' money more wisely. But we won't do that as long as we are awash in tax surpluses.
7. Today's federal tax burden is higher than it's been at any time in our nation's history. It's time to give tax relief to taxpayers, and lay the groundwork for a consumer-led expansion in the economy.

8. It's time to cut income taxes, so people keep more of what they earn, and decide for themselves how best to spend it.

Likely Questions:

1) If some agency budgets are growing faster than 4%, some other programs must be growing below that rate. You are cutting some programs, are you not? Which ones?

   There is plenty of duplication throughout the federal budget. We have dozens of programs in various departments all targeting the same problem. We need to figure out which ones are working, and target our resources accordingly.

2) Are you cutting Customs funding and letting up on the war on drugs?

   We are beefing up the war on drugs. The President's budget spends $35 million on the Western Hemisphere Drug Elimination Act to improve interdiction.

3) You say the "non-retireable" debt is $1.2 trillion, while CBO puts it at only $800 billion. Why the difference?

   OMB and CBO have different assumptions about buybacks over the next 5 years. OMB continues the previous Administration's insistence that we not project buybacks beyond the current year. We haven't adjusted that position because I do not have all my debt management officials in place yet at Treasury to conduct a full review. In either case, a substantial amount of debt remains in 2011. More importantly, even the CBO's estimate of a higher amount of potential debt reduction does not alter the allocation of the $5.6 trillion surplus. We have committed to locking away the $2.6 trillion Social Security surplus is locked away where it can only be used to pay down the debt. That $2.6 trillion in Social Security surplus would cover all possible debt retirement even if the CBO estimates turn out to be accurate.

4) But if CBO is right, that means there is less money for individual Social Security accounts.

   That's a question for another day. I'm looking forward to Social Security reform as much as you are, but first things first. Let's retire as much of the debt as we can and eliminate the structural overtaxation that puts today's federal tax burden at an all time high. That's enough to keep us busy for a while—then we can turn our attention to Social Security reform.

5) Why are we just now finding out about this so-called 'unretireable' debt?

This is a new policy area for all of us—we've never had the huge surpluses we have today.

6) If you are worried about the economy, why not include business tax cuts?

First of all, small businesses are the engine of growth in our economy, and a majority of small businesses are taxed under the individual income tax. Cutting rates at the high end will mean small businesses will keep more of what they earn, and plow it back into their firms to hire more workers or to increase productivity, which in turn increases wages. Second, allowing people to keep more of what they earn will help to lay the groundwork for another consumer-led expansion.

7) What do you think of the House plan to break up the tax bill into several pieces?

We'll work with the Congress on legislative strategy. I'm glad the House is eager to get to work on this right away, and I'm looking forward to working with them to achieve the President's goals of cutting income tax rates across the board and making our tax code more pro-family.

8) If you are worried about the economy, why not make the tax cut bigger?

It may turn out that the surplus will be much larger over the next 10 years than it is projected to be. When that becomes clear, I'll be more than happy to cut taxes again. In fact, I hope that we will turn our attention in the future to overall tax reform, and create a system that is simpler and fairer than what we have today. For now, let's enact the President's tax relief plan. We know there's plenty of tax surplus to make this plan possible. If more materializes, we can always do more tax cuts later.

★ APPENDIX B ★

O'NEILL GOES ON *MEET THE PRESS*

In another communications memo from January 4, 2002, released by Suskind, which is reproduced here, Davis coaches O'Neill on how to handle host Tim Russert during an upcoming appearance on NBC's *Meet the Press,* which is considered one of Washington's most challenging Sunday interview shows.

SUNDAY TV—MEET THE PRESS

8:30 AM
10 minute segment

Other guests: McCain and Lieberman from Uzbekistan
                        Karzai

MESSAGE

FIRST ANSWER, no matter the question:
We must act to ensure our economy recovers and people get back to work.

KEY LINES TO DELIVER:

An economic security package to make the recession shorter and put people back to work faster.

Creating jobs is the key to success.

a growing economy creates a budget surplus, not the other way around

If the Senate Majority Leader is serious about helping put people back to work, then we should have TPA and the economic security package on the President's desk by March 1.

WORD CHOICES:

"Economic Security" not "stimulus"
talk about people, and their jobs, not "growth" and "surplus"

TONE:

The economy is showing some signs of recovery, but they haven't yet solidified and we need to act to speed the recovery, because there's no reason people should be out of work for any longer than is necessary.

On questions about the state of the economy, we can't just cite good stats, we need to talk about both the good and bad signs:

- Unemployment went up, but not as much as it could be
- WSJ poll, average expect 0.9% growth in Q1
- Car and truck sales had the second strongest year to date, but they slowed in December

Likely Questions:

1. State of the Economy

   The first several questions are likely to be about the state of the economy—without Russert mentioning the President's agenda or anything else related to Washington. You need to interject the President's message, even if the question has nothing to do with that.

   EXAMPLE: "What is the state of the economy today?"

   A. We're seeing hopeful signs of a recovery, but they aren't as strong as we'd like them to be. Too many people are without a job right now. But confidence is up, which is a good sign. I saw in the WSJ that a consensus estimate on growth is something like 0.9% for the first quarter. That's growth, but it's just not good enough. The President doesn't want us to sit on my hands and hope this recovery takes root. We need to act, to get people back to work more quickly and get the economy growing again.

2. Daschle's accusations.

Russert will ask about Daschle's accusations that the tax cut created the deficit. You need to say in a very succinct sentence that the terrorist attacks and the recession caused the deficit. You can give the numbers (attached), but don't only give the numbers. First, give a clear succinct sentence. Russert likely will ask a series of questions about the deficit. You shouldn't make any projections—budget numbers are still weeks away.

Q. Are you willing to increase the deficit to pay for a stimulus package we may not need, since the economy is already showing signs of recovery.

A. (You need to respond very strongly that our primary concern is putting people back to work.) Millions of people don't have jobs right now, because our economy isn't growing. That has to be our primary concern. When people go back to work, the economy grows and the deficits disappear.

Q. Let me follow up to that: does the deficit not matter at all? Should we repeal the cut in the top tax rate to fill that hole?

A. Even Senator Daschle didn't suggest that. Because everyone knows, raising taxes slows the economy—exactly the medicine we don't need right now.

Q. Is this the old, failed 1980s rhetoric about growing our way out of a deficit?

A. In the 1980s, the economy grew and revenues to the Treasury grew a lot. The problem was that government spending grew even faster. What we learned from the mid 1990s is that economic growth, combined with spending discipline, is the path to budget surpluses.

Q. Your asking for an increase in the debt ceiling, too. Isn't that an admission that the tax cut was too big?

A. We need an increase in the debt ceiling because of the recession and the war. We are going to defeat terrorism abroad and we are going to create jobs here at home. That requires the government to borrow more money this year, an obvious price we are willing to pay to ensure our safety and prosperity here at home.

Q. In 1997, the Republican Congress refused to raise the debt ceiling when Rubin asked them to do so. Will you get the same reaction?

A. It's inconceivable that they won't raise the debt ceiling. Our economy was wracked by a terrorist attack and a recession. We need the tools to defeat terrorists abroad and reignite growth at home.

3. Daschle's proposals

Expect a series of questions about any of the particulars of Daschle's proposals. But don't answer only by critiquing that proposal. Instead, flip the question to talk about why the President's proposal is the right way to ensure a stronger recovery.

Q. Would you consider a new-worker tax credit, to encouraging hiring?

A. Do you think NBC might just fire everyone and rehire them to get a tax credit? Wouldn't that be nuts? The President has proposed the right tax incentives to create jobs—reducing income taxes on millions of small businesses, accelerating expensing of new investments, and fixing the corporate AMT so it doesn't raise taxes on companies when they are doing their best to avoid laying off workers.

4. Likelihood of enacting anything.

Senator Daschle said "We should move quickly to pass a bill that boosts demand, encourages investments, and creates jobs." Those are words the President has said many times. So you should welcome Senator Daschle's <u>new willingness</u> to enact an economic security package. You should also bring up dislocated workers as a reason you think we will get something done. And then give your deadline.

Q. Isn't this just posturing? You guys want to show the unemployed that you care. Will anything actually get done?

A. There's only one way to find out, Tim. Senator Daschle showed new willingness to enact an economic security package. He called for action to help strengthen our recovery. He's in charge in the Senate. So if he's serious, he will have Trade Promotion Authority and the economic stimulus package through the Senate by March 1.

Q. Would you be willing to drop the tax rate cuts to get the rest of the package done?

A. Millions of small businesses pay individual income taxes—not corporate income taxes. And those small businesses are the engines of job creation in our economy. We need to give them relief so they can invest and hire.

Q. Since you all can't agree on tax cuts, why not just do the package for dislocated workers?

A. People don't just want help while they are out of work, they want jobs. And even on the dislocated worker packages, in December Senator Daschle objected to our proposal to give unemployed Americans a tax credit to pay for 60% of their health insurance costs. Insurance is enormously expensive for so many of these families—that's got to be part of the help we give.

★ APPENDIX C ★

THE "TRIFECTA"

As we document in this book, President Bush repeatedly made false claims that he had listed three exceptions that would justify budget deficits at an appearance in Chicago during the 2000 campaign. We reproduce the months-long sequence of statements here for readers—and history—to judge.

PRESIDENT BUSH'S REPETITIONS OF THE CHICAGO STORY:

1) Remarks by the President in Photo Opportunity with Business Leaders, New York, New York, October 3, 2001:

"Well, as I said in Chicago during the campaign, when asked about should the government ever deficit spend, I said only under these circumstances should government deficit spend: if there is a national emergency, if there is a recession, or if there's a war."

2) Remarks by the President to Robin Hayes for Congress and Elizabeth Dole for Senate, North Carolina Republican Party Luncheon, Charlotte, North Carolina, February 27, 2002:

"You know, I was campaigning in Chicago and somebody asked me, is there ever any time where the budget might have to go into deficit? I said only if we were at war or had a national emergency or were in recession. Little did I realize we'd get the trifecta."

3) Remarks by the President to Iowa Republican Party Victory 2002 and Latham for Congress Luncheon, Des Moines, Iowa, March 1, 2002:

"You know, I remember campaigning in Chicago and somebody said, would you ever spend a deficit? And I said, only if we're at war or we had a recession or there was a national emergency. Little did I realize we'd get the trifecta."

4) Remarks by the President at the Graham for Senate Luncheon, Greenville, South Carolina, March 27, 2002:

"I was campaigning in Chicago one time and a fellow said, would you ever allow for deficit spending, would that ever enter your vocabulary? I said, well, under certain circumstances: only if we're at war or there was a national emergency or there was a recession. Little did I realize we'd draw the trifecta."

5) Remarks by the President at Saxby Chambliss for Senate Dinner, Atlanta, Georgia, March 27, 2002:

"I'll never forget one time in Chicago when a reporter said, would you ever deficit spend? And I said, well, only—only if we were at

war, only if there were a national emergency, or only if there is a re-cession. Never did I believe we'd get the trifecta. But we're dealing with it."

6) Remarks by the President to the Republican Party of Texas-Victory 2002 and Cornyn for Senate Luncheon, Dallas, Texas, March 28, 2002:

"You know, when I was campaigning in Chicago, in the general election, somebody said, would you ever deficit spend? I said, well, only if we were at war, or there was a national emergency, or we were in a recession. Little did I realize we'd get the trifecta."

7) Remarks by the President at Fisher for Governor Reception, Philadelphia, Pennsylvania, April 3, 2002:

"I remember campaigning in Chicago one time, and the guy said, would you ever deficit spend? I said, well, only if we were at war, or the country was in recession, or there was a national emergency. I didn't realize we were going to get the trifecta."

8) Remarks by the President at Heather Wilson for Congress Luncheon, Albuquerque, New Mexico, April 29, 2002:

"You know, when I was campaigning in Chicago one time, they said, would you ever have a deficit? I said, I hope not. I said, I think it's important for us to make—to work hard to have a balanced budget. But I said, yes, I'd have a deficit if I were the President only

if we were at war, or in a recession, or in times of emergency. I didn't think I was going to draw the trifecta."

9) Remarks by the President at Simon for Governor Luncheon, Santa Clara, California, April 30, 2002:

"I remember in Chicago they said to me, would you ever have deficit spending? I said, only if there was a war, or a national emergency, or a recession. Never did I realize we'd get the trifecta."

10) Remarks by the President at Taft for Governor Luncheon, Columbus, Ohio, May 10, 2002:

"You know, when I was running for President, in Chicago, somebody said, would you ever have deficit spending? I said, only if we were at war, or only if we had a recession, or only if we had a national emergency. Never did I dream we'd get the trifecta."

11) Remarks by the President in Ryan for Governor Luncheon, Chicago, Illinois, May 13, 2002:

"By the way, right here in Chicago, I was asked when I was campaigning here, they said, hey, Mr. President, would you ever have a deficit? I said, only if there was a war, or a recession, or a national emergency. Yeah, we've got one right now."

12) Remarks by the President at 2002 Republican National Committee Presidential Gala, Washington, D.C., May 14, 2002:

"I was in Chicago in 2002 [sic]*; some guy said—a reporter, excuse me, said—a male reporter said—would you ever allow a deficit? I said, only if we're at war, or only if the nation were in recession, or only if we had a national emergency would I allow a deficit. Well, this administration got all three."*

13) Remarks by the President to the 14th Annual World Pork Expo, Des Moines, Iowa, June 7, 2002:

"I remember—I remember campaigning in Chicago, and one of the reporters said, would you ever deficit spend? I said only—only in times of war, in times of economic insecurity as a result of a recession, or in times of national emergency. Never did I dream we'd have a trifecta."

14) Remarks by the President in Texans for Rick Perry Reception, Houston, Texas, June 14, 2002:

"You know, when I was one time campaigning in Chicago, a reporter said, would you ever have a deficit? And I said, I can't imagine it, but there would be one if we had a war, or a national emergency, or a recession. Never did I dream we'd get the trifecta."

SIMILAR STATEMENTS BY BUSH
THAT DON'T MENTION CHICAGO SPECIFICALLY:

1) Remarks by the President in Photo Opportunity with His Economic Advisors and Fed Chairman Alan Greenspan, January 7, 2002:

"I said to the American people that this nation might have to run deficits in time of war, in times of national emergency, or in times of a recession."

2) Remarks by the President at Meeting of the Leaders of the Fiscal Responsibility Coalition, April 16, 2002:

"The recession—no question, I remember when I was campaigning, I said, would you ever deficit spend? And I said, yes, only if there were a time of war, or recession, or a national emergency. Never thought we'd get—and so we have a temporary deficit in our budget, because we are at war, we're recovering, our economy is recovering, and we've had a national emergency. Never did I dream we'd have the trifecta."

3) President Comments on New Economic Numbers and Middle East, Crawford, Texas, April 26, 2002:

"I remind—I want to remind you what I told the American people, that if I'm the President—when I was campaigning, if I were to become the President, we would have deficits only in the case of war, a recession or a national emergency. In this case, we got all three."

4) Remarks by the President at the 21st Century High Tech Forum, June 13, 2002:

"You know, we—these are extraordinary times. I remember campaigning and somebody said, would you ever deficit spend? I said,

only if there was a war, or a recession, or a national emergency. I didn't think we were going to get the trifecta."

5) Remarks by the President at Ferguson for Congress Luncheon, Newark, New Jersey, June 24, 2002:

"You know, when I was running, I said—they asked me, would you ever deficit spend? I said, well, only if we had a recession, or a national emergency, or a war."

★ SOURCES AND METHODS ★

We have sought to document all of our factual claims and sources in this book as completely as possible. We do not provide citations for statements or articles explicitly referenced in the text itself (for example, a White House press briefing on a specific date), but all other sources are cited and documented in the Notes section so that readers can verify our claims for themselves.

To maximize readability, we have consolidated our footnotes whenever possible, particularly when drawing on the same source in more than one sentence. In these cases, a single footnote is often included at the end of a paragraph. Some material in the book also draws broadly on past work published on our website, but we do not cite our own articles here.

We have relied on primary sources as much as possible in our research. Citations of statements by President Bush, Vice President Cheney, administration spokesmen, and other White House officials are generally taken from official White House transcripts, with the title that is used on the whitehouse.gov website, the location (if it is outside Washington, D.C.), and the date. When White House transcripts are not available, we have cited specific transcripts when necessary, but otherwise we simply cite the testimony and the date it took place. Finally, it is worth noting that Bryan Keefer is the assistant managing editor of *Columbia Journalism Review*'s Campaign Desk weblog, which we cite in several instances.

When possible, we have drawn on professional news outlets and relatively neutral commentators in our research. However, we have made limited use of quotations or factual criticisms drawn from other sources. In particular, we have cited a number of analyses of President Bush's tax and budget proposals from the Center on Budget and Policy Priorities, Citizens for Tax Justice, and the Urban-Brookings Tax Policy Center. These groups are all left-of-center, but their technical analysis is highly respected and they provide some of the most detailed distributional and budget analyses available in Washington. We have noted the data used in their analyses wherever possible. We also use so-called "static" scoring estimates of the cost of tax cuts, which remain the standard for Congressional budgeting in the absence of more reliable "dynamic" estimates that incorporate feedback effects.

We have fact-checked this book. However, we take full responsibility for any mistakes that may have been made and will post any necessary corrections or clarifications at http://www.spinsanity .com/book/corrections.html. To notify us of an error, please e-mail corrections@spinsanity.com. We are tough critics of inaccuracy, and will hold ourselves to the same standard we apply to others.

★ NOTES ★

INTRODUCTION

1. David Yepsen, "Bush plan to cut taxes draws fire," *Des Moines Register,* December 2, 1999.

2. Brooks Jackson, CNN *Inside Politics,* August 22, 2000; Jonathan Chait, "Going for gold: The Bush tax cut is a lie, Part II," *New Republic,* May 21, 2001.

3. FDCH political transcripts, "U.S. Senator Edward Kennedy (D-MA) Holds Hearing on Stem Cell Research," September 5, 2001.

4. Remarks by the President at Taft for governor luncheon, Columbus, Ohio, May 10, 2002.

5. Remarks by the President on Iraq, Cincinnati, Ohio, October 7, 2002.

6. Interview of the President by TVP, Poland, May 29, 2003.

7. Remarks by the President to Veterans of Foreign Wars, August 20, 2001.

8. "President's spending for ex-soldiers falls short of promise to give them 'priority' treatment," *Daily Mislead,* October 21, 2003.

9. "Funding for veterans up 27%, but Democrats call it a cut," FactCheck.org, February 18, 2004.

1. Sidney Blumenthal, *The Permanent Campaign* (Boston: Beacon Press, 1980), 7.

2. Jeffrey K. Tulis, *The Rhetorical Presidency* (Princeton, New Jersey: Princeton University Press, 1987), 95–116.

3. Stuart Ewen, *PR! A Social History of Spin* (New York: Basic Books, 1996), 107–127.

4. Scott M. Cutlip, *The Unseen Power* (Hillsdale, New Jersey: Lawrence Erlbaum Associates, 1994), 107–127.

5. Walter Lippmann, *Public Opinion* (New York: Macmillan Company, 1956 [fifth edition]), 248; see Stuart Ewen, *PR! A Social History of Spin* (New York: Basic Books, 1996), 146–173.

6. Edward L. Bernays, *Propaganda* (New York: Liveright Publishing Corporation, 1928), 9.

7. John A. Morello, *Selling the President, 1920: Albert D. Lasker, Advertising, and the Election of Warren G. Harding* (Westport, Connecticut: Praeger, 2001), 49–58.

8. Betty Winfield, *FDR and the News Media* (Urbana, Illinois: University of Illinois Press, 1990), 103–111, 27–125; Lawrence R. Jacobs and Robert Y. Shapiro, "The rise of presidential polling: The Nixon White House in historical perspective," *Public Opinion Quarterly* (Vol. 59, No. 2, Summer 1995), 164.

9. Lawrence R. Jacobs and Robert Y. Shapiro, "The rise of presidential polling: The Nixon White House in historical perspective," *Public Opinion Quarterly* (Vol. 59, No. 2, Summer 1995), 163–195.

10. John Anthony Maltese, *Spin Control* (Chapel Hill: University of North Carolina Press, 1994 [second edition]), 16–17.

11. John Anthony Maltese, *Spin Control* (Chapel Hill: University of North Carolina Press, 1994 [second edition]), 3, 44, 58–60.

12. Mark Hertsgaard, *On Bended Knee* (New York: Farrar Straus Giroux,

1988), 37–38; John Anthony Maltese, *Spin Control* (Chapel Hill: University of North Carolina Press, 1994 [second edition]), 3, 94.

13. John Anthony Maltese, *Spin Control* (Chapel Hill: University of North Carolina Press, 1994 [second edition]), 93.

14. Mark Hertsgaard, *On Bended Knee* (New York: Farrar Straus Giroux, 1988), 23.

15. Mark Hertsgaard, *On Bended Knee* (New York: Farrar Straus Giroux, 1988), 48.

16. Martin F. Nolan, "How movers move and shakers shake," *New York Times,* March 24, 1988; Michael Deaver, *The News with Brian Williams,* MSNBC, February 5, 2001; Seth Gitell, "Robert Reich's guerrilla campaign," *Boston Phoenix,* July 25, 2002; Michael Deaver, *The News with Brian Williams,* CNBC, June 2, 2003.

17. Robert Parry, *Fooling America* (New York: William Morrow and Company Inc., 1992), 173–188.

18. Robert Parry, *Fooling America* (New York: William Morrow and Company Inc., 1992), 214, 216–217; Scott Peterson, "In war, some facts less factual," *Christian Science Monitor,* September 6, 2002.

19. Scott Peterson, "In war, some facts less factual," *Christian Science Monitor,* September 6, 2002; Robert Parry, *Fooling America* (New York: William Morrow and Company, Inc., 1992), 217; letter from Comptroller General of the United States to Reps. Jack Brooks and Dante B. Powell, September 30, 1987, published on National Security Archive website, March 2, 2001.

20. Wynton C. Hall, " 'Reflections of yesterday': George H. W. Bush's instrumental use of public opinion research in presidential discourse," *Presidential Studies Quarterly* (Vol. 32, No. 3, September 2002), 531–558.

21. Scott Peterson, "In war, some facts less factual," *Christian Science Monitor,* September 6, 2002.

22. Michael E. O'Hanlon, "A flawed masterpiece," *Foreign Affairs,* May/June 2002; Fred Kaplan, "Patriot games," *Slate,* March 24, 2003.

23. Lawrence R. Jacobs and Robert Y. Shapiro, *Politicians Don't Pander* (Chicago: University of Chicago Press, 2000), 103–105, 109–110, 112, 105.

24. Howard Kurtz, *Spin Cycle* (New York: Touchstone Books, 1998), 23–24.

25. Howard Kurtz, *Spin Cycle* (New York: Touchstone Books, 1998).

26. Lawrence R. Jacobs and Robert Y. Shapiro, *Politicians Don't Pander* (Chicago: University of Chicago Press, 2000), 270–288.

27. Richard Stengel and Eric Pooley, "Masters of the message," *Time*, November 6, 1996.

28. John C. Stauber and Sheldon Rampton, *Trust Us, We're Experts!* (New York: J.P. Tarcher, 2002), 2.

29. Benjamin I. Page and Robert Y. Shapiro, *The Rational Public: Fifty Years of Trends in American Politics* (Chicago: University of Chicago Press, 1992).

30. John C. Stauber and Sheldon Rampton, *Toxic Sludge Is Good for You* (Monroe, Maine: Common Courage Press, 1995), 105–107.

31. Dana Milbank, "Shifts predicted after Hughes's exit," *Washington Post*, April 24, 2002; Karen Hughes, *Ten Minutes From Normal* (New York: Viking, 2004), 134.

32. David Frum, *The Right Man: The Surprise Presidency of George W. Bush* (New York: Random House, 2003), 38, quoted in Ryan Lizza, "Run on," *New Republic*, February 10, 2003.

33. Elisabeth Bumiller, "Keepers of Bush image lift stagecraft to new heights," *New York Times*, May 16, 2003.

34. Karen Hughes, *Ten Minutes From Normal* (New York: Viking, 2004), 189–190.

35. Martha Joynt Kumar, "Communications operations in the White House of President George W. Bush: Making news on his terms," *Presidential Studies Quarterly* (Vol. 33, No. 2, June 2003), 366–393.

36. Jacob M. Schlesinger, "Budget chief fights to curb spending, to the enduring chagrin of Congress," *Wall Street Journal*, August 15, 2001.

37. Mike Allen, "Bush picks CSX Corp. chief for Treasury," *Washington Post,* December 9, 2002.

38. ABCNews.com, "Bush's first 100 Days: Michael Deaver interview," March 8, 2001.

39. Ken Auletta, "Fortress Bush," *New Yorker,* January 19, 2004; Elisabeth Bumiller, "Keepers of Bush image lift stagecraft to new heights," *New York Times,* May 16, 2003.

40. Elisabeth Bumiller, "Keepers of Bush image lift stagecraft to new heights," *New York Times,* May 16, 2003.

41. Elisabeth Bumiller, "Keepers of Bush image lift stagecraft to new heights," *New York Times,* May 16, 2003.

42. Elisabeth Bumiller, "Keepers of Bush image lift stagecraft to new heights," *New York Times,* May 16, 2003.

43. Dana Milbank and Bradley Graham, "With crisis, more fluid style at White House," *Washington Post,* October 10, 2001; Martha Joynt Kumar, "Communications operations in the White House of President George W. Bush: Making news on his terms," *Presidential Studies Quarterly* (Vol. 33, No. 2, June 2003), 374.

44. Martha Joynt Kumar, "Communications operations in the White House of President George W. Bush: Making news on his terms," *Presidential Studies Quarterly* (Vol. 33, No. 2, June 2003), 377.

45. Ken Auletta, "Fortress Bush," The *New Yorker,* January 19, 2004.

46. Mike Allen, "President says economy will overcome 'problems,'" *Washington Post,* August 14, 2002.

47. CBSNews.com, "Dear Taxpayer . . .", June 19, 2001.

48. See, for instance, Frank Bruni, "Bush cites news article to renew attack on Gore's fund-raising," *New York Times,* September 15, 2000.

49. John DiIulio, letter to Ron Suskind, published on Esquire.com, October 24, 2002.

50. *Christian Science Monitor,* "West Wing loyalty: A fine line," December 17, 2002.

51. See, for instance, Rick Pearson, "Bush endorses GOP's attack ad," *Chicago Tribune,* September 1, 2000.

52. Joshua Green, "The other War Room," *Washington Monthly,* April 2002.

53. Adam Nagourney, "Bush takes strategic no-remorse stance," *New York Times,* April 15, 2004.

54. Ari Fleischer, White House press briefing, May 16, 2001.

55. Dana Milbank, "A sound bite so good, the President wishes he had said it," *Washington Post,* July 2, 2002; Mike Allen, "Bush: 'We found' banned weapons," *Washington Post,* May 31, 2003.

56. *Meet the Press,* NBC, September 8, 2002; *Late Edition with Wolf Blitzer,* CNN, September 8, 2002; President's remarks at the United Nations General Assembly, September 12, 2002.

CHAPTER 2

1. Ken Auletta, "Fortress Bush," *New Yorker,* January 19, 2004.

2. Howard Kurtz, *Spin Cycle* (New York: Touchstone, 1998), xvii.

3. James T. Hamilton, *All the News That's Fit to Sell* (Princeton, New Jersey: Princeton University Press, 2004), 165.

4. Mark Hertsgaard, *On Bended Knee: The Press and the Reagan Presidency* (New York: Farrar Straus Giroux, 1988), 4.

5. Pew Research Center for the People and Press, "News media's improved image proves short-lived," August 4, 2002.

6. Darrell M. West, *The Rise and Fall of the Media Establishment* (Boston: Bedford/St. Martin's, 2001), 51.

7. Brent Cunningham, "Re-thinking objectivity," *Columbia Journalism Review,* April 2003.

8. Brent Cunningham, "Re-thinking objectivity," *Columbia Journalism Review,* April 2003; "Striking the balance, audience interests, business pressures and journalists' values," Pew Research Center on the People and the Press, March 30, 1999.

9. Michael Massing, "Now they tell us," *New York Review of Books,* February 26, 2004; Judith Miller and Michael Massing, " 'Now they tell us': An exchange," *New York Review of Books,* March 25, 2004.

10. Dana Milbank, "For Bush, a tactical retreat on Iraq," *Washington Post,* February 2, 2004.

11. Michael Massing, "Now they tell us," *New York Review of Books,* February 26, 2004.

12. "Dana Milbank and covering the White House . . . ," *Columbia Journalism Review* Campaign Desk, February 20, 2004.

13. Ken Auletta, "Fortress Bush," *New Yorker,* January 19, 2004.

14. Bob Woodward, *Bush at War* (New York: Simon & Schuster, 2002); Bill Sammon, *Fighting Back* (Washington, DC: Regnery, 2002).

15. Ken Auletta, "Fortress Bush," *New Yorker,* January 19, 2004; "Woodward defends book about Bush war strategy," MSNBC.com, April 20, 2004.

16. Dana Milbank, " 'Background' moves to forefront," *Washington Post,* April 6, 2004.

17. *Late Edition,* CNN, July 13, 2003; Stephen Hadley, White House press briefing, July 22, 2003.

18. February 27, 2001 memo from Secretary of the Treasury for Public Affairs Michele Davis to Treasury Secretary Paul O'Neill. Released by author Ron Suskind, RonSuskind.com.

19. January 4, 2002 memo from Secretary of the Treasury for Public Affairs Michele Davis to Treasury Secretary Paul O'Neill. Released by author Ron Suskind, RonSuskind.com.

20. Jonathan Chait, "Defense Secretary," *New Republic,* June 10, 2002.

21. Howard Kurtz, "Straight man," *Washington Post Magazine,* May 19, 2002.

22. Harry Jaffe, "White House press secretary lashes out at reporter: 'There's a difference between trashy rumors and journalism,' " *Washingtonian* Online, February 13, 2004.

23. Ken Auletta, "Fortress Bush," *New Yorker,* January 19, 2004.

24. Ken Auletta, "Fortress Bush," *New Yorker,* January 19, 2004.

25. " 'Scripted' Bush Press Conference Continues to Rankle Some White House Reporters," *White House Bulletin,* March 11, 2003.

26. Paul Bedard and Mark Mazzetti, "Washington whispers," *U.S. News & World Report,* March 15, 2004.

27. Ken Auletta, "Fortress Bush," *New Yorker,* January 19, 2004.

28. Eric Boehlert, "The Press vs. Al Gore," *Rolling Stone,* December 6, 2001.

29. Alec MacGillis, "Coaxing straight talk from masters of spin," *Baltimore Sun,* March 22, 2004.

30. Howard Kurtz, *Spin Cycle* (New York: Touchstone, 1998), 46.

31. Mark Hertsgaard, *On Bended Knee: The Press and the Reagan Presidency* (New York: Farrar Straus Giroux, 1988), 7–8.

32. Nicholas Confessore, "Beat the Press," *American Prospect,* March 11, 2002.

33. Ken Auletta, "Fortress Bush," *New Yorker,* January 19, 2004.

34. Mark Halperin, Elizabeth Wilner, and Marc Ambinder, "Teflon maintenance," *The Note,* ABCNews.com, October 22, 2002.

35. Nicholas Confessore, "Beat the Press," *American Prospect,* March 11, 2002.

36. Harry Jaffe, "Pentagon to Washington Post reporter Ricks: Get lost," *Washingtonian* Online, December 29, 2003.

CHAPTER 3

1. Nexis search for "fuzzy math" and all available publications for October 4, 2000, conducted April 18, 2004.

2. More detail on the media's treatment of Gore can be found in Eric Boehlert, "The Press vs. Al Gore," *Rolling Stone,* December 6, 2001, and Paul Waldman, "Gored by the media bull," *American Prospect,* January 13, 2003.

3. Project for Excellence in Journalism, "A question of character," July 2000.

4. Citizens for Tax Justice, "Summary and analysis of George W. Bush's tax plan," August 2000.

5. Ken Herman, "Bush, Gore draw battle lines," *Atlanta Journal-Constitution,* October 4, 2000; Scott MacKay, "Their first confrontation—Both Bush, Gore use debate in Boston to highlight differences," *Providence Journal-Bulletin,* October 4, 2000; Zachary Coile, "Flop-free debate focuses on policy," *San Francisco Examiner,* October 4, 2000.

6. *Larry King Live,* CNN, October 4, 2000.

7. Maria L. LaGanga and Mark Z. Barabak, "Bush camp's 'iron triangle' steels for a changing fight," *Los Angeles Times,* October 16, 2000.

8. Terry M. Neal and Thomas B. Edsall, "Bush tries to grab tag of reformer," *Washington Post,* February 8, 2000.

9. Jonathan Chait, "Don't worry, cut taxes," *New Republic,* December 27, 1999.

10. Eric Pianin and Terry Neal, "Bush to offer $483 billion tax-cut plan; working poor, middle class would get much of relief," *Washington Post,* December 1, 1999.

11. Terry Neal and Eric Pianin, "Bush draws criticism from rivals over his tax-cut plan," *Washington Post,* December 2, 1999.

12. "Truth in politics," *Washington Post,* October 15, 2000.

13. Presidential debate, October 17, 2000.

14. "Truth in politics," *Washington Post,* October 15, 2000.

15. Robert S. McIntyre, "Winners and losers from the Bush and Gore tax plans," *American Prospect,* October 23, 2000.

16. David Yepsen, "Bush plan to cut taxes draws fire," *Des Moines Register,* December 2, 1999.

17. Maria L. LaGanga, "The battle over single mothers," *Los Angeles Times,* June 6, 2000.

18. Jonathan Chait, "Going for gold: The Bush tax cut is a lie, Part II," *New Republic,* May 21, 2001.

19. Maria L. LaGanga, "The battle over single mothers," *Los Angeles Times,* June 6, 2000.

20. Wayne Slater, "New style energizes Bush camp," *Dallas Morning News,* January 23, 2000.

21. Mike Allen, "For Bush's 'typical' family, lots of tax restrictions," *Washington Post,* September 13, 2000.

22. Mike Allen, "For Bush's 'typical' family, lots of tax restrictions," *Washington Post,* September 13, 2000.

23. Robert S. McIntyre, "Winners and losers from the Bush and Gore tax plans," *American Prospect,* October 23, 2000.

24. Alison Mitchell, "Bush derides Gore for rejecting debate plan," *New York Times,* September 5, 2000.

25. Paul Krugman, "Bush gives no quarter," *New York Times,* September 13, 2000.

26. Alan Fram, "Bush now sees bigger budget surplus," Associated Press Online, May 2, 2000.

27. Robert S. McIntyre, "The taxonomist," *American Prospect,* June 19, 2000.

28. Robert S. McIntyre, "The taxonomist," *American Prospect,* June 19, 2000.

29. David Royse, "With presidential race hanging in balance, Florida recount set to begin," Associated Press, November 8, 2000.

30. Ford Fessenden and Christopher Drew, "Alas, vote-count machines are only human," *New York Times,* November 17, 2000.

31. "Text of comments by Bush," Associated Press, November 15, 2000.

32. "Bush spokespeople call Florida counties' manual counts 'fundamentally flawed,' " CNN, November 18, 2000.

33. "Cheney holds news briefing with Republican House leaders," CNN, December 5, 2000.

CHAPTER 4

1. CBSNews.com, "A casual Bush presses the flesh," September 8, 2000.

2. Judy Keen, "Bush wants second wind for economy," *USA Today,* November 3, 2000.

3. Alison Mitchell, "Saying downturn is possible, Bush trumpets tax cut," *New York Times*, December 16, 2000.

4. Remarks by the President to Southwest Michigan First Coalition/ Kalamazoo Chamber of Commerce joint event on the economy, Kalamazoo, Michigan, March 27, 2001.

5. The White House, "The President's agenda for tax relief," February 8, 2001.

6. Iris J. Lav and Joel Friedman, "Estate tax repeal: A costly windfall for the wealthiest Americans," Center on Budget and Policy Priorities, May 25, 2000, revised February 6, 2001.

7. Citizens for Tax Justice, "CTJ analysis of Bush plan updated to 2001 levels," February 27, 2001.

8. The White House, "The President's agenda for tax relief," February 8, 2001.

9. Remarks by the President on tax cut plan, February 5, 2001.

10. Remarks by the President after passage of the tax cut plan, May 26, 2001.

11. Robert Greenstein and Isaac Shapiro, "Taking down the tollbooth to the middle class?" Center on Budget and Policy Priorities, February 5, 2001, revised February 6, 2001.

12. Radio address by the President to the nation, February 17, 2001; remarks by the President at tax family event, St. Louis, Missouri, February 17, 2001; remarks by the President to the Greater Portland Chambers of Commerce meeting, Portland, Maine, March 23, 2001; remarks by the President to the United States Chamber of Commerce, April 16, 2001.

13. Alan Fram, "Bush faces hurdles in muscling tax cut through Congress," Associated Press, February 17, 2001.

14. Kelly Wallace, *CNN Saturday*, CNN, February 24, 2001.

15. Isaac Shapiro and Robert Greenstein, Center on Budget and Policy Priorities, "Reducing the top rates: How much benefit to small business?" May 3, 2001.

16. Remarks by the President in Sioux Falls, South Dakota send-off, March 9, 2001.

17. Treasury Department press release, "Treasury releases latest number of income tax returns filed by small business owners and entrepreneurs," March 16, 2001.

18. Treasury Department, "Individual income tax returns filed for 1999 with non-farm proprietor income," March 16, 2001.

19. Jodi Enda, "Bush says his proposed tax cuts will be 'a second wind for economic growth,'" Knight Ridder, March 15, 2001.

20. Jack Torry, "Bush says tax cut will help business," *Columbus Dispatch*, March 17, 2001.

21. Remarks by the President at Republican congressional retreat, Williamsburg, Virginia, February 2, 2001; remarks by the President at welcome event, Atlanta, Georgia, March 1, 2001; remarks by the President during meeting with small business owners, March 16, 2001; radio address by the President to the nation, February 3, 2001; remarks by the President on tax cut proposal, February 8, 2001; address of the President to the joint session of Congress, February 27, 2001.

22. Robert Greenstein and Isaac Shapiro, "Taking down the tollbooth to the middle class?" Center on Budget and Policy Priorities, February 5, 2001, revised February 6, 2001.

23. Steven Thomma and Ken Moritsugu, "Bush tax-cut plan gains allies; momentum building for even greater reductions," *Philadelphia Inquirer*, February 5, 2001.

24. President George W. Bush, "A blueprint for new beginnings," Fiscal Year 2002 budget, February 28, 2001, 33.

25. Radio address by the President to the nation, February 3, 2001; radio address by the President to the nation, February 17, 2001; radio address by the President to the nation, February 24, 2001; radio address by the President to the nation, March 3, 2001; remarks by President at tax family event, St. Louis, Missouri, February 20, 2001; address of the President to the joint session of Congress, February 27, 2001; re-

marks by the President to the United States Chamber of Commerce, April 16, 2001.

26. Citizens for Tax Justice, "Bush tax plan benefits are similar to campaign proposal: Skewed toward wealthy," February 8, 2001.

27. James Toedtman, "Figuring out Bush's tax plan," *Newsday,* April 16, 2001; Katherine Q. Seelye, "Bush's tax day wishes: A bigger trim and a Democratic ally," *New York Times,* April 17, 2001; Kevin Diaz and Craig Gustafson, "Bush details spending plan; it 'funds our needs without the fat,' " *Minneapolis Star-Tribune,* April 10, 2001, corrected April 12, 2001.

28. Iris J. Lav and Joel Friedman, "Estate tax repeal: A costly windfall for the wealthiest Americans," Center on Budget and Policy Priorities, May 25, 2000, revised February 6, 2001.

29. David Cay Johnston, "Talk of lost farms reflects muddle of estate tax debate," *New York Times,* April 8, 2001.

30. Treasury Department press release, "Treasury releases distribution table for the President's tax relief plan," March 8, 2001; Treasury Department, "Major individual income tax provisions of the President's tax proposal," March 8, 2001.

31. Citizens for Tax Justice, "CTJ analysis of Bush plan updated to 2001 levels," February 27, 2001.

32. Julie-Anne Cronin, U.S. Department of Treasury, Office of Tax Analysis, "U.S. Treasury distributional analysis methodology," OTA Paper 85, September 1999, quoted in Isaac Shapiro, "New Treasury table departs sharply from previous Treasury methodology," Center on Budget and Policy Priorities, March 8, 2001, revised March 9, 2001.

CHAPTER 5

1. Sheldon Rampton and John Stauber, *Trust Us, We're Experts!* (New York: J.P. Tarcher, 2002), 44–45.

2. Luntz Research Companies, "The environment: A cleaner, safer, healthier America," 132, published on the website of the Environmental Working Group.

3. Luntz Research Companies, "The environment: A cleaner, safer, healthier America," 137, published on the website of the Environmental Working Group.

4. Luntz Research Companies, "The environment: A cleaner, safer, healthier America," 138, published on the website of the Environmental Working Group.

5. Randy Lee Loftis, "U.S. global warming policy hinging on election," *Dallas Morning News,* October 27, 2000; *Oil & Gas Journal,* "A Bush misstep on CO_2," October 16, 2000, quoted in Ron Suskind, *The Price of Loyalty* (New York: Simon & Schuster, 2004), 99.

6. Second presidential debate, Winston-Salem, North Carolina, October 11, 2000, quoted in Ron Suskind, *The Price of Loyalty* (New York: Simon & Schuster, 2004), 99.

7. Paul O'Neill, "Global climate change," memo to President George W. Bush, February 27, 2001, quoted in Ron Suskind, *The Price of Loyalty* (New York: Simon & Schuster, 2004), 104–106, and published on Suskind's website RonSuskind.com; Christie Todd Whitman, memo to President George W. Bush, March 6, 2001, quoted in Ron Suskind, *The Price of Loyalty* (New York: Simon & Schuster, 2004), 113, and published on Suskind's website, RonSuskind.com.

8. Quoted in Ron Suskind, *The Price of Loyalty* (New York: Simon & Schuster, 2004), 102.

9. Ron Suskind, *The Price of Loyalty* (New York: Simon & Schuster, 2004), 102–103, 109–110.

10. Ari Fleischer, White House press briefing, March 28, 2001.

11. Letter from John M. Bridgeland and Gary Edson to Dr. Bruce Alberts, May 11, 2001 in Commission on Geosciences, Environment and Resources, *Climate Change Science: An Analysis of Some Key Questions* (Washington, DC: National Academies Press, 2001), 27.

12. Commission on Geosciences, Environment and Resources, *Climate Change Science: An Analysis of Some Key Questions* (Washington, DC: National Academies Press, 2001), 1.

13. United Nations Intergovernmental Panel on Climate Change, "Climate change 2001: The scientific basis," January 22, 2001.

14. Commission on Geosciences, Environment and Resources, *Climate Change Science: An Analysis of Some Key Questions* (Washington, DC: National Academies Press, 2001), 1.

15. Commission on Geosciences, Environment and Resources, *Climate Change Science: An Analysis of Some Key Questions* (Washington, DC: National Academies Press, 2001), 1–5; United Nations Intergovernmental Panel on Climate Change, "Climate Change 2001: The Scientific Basis," January 22, 2001, 10, 12–17.

16. Donald Kennedy, "An unfortunate u-turn on carbon," *Science,* March 30, 2001.

17. Eric Pianin, "NAS tells Bush global warming is real problem," *Washington Post,* June 7, 2001, quoted in Lindsay Sobel, "The year of the ostrich," *American Prospect* Online, June 7, 2001.

18. Commission on Geosciences, Environment and Resources, *Climate Change Science: An Analysis of Some Key Questions* (Washington, DC: National Academies Press, 2001), 4.

19. White House, "Climate change review—initial report," June 11, 2001, 21–25.

20. David Jackson, "Bush explains stance on global warming," *Dallas Morning News,* June 12, 2001; Richard Harris, "Bush administration environmental policies receive skepticism from European nations," National Public Radio, June 11, 2001.

21. President announces Clear Skies & Global Climate Change initiatives, Silver Spring, Maryland, February 14, 2002.

22. The Luntz Research Companies, "The environment: A cleaner, safer, healthier America," 142, published on the website of the Environmental Working Group.

23. National Institutes of Health, "Stem cell basics," National Institutes of Health website.

24. Rick Weiss, "Clinton hails embryo cell test rules," *Washington Post,* August 24, 2000.

25. Richard Lacayo, "How Bush got there," *Time,* August 20, 2001.

26. Howard Fineman, Debra Rosenberg, and Martha Brant, "Bush draws a stem cell line," *Newsweek,* August 20, 2001.

27. Howard Fineman, Debra Rosenberg, and Martha Brant, "Bush draws a stem cell line," *Newsweek,* August 20, 2001.

28. Katherine Q. Seelye with Frank Bruni, "A long process that led Bush to his decision," *New York Times,* August 11, 2001, cited in Stephen S. Hall, *Merchants of Immortality* (Boston: Houghton Mifflin Company, 2003), 296.

29. ABCNews.com, "Bush discusses decision," August 10, 2001.

30. Sheryl Gay Stolberg, "Disappointed by limits, scientists doubt estimate of available cell lines," *New York Times,* August 10, 2001.

31. Tommy Thompson, News conference on stem cell research, August 10, 2001.

32. Stephen S. Hall, "Bush's political science," *New York Times,* June 12, 2003.

33. Ceci Connolly, Justin Gillis, and Rick Weiss, "Viability of stem cell plan doubted," *Washington Post,* August 20, 2001.

34. "Statement By Tommy G. Thompson, Secretary of Health and Human Services, regarding stem cell lines," Department of Health and Human Services press release, August 27, 2001.

35. Paul Recer, "Some stem cell lines may be unusable," Associated Press Online, August 29, 2001.

36. FDCH Political Transcripts, "U.S. Senator Edward Kennedy (D-MA) holds hearing on stem cell research," September 5, 2001.

37. Sheryl Gay Stolberg, "Trying to get past numbers on stem cells," *New York Times,* September 7, 2001.

38. National Institutes of Health, "NIH Human Embryonic Stem Cell

Registry," National Institutes of Health website; Dan Vergano, "New stem cell lines available," *USA Today,* March 4, 2004.

39. Douglas Waller, "Some shaky figures on ANWR drilling," *Time,* August 31, 2001.

40. Michael Grunwald, "Departmental differences show over ANWR drilling," *Washington Post,* October 19, 2001.

41. United States House of Representatives Committee on Government Reform Minority Staff, "Politics and science in the Bush Administration," August 2003; National Cancer Institute, "Abortion and breast cancer," National Cancer Institute website, March 6, 2002, published on the website of the United States House of Representatives Committee on Government Reform Minority Staff; Judy Peres, "Scientists reject abortion, breast cancer link," *Chicago Tribune,* February 27, 2003.

42. United States House of Representatives Committee on Government Reform Minority Staff, "Politics and science in the Bush Administration," August 2003; National Cancer Institute, "Early reproductive events and breast cancer," National Cancer Institute website, November 25, 2002, published on the website of the United States House of Representatives Committee on Government Reform Minority Staff; Judy Peres, "Scientists reject abortion, breast cancer link," *Chicago Tribune,* February 27, 2003.

43. National Cancer Institute, "Abortion, miscarriage, and breast cancer risk," March 21, 2003, editorial changes made May 30, 2003.

CHAPTER 6

1. Noelle Straub and Melanie Fonder, "Senate Dems avoid attacks on Ashcroft," *The Hill,* December 5, 2001.

2. Mark Benjamin, "DOJ lashes out at reports on lashing out," United Press International, December 7, 2001.

3. Representative Dick Gephardt, press conference, Capitol Hill, May 16, 2002.

4. Senate Majority Leader Tom Daschle, press conference, May 16, 2002.

5. *Live at Daybreak,* report by David Ensor, CNN, May 17, 2002; Karen Tumulty, "Behind all the finger-pointing," *Time,* May 27, 2002.

6. First Lady Laura Bush in response to a media inquiry regarding May 16th news accounts of intelligence briefings in August 2001, May 17, 2002.

7. Juliet Eilperin, "Democrat implies Sept. 11 administration plot," *Washington Post,* April 12, 2002.

8. Representative Cynthia McKinney, "Terrorist warnings," press release, May 16, 2002.

9. Senator Hillary Rodham Clinton, "Investigate 9/11," Senate floor statement, May 16, 2002.

10. Dan Balz, "Bush and GOP defend White House response," *Washington Post,* May 18, 2002.

11. Dan Balz, "Bush and GOP defend White House response," *Washington Post,* May 18, 2002.

12. Bush remarks in Orlando, Florida, December 4, 2001; statement by the President, December 7, 2001; President's radio address, December 15, 2001; statement by the President, December 20, 2001; remarks by Counselor to the President Karen Hughes to White House press pool (includes such remarks by both Hughes and Scott McClellan), January 4, 2002; Bush remarks in Charleston, West Virginia, January 22, 2002; State of the Union address, January 29, 2002; statement by the President, January 30, 2002.

13. Governor George W. Bush delivers acceptance speech at Republican National Convention, August 3, 2000, cited in James A. Barnes, "It's all about leadership," *National Journal,* August 5, 2000.

14. *The Early Show,* Jane Clayton interview with President Bush, CBS, April 25, 2001.

15. Remarks by the President at Republican National Committee gala, May 22, 2001.

16. Remarks by the President at 2002 Republican National Committee presidential gala, May 14, 2002.

17. Ari Fleischer, White House press gaggle, October 18, 2002.

18. Remarks by the President at Anne Northrup for Congress luncheon, Louisville, Kentucky, September 5, 2002.

19. Quoted in Dana Milbank, "In President's speeches, Iraq dominates, economy fades," *Washington Post,* September 25, 2002.

20. *Today,* NBC, September 26, 2002; *Late Edition,* CNN, September 29, 2002; "Daschle's tantrum," *Washington Times,* September 29, 2002 (corrected October 1, 2002).

21. Adam Nagourney, "Eyes on 2004 vote, Democrats fault U.S. terror defense," *New York Times,* December 26, 2002.

CHAPTER 7

1. Ryan Lizza, "Raising Keynes," *New Republic,* September 10, 2001; Richard W. Stevenson, "A political straitjacket," *New York Times,* August 24, 2001.

2. Jonathan Chait, "Red handed," *New Republic,* May 13, 2002.

3. President comments on new economic numbers and Middle East, April 26, 2002.

4. Ron Fournier, "Bush defends tax cuts, deficit," Associated Press Online, January 7, 2002; Elizabeth Bumiller, "Bush says he may not seek balanced budget this year," *New York Times,* January 8, 2002.

5. "Notebook," *New Republic,* April 29, 2002.

6. Dana Milbank, "Karl Rove, adding to his to-do list," *Washington Post,* June 25, 2002; *Meet the Press,* NBC, June 16, 2002; Jonathan Chait, "Red handed," *New Republic,* May 13, 2002; "Notebook," *New Republic,* June 3, 2002; "Notebook," *New Republic,* June 24, 2002; "Notebook," *New Republic,* July 1, 2002.

7. Nexis search for "Bush AND Chicago AND deficit AND recession," all

available news sources for May 1, 2002, through June 24, 2002, conducted April 18, 2004.

8. Edwin Chen, "Deficit will hit $165 billion, White House says," *Los Angeles Times,* July 13, 2002.

9. Dana Milbank, "A sound bite so good, the President wishes he had said it," *Washington Post,* July 2, 2002.

10. Jeff Zeleny, "Chicago tale? Bush camp can't verify it," *Chicago Tribune,* July 14, 2002.

11. Searches in archives of *New York Times* and CNN stories in the Nexis database for "Bush AND trifecta AND Chicago" and "Bush AND ("national emergency" w/5 recession w/5 war) AND Chicago," all available dates, conducted April 18, 2004.

12. Alan Fram, "Democrats blame Bush for deficits," Associated Press, November 29, 2001.

13. *Novak, Hunt & Shields,* interview with Lawrence Lindsey, CNN, January 12, 2002.

14. Richard Kogan, Robert Greenstein, and Joel Friedman, "The new CBO projections: What do they tell us?" Center on Budget and Policy Priorities, January 23, 2002, revised January 29, 2002.

15. Miles Benson, "Bush charts centrist course with budget proposal," Newhouse News Service, February 5, 2002.

16. "Budget of the United States Government, Fiscal Year 2003," 37.

17. "Budget of the United States Government, Fiscal Year 2003," 32.

18. Robert Greenstein, "President's budget uses accounting devices and implausible assumptions to hide hundreds of billions of dollars in costs," Center on Budget and Policy Priorities, February 4, 2002, revised February 5, 2002.

19. Richard Kogan, Robert Greenstein, and Joel Friedman, "The new CBO projections: What do they tell us?" Center on Budget and Policy Priorities, January 23, 2002, revised January 29, 2002.

20. "Fiscal Year 2003: Mid-session review," Office of Management and Budget, July 12, 2002, 12.

21. Richard Kogan and Robert Greenstein, "What OMB's mid-session review tells us—and what it obscures," Center on Budget and Policy Priorities, July 25, 2002, revised August 14, 2002.

22. "OMB Director Mitchell E. Daniels, Jr. previews mid-session review," Office of Management and Budget press release, July 12, 2002.

23. Richard Kogan and Robert Greenstein, "What OMB's mid-session review tells us—and what it obscures," Center on Budget and Policy Priorities, July 25, 2002, revised August 14, 2002.

24. Paul Krugman, "The memory hole," *New York Times,* August 6, 2002; Trent Duffy, "Budget office error," letter to the editor, *New York Times,* August 3, 2002.

25. "Statement of OMB Director Mitchell E. Daniels, Jr.," Office of Management and Budget press release, August 27, 2002; Richard Kogan and Robert Greenstein, "The new Congressional Budget Office forecast and the remarkable deterioration of the surplus," Center on Budget and Policy Priorities, September 3, 2002.

26. Remarks by the President after meeting with the Cabinet, November 13, 2002.

27. Dana Milbank, "This time a Bush embraces 'voodoo economics' theory," *Washington Post,* November 14, 2002.

28. Edmund L. Andrews, "Who's afraid of the deficit? Cassandras are out of style," *New York Times,* November 19, 2002; *Late Edition,* report by Bruce Morton, CNN, November 17, 2002.

29. "Economic Report of the President," February 2003, 57–58.

30. "Fiscal year 2003: Mid-session review," Office of Management and Budget, July 12, 2002, 12; Mitch Daniels press conference, July 12, 2002.

31. "The price of profligacy," *Economist,* January 23, 2003.

32. William G. Gale and Peter R. Orszag, "The economic effects of long-term fiscal discipline," Urban-Brookings Tax Policy Center discussion paper, April 2003.

33. Richard W. Stevenson, "Bush's way clear to press agenda for economy," *New York Times*, November 11, 2002; Bob Davis, "Bush White House argues that federal debt doesn't matter and derides 'Rubinomics,'" *Wall Street Journal*, December 17, 2002; J. Bradford DeLong, "It's time for Glenn Hubbard to quit as CEA Chair," January 7, 2003 post at j-bradford-delong.net.

34. Mitch Daniels, press briefing, February 3, 2003.

35. Gregory Mankiw, speech to the annual meeting of the National Association of Business Economists, September 15, 2003; see also Gregory Mankiw, Whitehouse.gov online chat, January 22, 2004; Gregory Mankiw, Whitehouse.gov online chat, February 9, 2004; remarks at the National Association of Business Economists 2004 Washington economic policy conference, March 25, 2004.

36. President discusses job training and the economy in New Hampshire, March 25, 2004.

37. "Budget of the United States Government, fiscal year 2004," 1, 26.

38. "Notebook," *New Republic*, February 24, 2003.

39. *Late Edition*, CNN, February 25, 2001.

40. "Budget of the United States Government: Fiscal year 2003," 37; Mitch Daniels, press briefing on the federal budget, February 4, 2002.

41. Mitch Daniels, testimony before Senate Budget Committee, February 5, 2003.

42. Dana Milbank, "With '04 in mind, Bush team saw economic, political peril," *Washington Post*, December 7, 2002.

43. Mike Allen, "Bush picks CSX Corp. Chief for Treasury," *Washington Post*, December 9, 2002; Bob Davis, "Treasury Chief struggles to sell tax plan," *Wall Street Journal*, May 5, 2003.

44. Edmund Andrews, "White House officials launch a defense of Bush tax plan," *New York Times*, January 7, 2003.

45. Radio address of the President to the nation, January 11, 2003.

46. "President Bush taking action to strengthen America's economy,"

White House fact sheet, January 7, 2003; remarks by the President on the economy, St. Louis, Missouri, January 22, 2003.

47. Remarks by the President on the economy, St. Louis, Missouri, January 22, 2003.

48. Urban-Brookings Tax Policy Center, "2003 Tax Act: Administration proposal," May 2, 2003, table T03-0020.

49. Joel Friedman, "Impact of administration 'growth' package on the elderly," Center on Budget and Policy Priorities, January 7, 2003, revised January 28, 2003; Andrew Lee, "President's radio address and other administration statements exaggerate tax plan's impact on small business," January 18, 2003, revised January 21, 2003.

50. Diego Ibarguen and James Kuhnhenn, "Bush's economic medicine," *Philadelphia Inquirer,* January 8, 2003.

51. "President Bush taking action to strengthen America's economy," White House fact sheet, January 7, 2003.

52. Bush speech in Chicago, Illinois, January 7, 2003; remarks by the President to the employees of United Defense Industries, May 2, 2003.

53. Remarks by the President to the press pool, January 2, 2003.

54. Ari Fleischer, White House press gaggle, January 7, 2003.

55. Remarks by the President on the jobs and growth package, St. Louis, Missouri, January 9, 2003.

56. Dana Milbank, "Bush administration using war to justify its tax cut," *Washington Post,* March 26, 2003.

57. Remarks by the President to the Tax Relief Coalition, May 6, 2003.

58. Richard Kogan, "Are tax cuts a major or minor factor in the return of deficits? What the CBO data show," Center on Budget and Policy Priorities, February 12, 2003.

59. Remarks by the President on the economy, September 5, 2003; remarks by the President on the economy, October 3, 2003.

60. "Fiscal year 2004: Mid-session review," Office of Management and Budget, July 15, 2003.

61. Gregory Mankiw, Whitehouse.gov online chat, October 10, 2003.

62. Remarks by the Vice President at the Celebrating Women in Business breakfast, September 18, 2003; remarks by the Vice President at the State of Commerce luncheon, September 30, 2003.

63. Richard Kogan, David Kamin, and Joel Friedman, "Deficit picture grimmer than new CBO projections suggest," Center on Budget and Policy Priorities, January 28, 2004, revised February 1, 2004.

64. Edmund L. Andrews, "Deficit study disputes role of economy," *New York Times,* March 16, 2004; President discusses job training and the economy in New Hampshire, March 25, 2004.

65. "Mid-session review: Fiscal year 2004," July 15, 2003, 2.

66. Richard Kogan, "Does the Administration really have a plan to cut the deficit in half?" Center on Budget and Policy Priorities, September 11, 2003, revised September 16, 2003.

67. Scott McCellan, White House press briefing, July 15, 2003.

68. President's radio address, July 19, 2003; President discusses economy, jobs in Michigan, July 24, 2003; remarks by the President on the jobs and growth plan, July 24, 2003; press conference of the President, July 30, 2003.

69. President's radio address, August 30, 2003; Scott McClellan, White House press briefing, September 2, 2003; remarks by the President at Kansas City Convention Center, Kansas City, Missouri, September 4, 2003; remarks by the President on the economy, September 5, 2003; remarks by the Vice President at the Celebrating Women in Business breakfast, September 18, 2003; remarks by the President after meeting with members of the Congressional Conference on Medicare Modernization, September 25, 2003.

70. Stephen Friedman, Whitehouse.gov online chat, October 27, 2003; Scott McClellan, White House press briefing, November 6, 2003; Joshua Bolten, CNBC, *Titans with Maria Bartiromo,* December 8, 2003; Gregory Mankiw, CNBC, *Titans with Maria Bartiromo,* December 8, 2003; Joshua Bolten, "We can cut the deficit in half," *Wall*

Street Journal, December 10, 2003; press conference of the President, December 15, 2003.

71. *Titans with Maria Bartiromo,* CNBC, December 8, 2003.

72. "2003: A year of accomplishment for the American people," fact sheet, White House Office of the Press Secretary, December 13, 2003.

73. For example, see Factcheck.org, "Here we go again: Bush exaggerates tax cuts," February 20, 2004; Andrew Lee and Joel Friedman, "Administration continues to rely on misleading use of 'averages' to describe tax-cut benefits," Center on Budget and Policy Priorities, May 28, 2003.

CHAPTER 8

1. Hendrick Hertzberg, "Grinding axis," *New Yorker,* February 11, 2002.

2. Dana Priest, "No evidence CIA slanted Iraq data," *Washington Post,* January 31, 2004; David Kay testimony to Senate Armed Services Committee, January 28, 2004.

3. Seth Ackerman, "A legacy of lies," *Mother Jones,* January/February 2004.

4. Richard Morin and Claudia Deane, "71% of Americans support war, poll shows," *Washington Post,* March 9, 2003.

5. UNMOVIC working document, "Unresolved Disarmament Issues: Iraq's Proscribed Weapons Programmes," March 6, 2003.

6. Barton Gellman, "Iraq's arsenal was only on paper," *Washington Post,* January 7, 2004.

7. This is the version that appeared in the Federal Documents Clearinghouse transcript of the Republican primary debate, December 2, 1999. Other accounts reported the quote as "And if I found, in any way shape or form, that he was developing weapons of mass destruction, I'd take him out," though Bush's response to Hume, "Take out the weapons of mass destruction," is not in dispute.

8. Ron Suskind, *The Price of Loyalty* (New York: Simon & Schuster, 2004), 72–75, 82–86, 95–97.

9. Letter to William J. Clinton, Project for the New American Century, January 26, 1998.

10. "Plan for Iraq attack began on 9/11," CBSNews.com, September 4, 2002.

11. Bob Woodward, *Plan of Attack* (New York: Simon & Schuster, 2004), 25.

12. John B. Judis and Spencer Ackerman, "The first casualty," *New Republic,* June 30, 2003.

13. As of this printing, the most complete argument for such a connection is found in Stephen Hayes, "Case closed," *Weekly Standard,* November 24, 2003. However, even this article, which reports on a leaked classified memo from Undersecretary of Defense for Policy Douglas Feith to the Senate Intelligence Committee, does not provide definitive evidence of such a connection.

14. Sam Tanenhaus, "Bush's brain trust," *Vanity Fair,* July 2003.

15. Bob Woodward, *Plan of Attack* (New York: Simon & Schuster, 2004), 1–3.

16. David Frum, *The Right Man: The Surprise Presidency of George W. Bush* (New York: Random House, 2002), 221–245; Bob Woodward, *Plan of Attack* (New York: Simon & Schuster, 2004), 86.

17. Bob Woodward, *Plan of Attack* (New York: Simon & Schuster, 2004), 108–109.

18. Michael Elliott and James Carney, "First stop, Iraq," *Time,* March 31, 2003.

19. Daniel Eisenberg, "We're taking him out," *Time,* May 13, 2002.

20. Fred Kaplan, "The Rumsfeld Intelligence Agency," *Slate,* October 28, 2003.

21. Seymour Hersh, "Selective intelligence," *New Yorker,* May 12, 2003; Robert Dreyfuss and Jason Vest, "The lie factory," *Mother Jones,* January/February 2004; Karen Kwiatkowski, "The new Pentagon Papers," *Salon,* March 10, 2004.

22. Seymour Hersh, "The stovepipe," *New Yorker,* October 27, 2003; Robert Dreyfuss and Jason Vest, "The lie factory," *Mother Jones,* January/February 2004.

23. George Tenet, remarks as prepared for delivery, Georgetown University, February 5, 2004.

24. Seymour Hersh, "Selective intelligence," *New Yorker,* May 12, 2003.

25. Elisabeth Bumiller, "Traces of terror: The strategy," *New York Times,* September 7, 2002.

26. Barton Gellman and Walter Pincus, "Depiction of threat outgrew supporting evidence," *Washington Post,* August 10, 2003.

27. Deputy Secretary of Defense Paul Wolfowitz, interview with Sam Tannenhaus, May 9, 2003.

28. Barton Gellman and Walter Pincus, "Depiction of threat outgrew supporting evidence," *Washington Post,* August 10, 2003.

29. Karen Kwiatkowski, "The new Pentagon Papers," *Salon,* March 10, 2004.

30. Elisabeth Bumiller, "Traces of terror: The strategy," *New York Times,* September 7, 2002.

31. Seymour Hersh, "The stovepipe," *New Yorker,* October 27, 2003.

32. Barton Gellman and Walter Pincus, "Depiction of threat outgrew supporting evidence," *Washington Post,* August 11, 2003.

33. General Tommy Franks delivers remarks about possible war against Iraq, West Palm Beach, Florida, November 12, 2002.

34. Remarks by the Vice President to the Veterans of Foreign Wars 103rd National Convention, August 26, 2002; Vice President honors Veterans of Korean War, August 29, 2002.

35. Fred Kaplan, "The Iraq sanctions worked," *Slate,* October 7, 2003.

36. President discusses Iraq and North Korea with reporters, December 31, 2002.

37. Dana Milbank, "Cheney Says Iraqi Strike Is Justified," *Washington Post,* August 27, 2002.

38. Elisabeth Bumiller and James Dao, "Cheney Says Peril of a Nuclear Iraq Justifies Attack," *New York Times,* August 27, 2002; "In Cheney's

Words: The Administration Case for Removing Saddam Hussein," *New York Times*, August 27, 2002.

39. Mike Allen, "Bush Sees Resolution on N. Korea," *Washington Post*, January 1, 2003.

40. Remarks by the Vice President to the Veterans of Foreign Wars 103rd National Convention, August 26, 2002.

41. Seymour Hersh, "Selective intelligence," *New Yorker*, May 12, 2003; Seth Ackerman, "A Legacy of Lies," *Mother Jones*, January/February 2004.

42. Barton Gellman and Walter Pincus, "Depiction of threat outgrew supporting evidence," *Washington Post*, August 10, 2003.

43. Seth Ackerman, "A legacy of lies," *Mother Jones*, January/February 2004.

44. Douglas Jehl and David E. Sanger, "Powell's case, a year later: Gaps in picture of Iraq arms," *New York Times*, February 1, 2004.

45. President Bush, Prime Minister Blair discuss keeping the peace, Camp David, Maryland, September 7, 2002.

46. United Nations Security Council, Sixth consolidated report of the Director General of the International Atomic Energy Agency under Paragraph 16 of Security Council Resolution 1051 (1996)," Document S/1998/927, October 7, 1998.

47. Joseph Curl, "Agency disavows report on Iraq arms," *Washington Times*, September 27, 2002.

48. Dana Milbank, "For Bush, facts are malleable," *Washington Post*, October 22, 2002.

49. Michael R. Gordon and Judith Miller, "Threats and responses: The Iraqis; U.S. says Hussein intensifies quest for A-bomb parts," September 7, 2002.

50. *Meet the Press*, NBC, September 8, 2002.

51. *Late Edition with Wolf Blitzer*, CNN, September 8, 2002.

52. President's remarks at the United Nations General Assembly, September 12, 2002.

53. Barton Gellman and Walter Pincus, "Depiction of threat outgrew supporting evidence," *Washington Post,* August 10, 2003.

54. John B. Judis and Spencer Ackerman, "The first casualty," *New Republic,* June 30, 2003; Barton Gellman and Walter Pincus, "Depiction of threat outgrew supporting evidence," *Washington Post,* August 10, 2003.

55. Joby Warrick, "U.S. claim on Iraqi nuclear program is called into question," *Washington Post,* January 24, 2003.

56. Institute for Science and International Security, "Aluminum tubing is an indicator of an Iraqi gas centrifuge program: But is the tubing specifically for centrifuges?" September 23, 2002 (updated October 9, 2002); "Iraq's weapons of mass destruction—the assessment of the British Government," United Kingdom, September 24, 2002.

57. President Bush outlines Iraqi threat, Cincinnati, Ohio, October 7, 2002.

58. Ari Fleischer, White House press briefing, December 2, 2002.

59. Colum Lynch, "No 'smoking guns' So far, UN told," *Washington Post,* January 10, 2003.

60. Michael R. Gordon, "Agency challenges evidence against Iraq cited by Bush," *New York Times,* January 10, 2003.

61. Barton Gellman and Walter Pincus, "Depiction of threat outgrew supporting evidence," *Washington Post,* August 10, 2003.

62. Quoted in Charles Henley, "Powell's case for war falls apart 6 months later," Associated Press, July 11, 2003.

63. Barton Gellman and Walter Pincus, "Depiction of threat outgrew supporting evidence," *Washington Post,* August 10, 2003.

64. This account draws heavily on Seymour Hersh, "The stovepipe," *New Yorker,* October 27, 2003.

65. Joseph C. Wilson IV, "What I didn't find in Africa," *New York Times,* July 6, 2003.

66. Walter Pincus, "Bush team kept airing Iraq allegation," *Washington Post,* August 8, 2003.

67. Walter Pincus, "U.S.-British differences show Iraq intelligence gap," *Washington Post,* September 30, 2003.

68. Walter Pincus and Mike Allen, "CIA got uranium reference cut in October," *Washington Post,* July 13, 2003; Seymour Hersh, "The stovepipe," *New Yorker,* October 27, 2003.

69. Walter Pincus, "White House faulted on uranium claim," *Washington Post,* December 24, 2003.

70. Condoleezza Rice, "Why we know Iraq is lying," *New York Times,* January 23, 2003.

71. John B. Judis and Spencer Ackerman, "The first casualty," *New Republic,* June 30, 2003.

72. John B. Judis and Spencer Ackerman, "The first casualty," *New Republic,* June 30, 2003.

73. "Pentagon: WMD report consistent with US case," CNN.com, June 6, 2003.

74. Colin Powell, Press remarks with Foreign Minister of Egypt Amre Moussa, February 24, 2001.

75. Glen Rangwala, "Claims and evaluations of Iraq's proscribed weapons," MiddleEastReference.org.uk.; UNMOVIC working document, "Unresolved Disarmament Issues: Iraq's Proscribed Weapons Programmes," March 6, 2003.

76. Anthony Cordesman, "Iraq's past and future biological weapons capabilities," Center for Strategic and International Studies, February 1998; Glen Rangwala, "Claims and evaluations of Iraq's proscribed weapons," MiddleEastReference.org.uk.

77. Dana Priest and Walter Pincus, "Bush certainty on Iraq arms went beyond analysts's views," *Washington Post,* June 7, 2003.

78. "Spooks: No reliable intel on Iraqi weapons," *U.S. News & World Report,* June 23, 2003.

79. President Bush discusses Iraq with congressional leaders, September 26, 2002.

80. Glen Rangwala, "Claims and evaluations of Iraq's proscribed weapons," MiddleEastReference.org.uk.

81. Press briefing by Ari Fleischer, February 6, 2003.

82. Carolyn Lochhead, "Resolute Bush says U.S. must be ready for war," *San Francisco Chronicle,* January 29, 2003.

83. Shelley Emling and Don Melvin, "U.S. spells out case against Iraq," *Atlanta Constitution-Journal,* February 6, 2003.

84. "The man who knew," CBSNews.com (from *60 Minutes*), October 15, 2003.

85. Robert Wright, "Verify first," *New Republic,* March 31, 2003; Charles Hanley, "Powell's case for Iraq war falls apart 6 months later," Associated Press, August 11, 2003.

86. President Bush discusses Iraq with congressional leaders, September 26, 2002; radio address by the President to the nation, September 28, 2002.

87. Walter Pincus, "U.S.-British differences show Iraq intelligence gap," *Washington Post,* September 30, 2003.

88. Charles Hanley, "Powell's case for Iraq war falls apart 6 months later," Associated Press, August 11, 2003.

89. Glenn Kessler and Walter Pincus, "A flawed argument in the case for war," *Washington Post,* February 1, 2004.

90. Colin Powell, *Fox News Sunday,* Fox News Channel, September 8, 2002; Condoleezza Rice, *Late Edition,* CNN, September 8, 2002.

91. Charles Hanley, "Powell's case for Iraq war falls apart 6 months later," Associated Press, August 11, 2003.

92. Bob Woodward, *Plan of Attack* (New York: Simon & Schuster, 2004), 309.

93. CBSNews.com, "The man who knew" (from *60 Minutes II*), October 15, 2003.

94. Seymour Hersh, "Selective intelligence," *New Yorker,* May 12, 2003.

95. Daniel Eisenberg, "We're taking him out," *Time,* May 13, 2002.

96. John B. Judis and Spencer Ackerman, "The first casualty," *New Republic,* June 30, 2003.

97. *Meet the Press,* NBC, December 9, 2001; Dana Priest and Glenn

Kessler, "Iraq, 9/11 still linked by Cheney," *Washington Post,* September 29, 2003.

98. Michael Isikoff, "The phantom link to Iraq," *Newsweek,* May 6, 2002 (published in late April).

99. "U.S. drops last link of Iraq to 9/11," *New York Times,* May 2, 2002.

100. James Risen, "Prague discounts an Iraqi meeting," *New York Times,* October 21, 2002; Peter S. Green, "Havel denies telephoning U.S. on Iraq meeting," *New York Times,* October 22, 2002.

101. Stephen F. Hayes, "Case closed," *Weekly Standard,* November 24, 2003.

102. Walter Pincus, "Alleged al Qaeda ties questioned," *Washington Post,* February 7, 2003.

103. Remarks by the President at Naval Station Mayport, Jacksonville, Florida, February 13, 2003.

104. Walter Pincus, "Report cast doubt on Iraq-al Qaeda connection," *Washington Post,* June 22, 2003.

105. Walter Pincus, "Report cast doubt on Iraq-al Qaeda connection," *Washington Post,* June 22, 2003.

106. Walter Pincus, "Report cast doubt on Iraq-al Qaeda connection," *Washington Post,* June 23, 2003.

107. Bruce Morton, "Selling an Iraq-al Qaida connection," CNN.com, March 11, 2003.

CHAPTER 9

1. Elisabeth Bumiller, "Keepers of the Bush image lift stagecraft to new heights," *New York Times,* May 16, 2003.

2. Dana Milbank, "Explanation for Bush's carrier landing altered," *Washington Post,* May 7, 2003; Eric Boehlert, "How the GOP struck gold with its permanent 'war on terrorism,' " *Salon,* May 8, 2003.

3. Ari Fleischer, White House press briefing, July 1, 2003.

4. Dana Milbank, "Bush revises views on 'combat' in Iraq," *Washington*

Post, August 19, 2003; Dana Milbank, "Not up to code? Embellishing the flag, then the web site," *Washington Post,* August 26, 2003.

5. Paul Bedard, David E. Kaplan, and Angie Cannon, "Washington whispers," *U.S. News & World Report,* September 29, 2003.

6. Elisabeth Bumiller, "Keepers of Bush image lift stagecraft to new heights," *New York Times,* May 16, 2003.

7. President holds press conference, October 28, 2003.

8. "Bush steps away from victory banner," *New York Times,* October 29, 2003.

9. Elisabeth Bumiller, "A proclamation of victory that no author will claim," *New York Times,* November 3, 2003.

10. Glenn Kessler and Dana Milbank, "Administration now turns to finding prohibited weapons," *Washington Post,* April 10, 2003; Dana Milbank, "Bush: Iraq may have destroyed weapons," *Washington Post,* April 25, 2003; President Bush announces major combat operations in Iraq have ended, May 1, 2003.

11. John Cochran, "Reason for war?" *ABC News,* April 25, 2003.

12. Remarks by the President on Iraq, September 26, 2002.

13. *Dateline NBC,* NBC, April 25, 2003.

14. President discusses national, economic security in California, Santa Clara, California, May 2, 2003.

15. President names envoy to Iraq, May 6, 2003.

16. President discusses Middle East, Iraq, and dollar in cabinet meeting, June 9, 2003.

17. Dana Milbank, "Bush remarks confirm shift in justification for war," *Washington Post,* June 1, 2003.

18. Judith Miller, "Trailer is a mobile lab capable of turning out bioweapons, a team says," *New York Times,* May 11, 2003.

19. Douglas Jehl, "State Department disputes CIA view of trailers as labs," *New York Times,* June 26, 2003.

20. Douglas Jehl and David E. Sanger, "Powell's case, a year later: Gaps in picture of Iraq arms," *New York Times,* January 31, 2004.

21. Ari Fleischer, Press gaggle aboard Air Force One en route to Crawford, Texas, May 22, 2003.

22. Interview of the President by TVP, Poland, May 29, 2003.

23. *Meet the Press*, NBC, September 14, 2003; *Morning Edition*, National Public Radio, January 22, 2004.

24. David E. Sanger, "Bush's risky options," *New York Times*, January 30, 2004.

25. George Tenet, testimony to Senate Armed Services Committee, March 9, 2004.

26. John King, *Wolf Blitzer Reports*, CNN, May 30, 2003.

27. "The bioweapons enigma," *New York Times*, June 1, 2003.

28. "Weapons hunt will shift to new sites, head of new search group says," Associated Press, May 31, 2003.

29. Mike Allen, "Bush: 'We found' banned weapons," *Washington Post*, May 30, 2003; John Walcott, "Questions linger over war in Iraq," *The State* (Columbia, SC), June 1, 2003.

30. Ari Fleischer, White House press briefing, June 10, 2003; Dana Milbank, "War in Iraq was 'right decision,' Bush says," *Washington Post*, June 10, 2003.

31. *All Things Considered*, National Public Radio, June 27, 2003, pointed out by Joshua Micah Marshall, TalkingPointsMemo.com, June 27, 2003.

32. *Meet the Press*, NBC, September 14, 2003.

33. Dr. Condoleezza Rice discusses Iraq in Chicago, Illinois, October 8, 2003.

34. *Primetime Live*, ABC, December 16, 2003.

35. Remarks by the President and United Nations Secretary General Kofi Annan in photo opportunity, July 14, 2003.

36. Nexis search of "Bush" *and* "did not let us in," all available news sources, January 27 to February 10, 2004, conducted May 18, 2004; Dana Milbank, "For Bush, a tactical retreat on Iraq," *Washington Post*, February 2, 2004.

37. David Kay, testimony before the House Permanent Select Committee on Intelligence, the House Committee on Appropriations, Subcommittee on Defense, and the Senate Select Committee on Intelligence, October 2, 2003.

38. Remarks by the President after a meeting with former New York City Police Commissioner Bernard Kerik, South Lawn, October 3, 2003.

39. Remarks by the Vice President to the Heritage Foundation, October 10, 2003.

40. Fred Kaplan, "The Iraq sanctions worked," *Slate*, October 7, 2003.

41. James Risen, "Ex-inspector says C.I.A. missed disarray in Iraqi arms program," *New York Times*, January 26, 2004.

42. *Meet the Press*, NBC, February 8, 2004.

43. Dana Milbank, "Bush hails al Qaeda arrest in Iraq," *Washington Post*, January 27, 2004.

44. Seymour Hersh, "The stovepipe," *New Yorker*, October 27, 2003.

45. Walter Pincus, "U.S.-British differences show Iraq intelligence gap," *Washington Post*, September 30, 2003.

46. Nicholas Kristof, "Missing in action: Truth," *New York Times*, May 6, 2003; Joseph C. Wilson IV, "What I didn't find in Africa," *New York Times*, July 6, 2003.

47. Joseph C. Wilson IV, "What I didn't find in Africa," *New York Times*, July 6, 2003; Ari Fleischer, White House press gaggle, July 7, 2003.

48. David Sanger and Carl Hulse, "Bush charge on Iraq arms had doubters," *New York Times*, July 9, 2003.

49. Walter Pincus and Mike Allen, "CIA got uranium reference cut in Oct.," *Washington Post*, July 13, 2003.

50. Dana Milbank and Mike Allen, "Iraq flap shakes Rice's image," *Washington Post*, July 27, 2003.

51. Dana Milbank and Mike Allen, "Iraq flap shakes Rice's image," *Washington Post*, July 27, 2003.

52. President Bush discusses top priorities for the U.S., White House, July 30, 2003.

53. *CBS Evening News,* July 10, 2003.

54. *World News Tonight with Peter Jennings,* ABC, July 11, 2003.

55. Nicholas Kristof, "16 Words and counting," *New York Times,* July 15, 2003; Harold Meyerson, "Inconvenient facts . . ." *Washington Post,* July 17, 2003.

56. Dana Milbank and Walter Pincus, "Bush team stands firm on Iraq policy," *Washington Post,* September 15, 2003; David Kay testimony to House Permanent Select Committee on Intelligence and the House Committee on Appropriations, Subcommittee on Defense, and the Senate Select Committee on Intelligence, October 2, 2003.

57. Dana Milbank and Walter Pincus, "Bush team stands firm on Iraq policy," *Washington Post,* September 15, 2003; October 2002 national intelligence estimate.

58. Dana Milbank and Walter Pincus, "Bush team stands firm on Iraq policy," *Washington Post,* September 15, 2003.

59. Colin Powell, press conference, January 8, 2004.

60. Mitch Potter, "Star finds documents linking bin Laden, Iraq," *Toronto Star,* April 27, 2003.

61. John J. Lumpkin, "Top Iraqi prisoners all denying Saddam had weapons of mass destruction," Associated Press, April 30, 2003.

62. John F. Burns, "Iraq's October surprise," *New York Times,* October 27, 2002.

63. President discusses progress in Afghanistan, Iraq, July 1, 2003; President discusses progress in Iraq, Portsmouth, New Hampshire, October 9, 2003.

64. Remarks by the Vice President to the Heritage Foundation, Washington, DC, October 10, 2003.

65. President discusses progress in Afghanistan, Iraq, July 1, 2003; *Primetime Live,* ABC, December 16, 2003.

66. *The Sean Hannity Show,* September 8, 2003; *Meet the Press,"* NBC, September 14, 2003; *Meet the Press,* NBC, November 2, 2003; *Fox News Sunday,* Fox News Channel, November 2, 2003; *This Week,*

ABC, November 2, 2003; for more, see Matthew Yglesias, "Rumsfeld, Ansar al-Islam and Saddam," the *American Prospect* Online's Tapped weblog, November 3, 2003.

67. Stephen F. Hayes, "Case closed," *Weekly Standard*, November 24, 2003.

68. "DoD news briefing—Secretary Rumsfeld and Gen. Pace," September 16, 2003; *Nightline*, September 16, 2003; remarks by the President after meeting with members of the Congressional Conference Committee on Energy Legislation, September 17, 2003.

69. M.E. Sprengelmeyer, "Transcript of interview with Vice President Dick Cheney," *Rocky Mountain News*, January 9, 2004.

70. Gwen Ifill, *NewsHour with Jim Lehrer*, PBS, July 30, 2003.

71. President Bush commends military in speech at Fort Stewart, Fort Stewart, Georgia, September 12, 2003.

72. Remarks by the Vice President, McChord Air Force Base, Tacoma, Washington, December 23, 2003.

73. Remarks by the Vice President at National Republican Congressional Committee Event, Rosemont, Illinois, February 8, 2004.

74. Remarks by the Vice President to troops and families, Caserma Ederle Army Base, Italy, January 27, 2004; remarks by the Vice President to Troops and Families, Aviano Air Base, Italy, January 27, 2004.

75. Elaine Sciolino, "Clinton overstates impact of raid, his aides warn," *New York Times*, June 29, 1993.

76. Remarks by the President at Bush-Cheney 2004 luncheon, Dallas, Texas, March 8, 2004.

77. President meets with small business owners in New Jersey, Elizabeth, New Jersey, June 16, 2003.

CHAPTER 10

1. Susan Q. Stranahan, "Is anybody looking for any facts?" *Columbia Journalism Review* Campaign Desk, January 31, 2004.

2. Dan Bartlett, Ask the White House chat, January 20, 2004; Gregory Mankiw, Ask the White House chat, January 22, 2004; Don Evans, Ask the White House chat, January 29, 2004; Scott McClellan, White House press briefing, January 23, 2004; Scott McClellan, White House press gaggle, January 26, 2004; Scott McClellan, White House press briefing, January 30, 2004; President Bush, State of the Union address, January 20, 2004; President Bush, remarks at Congress of Tomorrow luncheon, January 31, 2004; President Bush, radio address, January 31, 2004.

3. Richard Kogan, Joel Friedman, and John Springer, Center on Budget and Policy Priorities, "Does the President's 2005 budget really cut the deficit in half?" January 16, 2004, revised February 3, 2004.

4. President Bush discusses budget after cabinet meeting, February 2, 2004; Joel D. Kaplan, Ask the White House online chat, whitehouse.gov, February 2, 2004; OMB director discusses 2005 budget, February 2, 2004.

5. John F. Dickerson and Karen Tumulty, "Raising the volume," *Time,* March 22, 2004.

6. John F. Dickerson and Karen Tumulty, "Raising the volume," *Time,* March 22, 2004.

7. Perry Bacon, "E-mail from the trail: Inside the Kerry war room," *Time,* March 22, 2004; John F. Dickerson and Karen Tumulty, "Raising the volume," *Time,* March 22, 2004; Scott Shepard, "Kerry's tactics: Rapid 'pre-sponse,' " Cox News Service, March 16, 2004.

8. Dana Milbank, "The challenger gets mentioned early," *Washington Post,* March 9, 2004.

9. Jim Rutenberg, "90-Day media strategy by Bush's aides to define Kerry," March 20, 2004.

10. "A tough election ahead," Ken Mehlman, online chat at Bush-Cheney '04 website, February 9, 2004.

11. Eric Sundquist, "Kerry's campaign comes to Atlanta," *Atlanta Journal-Constitution,* February 22, 2004.

12. Ed Gillespie, speech at the Republican National Committee winter meeting, January 29, 2004; Mary Beth Cahill, "The GOP attacks begin!" email to John Kerry supporters, John Kerry for President, January 29, 2004.

13. Marc Racicot, "Bush-Cheney '04 Campaign Chairman Governor Marc Racicot's Letter to Senator John Kerry," Bush-Cheney '04 web site, February 22, 2004.

14. Fred Kaplan, "John Kerry's defense defense," *Slate*, February 25, 2004; "Did Kerry oppose tanks & planes? Not lately," Factcheck.org, February 26, 2004.

15. Brian C. Mooney, "Taking one prize, then a bigger one," *Boston Globe*, June 19, 2003.

16. Remarks by the Vice President at the Ronald Reagan Presidential Library and Museum, Simi Valley, California, March 17, 2004; remarks by Vice President Cheney at a reception for Bush-Cheney '04, Lakewood, New Jersey, March 23, 2004.

17. "Senator Kerry's specific record—again!" Republican National Committee research briefing, February 23, 2004.

18. Nedra Pickler, "Kerry says Bush will run away from his own record in new stump speech," Associated Press, February 23, 2004; "Did Kerry Oppose Tanks & Planes? Not Lately," Factcheck.org, February 26, 2004.

19. James Gerstenzang and Matea Gol, "Clash deepens over wartime leadership," *Los Angeles Times*, March 18, 2004; Ken Fireman, "Attacks over military, Iraq," *Newsday*, March 18, 2004.

20. Remarks by the President at Bush-Cheney 2004 luncheon, Dallas, Texas, March 8, 2004.

21. Fred Kaplan, "Bush insults Kerry's intelligence," *Slate*, March 9, 2004; "Bush strains facts re: Kerry's plan to cut intelligence funding in the '90s," FactCheck.org, March 15, 2004.

22. "Bush strains facts re: Kerry's plan to cut intelligence funding in the '90s," FactCheck.org, March 15, 2004.

23. "Biggest deficit in history? Yes and no," Factcheck.org, February 27, 2004.

24. "Keep our word," John Kerry for President internet ad, February 27, 2004.

25. "Kerry's attack video misleads on veterans, jobs," FactCheck.org, March 1, 2004.

26. "Funding for veterans up 27%, but Democrats call it a cut," Factcheck.org, February 18, 2004.

27. "Kerry's attack video misleads on veterans, jobs," FactCheck.org, March 1, 2004.

28. Telis Demose, "John Kerry reaches out to college-aged voters," *Columbia Spectator*, April 14, 2004.

29. Christopher Wills, "In Senate race, government experience comes in all flavors," Associated Press, March 3, 2004; Liz Sidoti, "Bush's New TV ads focus on last 3 years," Associated Press, March 4, 2004; Wendell Goler, *Special Report with Brit Hume*, Fox News, March 11, 2004; Ken Rudin, *Talk of the Nation*, National Public Radio, March 3, 2004; Laura Mecoy, "Boxer: Jones is on 'far wrong side,' " *Sacramento Bee*, March 17, 2004; William Hershey, "Kerry focuses on Ohio, Bush," Cox News Service, March 1, 2004; David L. Greene, "Democrats talking overtime about jobs," *Baltimore Sun*, February 28, 2004.

30. Jeff Mapes, "Bush's right-hand man defends his boss in Portland," *Oregonian*, March 12, 2004.

31. "In his words: John Kerry," *New York Times*, March 6, 2004.

32. Remarks by the President at Bush-Cheney 2004 reception, East Meadow, New York, March 11, 2004.

33. Remarks by the Vice President at a reception for Bush-Cheney '04, Lakewood, New Jersey, March 23, 2004; see also remarks by the Vice President at a reception for John Thune, Sioux Falls, South Dakota, March 9, 2004; remarks by the Vice President at a reception for Senator Jim Bunning, March 14, 2004; remarks by the Vice President at the Ronald Reagan Presidential Library and Museum, Simi Valley,

California, March 17, 2004; remarks by the Vice President at a luncheon for Bush-Cheney '04, Dayton, Ohio, March 26, 2004; remarks by the Vice President at a dinner for congressional candidate Mike Sodrel, Jeffersonville, Indiana, March 29, 2004.

34. "Vice President Cheney raises money for Thune, rallies Republicans," Associated Press, March 8, 2004; first pointed out by Zachary Roth, "A comedy of errors," *Columbia Journalism Review* Campaign Desk, March 2, 2004; Al Cross, "Backing Bunning, blasting Kerry," *Louisville Courier-Journal,* March 13, 2004.

35. Kerry campaign press release, "Kerry campaign responds to White House Press Secretary Scott McClellan attacks," March 15, 2004.

36. Remarks by the Vice President to the Veterans of Foreign Wars 103rd National Convention, August 26, 2002; remarks by the President in address to the nation, March 17, 2003.

37. Eugene Volokh, "Cheney's supposed lie," *National Review* Online, June 30, 2003; Dana Milbank, "Energy policy spurs affirmative action debate," *Washington Post,* May 20, 2003; interview with Dick Cheney, *Meet the Press,* NBC, September 14, 2003.

38. Ari Fleischer, White House press briefing, October 16, 2002; interview with White House communications director Dan Bartlett, *Late Edition with Wolf Blitzer,* CNN, January 26, 2003; Ari Fleischer, White House press briefing, May 7, 2003.

39. "Kerry seeks tax fairness for hard working americans," John Kerry for President press release, March 10, 2004.

40. "Bush-Cheney '04 announces new ad," Bush-Cheney '04 press release, April 1, 2004.

41. Dan Balz and Jim VandeHei, "In a war of words over numbers, both campaigns have problems," *Washington Post,* March 25, 2004.

42. Jim VandeHei and Brian Faler, "Kerry's spending, tax plans fall short," *Washington Post,* February 29, 2004; John F. Harris and Jim VandeHei, "N.Y. Debate, It's no more Mr. Nice Guys," *Washington Post,* March 1, 2004.

43. Howard Kurtz, "Campaign mantra is rapid response," *Washington Post,* March 20, 2004.

44. Dan Balz and Jim VandeHei, "In a war of words over numbers, both campaigns have problems," *Washington Post,* March 25, 2004.

45. Remarks by the President at Bush-Cheney 2004 reception, Boston, Massachusetts, March 25, 2004; see also remarks by the President at Florida rally, Orlando, Florida, March 20, 2004.

46. Tom Raum, "Bush campaign circle includes Rove, brother Jeb," Associated Press, March 22, 2004.

47. Howard Kurtz, "Campaign mantra is rapid response," *Washington Post,* March 20, 2004.

48. Howard Kurtz, "Campaign mantra is rapid response," *Washington Post,* March 20, 2004.

49. Bush-Cheney '04 troops ad, released March 16, 2004.

50. "Bush-Cheney '04 Ad Facts—'Troops,' " Bush-Cheney '04 press release, March 16, 2004.

51. Mike Glover, "Kerry criticizes Bush for failed policies," Associated Press, March 17, 2004.

52. Remarks by the President at Florida rally, Orlando, Florida, March 20, 2004.

53. Judy Woodruff's Inside Politics," CNN, interviews with Ken Mehlman, March 12 and 16, 2004; *Wolf Blitzer Reports,* CNN, interview with Don Evans, March 10, 2004.

54. "Bush accuses Kerry of 350 votes for 'higher taxes:' Higher than what?" FactCheck.org, March 23, 2004.

55. Michael Janofsky, "Cheney jabs on tax issues and Kerry fights back," *New York Times,* March 30, 2004.

56. "Bush-Cheney '04 ad facts—"Wacky," Bush-Cheney '04 press release, March 30, 2004.

57. "10 Million new jobs," John Kerry for President ad, April 1, 2004; "New Ad Highlights Kerry commitment to keeping jobs here," John Kerry for President press release, April 1, 2004.

58. Edmund L. Andrews, "Treasury Chief defends outsourcing of U.S. work," *New York Times,* March 31, 2004.

59. John Byczkowski, "Treasury's Snow says jobs coming," *Cincinnati Enquirer,* March 30, 2004; "Bush advisor backs off pro-outsourcing comment," CNN.com, February 12, 2004.

60. Remarks by President Bush and Prime Minister Balkenende of the Netherlands in a photo opportunity, March 16, 2004.

CONCLUSION

1. See, for instance, "The Times and Iraq," *New York Times,* May 26, 2004, and Daniel Okrent, "Weapons of Mass Destruction? Or Mass Deception?", *New York Times,* May 30, 2004.

2. Matt Bai, "Notion building," *New York Times Magazine,* October 12, 2003.

3. "What we're about," Center for American Progress website.

4. David Von Drehle, "Liberals get a think tank of their own," *Washington Post,* October 23, 2003.

5. Scott McClellan, White House press gaggle, February 10, 2003.

6. Paul Begala, *Crossfire,* CNN, January 30, 2004; Tim Russert, *Meet the Press,* NBC, March 14, 2004; Tim Russert, *Meet the Press,* NBC, March 21, 2004; Noam Scheiber, "Scott McClellan, not exactly coming clean," &c. blog, *New Republic* website, January 28, 2004; Dan Froomkin, "The President and the chocolate factory," WashingtonPost.com, January 30, 2004; Dan Froomkin, "Why the sudden turnaround?" WashingtonPost.com, February 2, 2004.

7. Marc Kaufman, "Whatever you think about Afghanistan is probably wrong," *Washington Post,* September 23, 2001; "Bad actors," *Newsday,* May 29, 2001.

8. Elise Labott, "U.S. gives $43 million to Afghanistan," CNN.com, May 17, 2001.

9. Rockridge Institute, "Rockridge Institute—Welcome," Rockridge Institute website.

10. Bonnie Azap Powell, "Framing the issues," UC Berkeley NewsCenter, University of California, Berkeley, website, October 27, 2003.

11. "The Frameworks Institute: Strategic frame analysis," FrameWorks Institute website.

12. "The Frameworks Institute: About us," FrameWorks Institute website; Bonnie Azap Powell, "Framing the issues," UC Berkeley NewsCenter, University of California, Berkeley, website, October 27, 2003.

13. See, for instance, Kathleen Hall Jamieson and Paul Waldman, *The Press Effect: Politicians, Journalists and the Stories That Shape the Political World* (New York: Oxford University Press, 2002), or Leonard Downie and Robert Kaiser, *The News About the News: American Journalism in Peril* (New York: Alfred A. Knopf, 2002).

14. Brit Hume, *Fox Special Report with Brit Hume,* Fox News Channel, October 6, 2003; Tony Snow and Brit Hume, *Fox News Sunday,* Fox News Channel, October 12, 2003.

15. Jake Tapper, "Meet the press, with David Letterman," Salon.com, October 20, 2000.

16. Pew Research Center for The People & The Press and the Pew Internet and American Life Project, "Cable and internet loom large in fragmented political news universe: Perceptions of partisan bias seen as growing—especially by Democrats," January 11, 2004.

17. Robert Pear, "U.S. videos, for TV news, come under scrutiny," *New York Times,* March 15, 2004; Eric Boehlert, "Lies, bribes and hidden costs," Salon.com, April 5, 2004.

18. Robert Pear, "U.S. videos, for TV news, come under scrutiny," *New York Times,* March 15, 2004; Eric Boehlert, "Lies, bribes and hidden costs," Salon.com, April 5, 2004.

19. Amy Goldstein, "Probe starts in Medicare drug cost estimates," *Washington Post,* March 17, 2004; Zachary Roth, "Karen Ryan: I feel like

political roadkill," *Columbia Journalism Review* Campaign Desk, March 18, 2004.

20. Robert Pear, "U.S. videos, for TV news, come under scrutiny," *New York Times,* March 15, 2004.

21. Doug Halonen, "News videos spark inquiry," *Television Week,* March 22, 2004.

22. Michael Doyle, "Medicare ad aired in Fresno draws scrutiny," *Fresno Bee,* March 20, 2004.

23. Robert Pear, "U.S. videos, for TV news, come under scrutiny," *New York Times,* March 15, 2004.

24. Zachary Roth, "Bring us the heads of 'Karen Ryan' and 'Alberto Garcia,' " *Columbia Journalism Review* Campaign Desk, March 15, 2004; Zachary Roth, "Bring us the heads of 'Karen Ryan' and 'Alberto Garcia,' Cont'd," *Columbia Journalism Review* Campaign Desk, March 16, 2004; Zachary Roth, "Time to check your checks and balances," *Columbia Journalism Review* Campaign Desk, March 18, 2004; Zachary Roth, "Karen Ryan: 'I feel like political roadkill,' " *Columbia Journalism Review* Campaign Desk, March 18, 2004; Zachary Roth, "CNN: Spinning PR into news," *Columbia Journalism Review* Campaign Desk, March 22, 2004.

25. Howard Kurtz, "Bush and Kerry, a running gag on Late Night," *Washington Post,* March 22, 2004; Zachary Roth, "CNN cracks down—on CNN," *Columbia Journalism Review* Campaign Desk, March 31, 2004.

26. Zachary Roth, "Karen Ryan, revisited," *Columbia Journalism Review* Campaign Desk.org, April 20, 2004.

27. Amy Goldstein, "GAO Says HHS Broke Laws With Medicare Videos," *Washington Post,* May 20, 2004; William L. Watts, "Medicare TV spots illegal, GAO claims," CBS.Marketwatch.com, May 19, 2004.

★ ACKNOWLEDGMENTS ★

Spinsanity has always been a collaborative enterprise, and that has been especially true with this book.

Thanks first to our agent Jonathan Pecarsky, who helped shape this project from the earliest version of the proposal to the final drafts of the manuscript. Without him, this book would still be nothing more than an idea. He and his former colleague Amy Paul believed in Spinsanity's potential from the very beginning—even when we weren't quite certain of it ourselves—and for that we are deeply grateful to both of them.

We would also like to thank Brett Valley, our editor at Touchstone, who helped us find our voice and served as an advocate for the book every step of the way.

All the President's Spin is the biggest project to result from our website, but it's not the first. We would like to express our gratitude to Kerry Lauerman and *Salon* for taking a chance on us in 2002, and John Timpane and the *Philadelphia Inquirer* for creating a weekly column for us this year.

We are also grateful to those who read early drafts of the manuscript, including Mike Hoyt, Robert O. Keohane, Chris Mooney, Gail Nyhan, Dave Offen, and Hillary Thompson. Their feedback vastly improved the writing and content of this book.

Another thank-you goes to all of the journalists and bloggers whose work we have drawn on here. Though the nation's press corps is hardly perfect, the dedicated reporters and commentators who provide public-spirited coverage of national politics deserve praise.

Finally, we'd like to thank the readers of Spinsanity, whose support and criticism have sustained us for over three years. We would be nowhere without them.

Ben extends a special thanks to his family, who have supported his every decision, smart and dumb, over the years; his close friends who constantly amuse and inspire him; and most of all Alicia, his dearest friend.

Bryan thanks Alan Keefer, who commented on an early draft and was always up for heading to the ball game; Lauren Cerand, who read drafts that were probably a little too rough and kept him on his toes with her acid wit; and last but certainly not least, his parents, whose support and encouragement made his portion of this book possible.

Brendan thanks his family and friends for all their support and encouragement, especially his wonderful wife Mary, who stood by his side through the long and arduous book production process and made it all worthwhile.

★ INDEX ★

postwar eagerness to criticize by,
190, 202–3, 206
Reagan and, 34, 46, 51, 237–39
rise of national, 11
seduced by false or misleading
narratives, 51, 73
uncritical responses of, 3, 36,
58–59, 68, 77, 79–80, 81, 82,
94, 117, 121–22, 124, 128, 132,
134, 141, 146, 156–57, 171–73,
190, 195, 199, 220, 225,
227–28, 229, 233, 240
as watchdog on public officials, 31,
32, 33, 36
press conferences:
of Clinton, 46
of G. H. W. Bush, 46
of G. W. Bush, 46–47, 68, 138,
198, 201, 205
of Reagan, 46
scripted order of, 44–45, 257–60
televised, 13
Price of Loyalty, The (Suskind), 257
Priest, Dana, 40
Project for Excellence in Journalism,
57
Propaganda (Bernays), 12
Providence Journal-Bulletin, 58
public opinion, stability of, 18
Public Opinion (Lippmann), 12
public relations, 10–17, 237
founding of, 87
in G. W. Bush staffing, 131–32
G. W. Bush's use of, ix, 3, 10, 56,
93, 103–4, 107, 237–41
Karen Ryan incident and, 252–54,
255
liberals and, 242–44
polls and, 18–19
Public Relations Society of America,
254

Racicot, Marc, 224–25
Raddatz, Martha, 206

Reagan, Ronald, 9, 10–11, 14–15, 27,
29, 144, 226
information flow controlled by, 15,
22, 23–24, 34, 35, 49
press and, 34, 46, 51, 237–39
visual imagery used by, 14, 22–23,
34, 35
Reagan administration, 41
recession, 119–26, 128, 130, 137–38,
263, 264
"reformer with results," 59–60
Republican National Committee, 21,
26, 57, 114–15, 224
Republican National Convention, of
2000, 71, 114
Republican Party, 10, 17, 40, 112,
115, 150, 224, 231, 254
environment as vulnerability of,
87–88
see also specific elections
"revisionist historians," 217
Rice, Condoleezza, 44, 150, 151, 153,
154, 159–60, 166–67, 182, 196,
204–5, 212–13, 217
ricin, 201
Ricks, Thomas, 50
Roberts, John, 46
Rockridge Institute, 244–45
Rocky Mountain News, 212
Romania, 163
Romenesko, James, 43
Roosevelt, Franklin Delano, 13
Roosevelt, Theodore, 11
Rove, Karl, 20, 22, 24, 26, 49, 56,
151, 223, 228
Rumsfeld, Donald, 148–49, 150–51,
177
Russert, Tim, 45, 156, 173, 179, 202,
211, 243, 261, 262
Russia, 163
Ryan, Karen, 252–54, 255

Sacramento Bee, 227
Sammon, Bill, 42

Veterans of Foreign Wars, 157, 169
Vienna, 167
Vietnam War, 33
visual imagery:
    in Gulf War, 15–16
    G. W. Bush White House and, 22–24, 145
    Reagan's use of, 14, 22–23, 34
Vlasto, Chris, 48
VX nerve agent, 170–71, 172

Wallace, Kelly, 77
Wall Street Journal, 21
war, deficits and, *see* defense spending
war on terror, 48, 112, 123, 124, 136, 149, 214, 225, 228–29, 238, 240
Washingtonian, 50
Washington Monthly, 26
Washington Post, 22, 24, 33, 39–40, 42, 43, 49–50, 61–62, 65, 92, 102, 111, 117, 122, 128, 132, 147, 152, 156–57, 158–59, 161, 163, 164, 166, 180, 181, 189, 195, 199, 204, 205, 206, 231–32, 247, 251
WashingtonPost.com, 243
Washington Times, 42, 117, 158
Watergate, 4, 11, 32, 33
Waxman, Henry, 102–3

weapons of mass destruction, 143
    claimed found, 193–95
    in Iraq, 2–3, 4, 6–7, 27, 28, 35–36, 49, 143–85, 190, 199–207, 229
    White House spin on, 191–202
weapons programs, 191–93, 195–98, 199–202, 219–20
Weekly Standard, 211
Weisman, Jonathan, 43
Western Hemisphere Drug Elimination Act, 259
White House, 5, 7, 13, 14, 15, 16, 17, 20, 22
    "war room" in, 16, 34
White House Iraq Group (WHIG), 151–52, 164
White House Office of Communications, 13, 188
White House Television Office, 13
Whitman, Christie Todd, 90
Wilkinson, James, 151
Wilson, Joseph, 51, 165, 203
Wilson, Woodrow, 11
Wolfowitz, Paul, 148, 149, 150–51, 152, 210
Woodward, Bob, 42, 149
Woolsey, James, 149
World News Tonight, 206
World War II, 144, 226

yellowcake, 164–65, 167

Zarqawi, Abu Musab al-, 179–81

★ ABOUT THE AUTHORS ★

B EN FRITZ, BRYAN KEEFER, and BRENDAN NYHAN are the founders and editors of Spinsanity (www.spinsanity.com), the nation's leading watchdog of manipulative political rhetoric. Since founding the site in April 2001, their award-winning analysis has been cited in scores of national and international media outlets, including CNN, Fox News Channel, the *New York Times*, and the *Washington Post*, and they have appeared on numerous radio and television shows. In 2002, they were featured in a regular column on *Salon*, and they can currently be found every Thursday on the commentary page of the *Philadelphia Inquirer*. Readers are invited to visit their website to see more of their work.

BEN FRITZ is a reporter for the entertainment trade paper *Variety*. He also edits the satirical website Dateline Hollywood (www.datelinehollywood.com) and was recently named one of the nation's top thirty business journalists under thirty. Originally from New York, Ben graduated from Swarthmore College and served for a year in the AmeriCorps* National Civilian Community Corps. He lives in Los Angeles and can be reached at ben@spinsanity.com.

BRYAN KEEFER is assistant managing editor of *Columbia Journalism Review*'s Campaign Desk (www.campaigndesk.org), which monitors the media's coverage of politics. He has worked at the

AFL-CIO and the Service Employees International Union. Bryan lives in New York City, but he left his heart in the San Francisco Bay Area, where he was raised. He can be reached at bryan@spin sanity.com.

BRENDAN NYHAN is a graduate student in the department of political science at Duke University in Durham, North Carolina. From 2001 to 2003, he managed new projects and later marketing and fundraising for Benetech (www.benetech.org), a Silicon Valley technology nonprofit. Brendan grew up in Mountain View, California, and attended Swarthmore College. In 2000, he served as the Deputy Communications Director for the Bernstein for U.S. Senate campaign in Nevada. In 2003, he received an Award of Distinction in the Paul Mongerson Prize for Investigative Reporting on News Coverage competition. Brendan can be reached at brendan@spinsanity.com.